Bloom's Modern Critical Views

Bloom's Modern Critical Views

SYLVIA PLATH
Updated Edition

Edited and with an introduction by
Harold Bloom
Sterling Professor of the Humanities
Yale University

BLOOM'S
LITERARY CRITICISM
An imprint of Infobase Publishing

Bloom's Modern Critical Views: Sylvia Plath—Updated Edition

Copyright © 2007 Infobase Publishing

Introduction © 2007 by Harold Bloom

Bloom's Literary Criticism
An imprint of Infobase Publishing
132 West 31st Street
New York NY 10001

ISBN-10: 0-7910-9431-6
ISBN-13: 978-0-7910-9431-0

Library of Congress Cataloging-in-Publication Data
Sylvia Plath / Harold Bloom, editor. — Updated ed.
    p. cm. —— (Bloom's modern critical views)
  Includes bibliographical references and index.
  ISBN 0-7910-9431-6 (hardcover)
  1. Plath, Sylvia--Criticism and interpretation. I. Bloom, Harold. II. Title. III. Series.
  PS3566.L27Z914 2007
  811'.54--dc22   2006033633

Contributing Editor: Amy Sickels
Cover designed by Takeshi Takahashi
Cover photo © Associated Press, AP

Printed in the United States of America
Bang EJB 10 9 8 7 6 5 4 3 2 1

Contents

Editor's Note

My Introduction, written in 1988, is presented here again. After rereading Plath's *Ariel*, my reservations as to her aesthetic eminence only have been enhanced. Readers of this critical volume will find that merely one of the eleven essays is in any agreement with me.

Bruce Bawer begins this volume's selection of essays with an indication of the limitations of "confessional poetry" in *Ariel*.

The litany of idolatry commences with Jacqueline Rose's fiercely Feminist exegesis of "Daddy," while Nancy D. Hargrove praises the poems of 1957 that point towards *Ariel*.

Sandra M. Gilbert, to me the most distinguished of Feminist critics, finds in Plath's "Berck-Plage" a modern version of Matthew Arnold's "Dover Beach," after which Caroline King Barnard Hall presents a consideration of *Crossing the Water* as a transition to Plath's major phase.

For Christina Britzolakis, Plath achieves a reversal of the male-originated myth of "the fatal woman," while Tim Kendall believes he discovers in Plath's final poems a sublimity that transcends our inadequate modes of reading.

Susan Gubar defends Plath's Holocaust poetry, whose palpable inauthenticity defeats me, after which Linda Wagner-Martin is triumphalist in saluting Plath's apotheosis of femaleness as such.

In this book's final essay, Susan Bassnett bestows her approval upon Plath's religiosity.

HAROLD BLOOM

Introduction

When I was much younger, I believed firmly that critics should not write about poetry that they did not love, indeed had not loved for a long time. I met and liked Sylvia Plath a half of a century ago in Cambridge, England, and remember then reading her earliest poems with respectful interest. Purchasing *The Colossus* in 1960, I expected a touch more than I received, and found the volume too derivative, though accomplished enough. Plath killed herself in 1963, and *Ariel* was published in 1965. I shied away from the book and did not purchase and read it until the early 1970s. Perhaps I would have liked it better then, or could now, if its few merits were not so grossly exaggerated by its many admirers. Perhaps not.

Plath was not Christina Rossetti or even Elizabth Barrett Browning. If we compare her to an original and powerful poet of her own generation, like the superb May Swenson, then she quite dwindles away. Contemporary reputation is a most inadequate guide to canonical survival. The more fanciful of Plath's admirers have ventured to link her to Emily Dickinson, the most original consciousness and most formidable intellect among all poets in the language since William Blake. A far better comparison would be to Mrs. Felicia Hemans, English Romantic versifier, whose tragic early death gave her a certain glamour for a time. Mrs. Hemans is rembered today solely for her dramatic lyric, "Casabianca," with its abrupt opening line, "The boy stood on the burning deck," most memorably parodied by the wag who completed the couplet with: "Eating peanuts by the peck." "Lady Lazarus" is the "Casabianca" of my generation and may endure, as such, in some future edition of that marvelous anthology *The Stuffed Owl.*

I do not intend to be contentious, and I have been preceded in my reservations by two critics who are very different both from one another and from myself, Irving Howe and Hugh Kenner. Dr. Samuel Johnson, the Sublime of criticism, took on his *Lives of the English Poets* with the understanding that the choice of poets was to be that of the booksellers, whose object was to satisfy the taste of the time. In that spirit, Johnson cheerfully suggested the inclusion of such mighty pens as Yalden and Pomfret to join such eminent hands as Stepney, Sprat, Tickell, Mallet, and Lyttleton. The fashions of each moment in literary history are not unlike each moment in sartorial tradition. Sprat went the way of the bustle. Hysterical insanity, whatever its momentary erotic appeal, is not an affect that endures in verse. Poetry relies upon trope and not upon sincerity. I have just reread *Ariel*, after some fifteen years, and spontaneously I find myself again murmuring Oscar Wilde's definitive apothegm: "All bad poetry springs from genuine feeling." There are the immensely celebrated pieces, including "Lady Lazarus" with its much-admired conclusion:

> Dying
> Is an art, like everything else.
> I do it exceptionally well.
>
> I do it so it feels like hell.
> I do it so it feels real.
> I guess you could say I have a call.
>
> It's easy enough to do it in a cell.
> It's easy enough to do it and stay put.
> It's the theatrical
>
> Comeback in broad day
> To the same place, the same face, the same brute
> Amused shout:
>
> "A miracle!"
> That knocks me out.
> There is a charge
>
> For the eyeing of my scars, there is a charge
> For the hearing of my heart—
> It really goes.

And there is a charge, a very large charge
For a word or a touch
Or a bit of blood

Or a piece of my hair or my clothes.
So, so, Herr Doktor.
So, Herr Enemy.

I am your opus,
I am your valuable,
The pure gold baby

That melts to a shriek.
I turn and burn.
Do not think I underestimate your great concern.

Ash, ash—
You poke and stir.
Flesh, bone, there is nothing there—

A cake of soap,
A wedding ring,
A gold filling.

Herr God, Herr Lucifer
Beware
Beware.

Out of the ash
I rise with my red hair
And I eat men like air.

Helen Vendler calls this "a tantrum of style" and "a centrifugal spin to further and further reaches of outrage." Those seem to me characteristically kind judgments from a severe student of poetic syntax, the most authoritative in my critical generation. I become lost, and doubt my competence to read Plath (or Adrienne Rich and other seers of the School of Resentment), when I encounter feminist defenses of Plath's final mode, as here in Mary Lynn Broe:

We lack a critical vocabulary for these rich tones. We lack a critical vocabulary precisely because our society lacks any definition of power which *transforms* rather than *coerces*.

This is to tell me, presumably, that I can write criticism of Emily Dickinson, Elizabeth Bishop, and May Swenson because they manifest a power of *coercion* while Plath, Rich, Alice Walker defeat me because I do not know how to describe and analyze a power of *transformation*. "Lady Lazarus" with its gratuitous and humanly offensive appropriation of the imagery of Jewish martyrs in Nazi death camps (an appropriation incessant in Plath) seems to me a pure instance of coercive rhetoric, transforming absolutely nothing. That the reader is harangued, not persuaded, is my baffled protest. Barbara Hardy, however, hears an "unfailing grim humor" and a "rationally alert intelligence" in "Lady Lazarus" and its companion poems:

> It is present in the great *Ariel* poems: "Lady Lazarus," "Daddy," "Death & Co.," "A Birthday Present," and "The Applicant," which are very outgoing, very deranged, very enlarged. In "Lady Lazarus" the persona is split, and deranged. The split allows the poem to peel off the personal, to impersonate suicidal feeling and generalize it. It is a skill, it is a show, something to look at. The poem seems to be admitting the exhibitionism of suicide (and death poetry?) as well as the voyeurism of spectators (and readers?). It is also a foul resurrection, stinking of death. This image allows her to horrify us, to complain of being revived, to attack God and confuse him with a doctor, any doctor (bringing round a suicide) and a Doktor in a concentration camp, experimenting in life and death. It moves from Herr Doktor to Herr Enemy and to miracle makers, scientists, the torturer who may be a scientist, to Christ, Herr God, and Herr Lucifer (the last two after all collaborated in experiments on Adam, Eve, and Job). They poke and nose around in the ashes, and this is the last indignity, forcing the final threat: "I eat men like air." It is a threat that can intelligibly be made by martyred victims (she has red hair, is Jewish), by phoenixes, by fire, by women. The fusion and dispersal, once more rational and irrational, makes the pattern of controlled derangement, creating not one mirror but a hall of mirrors, all differently distorting, and revealing many horrors.

The poem "Lady Lazarus," here as elsewhere, provokes a mode of criticism that Plath herself deeply contaminates. I have no desire to invoke "The Fallacy of Imitative Form," a legacy of the critic Yvor Winters. Plath's fate was poignant; whether "Lady Lazarus" is poignant, or a tantrum, or even a poignant tantrum, seems to me an aesthetic question to which a clear answer indeed can be made. If Plath's achievement (and Rich's) is indeed so original and so great that it calls for a new aesthetic, then let that aesthetic come down upon us. Until the aesthetic of Resentment has achieved itself, the later poetry of Sylvia Plath will abide with its admirers.

BRUCE BAWER

Sylvia Plath and the Poetry of Confession

Back when America was careening from the Eisenhower era—the "tranquillized Fifties," as Robert Lowell called them—toward the Age of Aquarius, American poetry was undergoing a dramatic shift as well. A period of highly controlled, formal, and impersonal poetry, dominated by the likes of Richard Wilbur and Anthony Hecht, gave way with surprising rapidity to one of unrestrained, exceedingly personal free verse, often about extreme emotional states, by such poets as John Berryman, Anne Sexton, and W. D. Snodgrass. So revolutionary did these effusions seem at the time that the critic M. L. Rosenthal found it necessary, in a review of Lowell's 1959 volume *Life Studies*, to coin a new name for them: confessional poetry. To be sure, although the confessionalists tended to be more explicit about their divorces, orgasms, and such than poets of earlier generations, there was nothing fundamentally new about verse that took the poet's private life and feelings for its material; accordingly, though Rosenthal's term gained widespread currency, there were from the beginning those who objected to it as unnecessary and even denigrating, and who maintained that to label a poem in this fashion was to draw inordinate attention to its often sensational subject matter and thereby to slight its literary merit.

Of course, the literary merit of confessional poetry varied widely; and perhaps the most unfortunate effect of the term's broad acceptance was

From *The New Criterion* 9, no. 6 (February, 1991): pp. 18–27. © 1991 *The New Criterion.*

that, in the years after *Life Studies*, many a poet and critic began thinking of confessionalism as something that aspired not to aesthetic excellence so much as to the total honesty of the psychiatrist's couch or—well—the church confessional, and that should therefore be judged by the degree not of its artistry but of its candor. What was lost sight of, by many, was that for such poetry to be of literary importance it must, through a concentration not on universals but on intimate particulars, awaken in all sorts of readers (whose lives might, needless to say, be extremely different from the poet's in those intimate particulars) a sense of common humanity, a mature recognition that the essentials of one life are the essentials of all. If bad confessional poetry, in other words, appeals to a reader superficially, soliciting his attention and empathy on the basis of shared background or politics or neuroses or sexual tastes—or, alternatively, taking him out of himself in much the same way as a lurid, gossipy supermarket tabloid—the best confessional poetry introduces him to individuals with whose social lives and ideas he might not identify at all, but whose personal testimony nonetheless manages somehow to draw him inward. Like the poetry of Wilbur and Hecht, moreover, the best confessional poetry is marked by balance, control, a sense of form and rhythm, and even a degree of detachment.

Though, of all the confessional poets, Robert Lowell earned the most substantial literary reputation, it was Sylvia Plath who, in the years following the posthumous publication of her second poetry collection, *Ariel* (1965), became the movement's chief icon. Yet while Lowell's fame needs no more explanation than the aesthetic merit of his work, Plath's quick rise to near-legendary status owes much to other factors. For one thing, Plath's notion of herself as a victim of two domineering men—her father, who died when she was a child, and her husband, the poet Ted Hughes, from whom she was separated at the time of her suicide in London in 1963—made her extremely useful to the women's movement. (Perhaps no one has more memorably expressed the feminist position on Plath than Robin Morgan, who in a poem entitled "Arraignment" accuses Hughes of Plath's murder and envisions a group of women entering his home, "disarm[ing] him of that weapon with which he tortured us, / stuff[ing] it into his mouth, sew[ing] up his poetasting lips around it, / and blow[ing] out his brains.") Meanwhile, Plath's proudly flaunted self-destructiveness, and her romantic image of herself as a sensitive genius in a brutal and indifferent world, made her a natural idol for many a young person in the throes of adolescent torment. (What, after all, could be more irresistible to a saturnine, self-romanticizing teenager than a passage like this, from Plath's college journal: "nothing is real, past or future, when you are alone in your room with the clock ticking loudly into the false cheerful brilliance of the electric light. And if you have no past or future, which, after all, is all that the present is made of, why then you may as well dispose of the empty shell of present and commit suicide.") I think it is safe to say that these two groups account for the majority of Plath's devotees and that neither group cherishes her work chiefly for its literary merit.

For such readers, patently, the real interest lies not in Plath's art but in her life. And her life—from her childhood in Jamaica Plain, Winthrop, and Wellesley, Massachusetts, through her undergraduate career at Smith and two Fulbright years at Cambridge, to marriage, motherhood in Devon and London, the beginnings of literary prominence, marital estrangement, and self-slaughter at thirty—*is* fascinating, though not on the superficial level that such readers tend to focus upon. It is fascinating, rather, as a study in the nexus among art, ambition, and abnormal psychology, and, more specifically, in the formation of an author whose most anguished poems, composed only weeks before her suicide, are widely considered to be the quintessence of confessional poetry. The story of this formation must begin with Plath's parents, Otto Emil Plath, an authoritarian, German-born entomology professor, and his submissive wife, Aurelia, a second-generation Austrian-American. Both parents shared a belief in discipline, a disinclination to make (or to allow their children to make) close friends, and—in the words of Anne Stevenson, author of the biography *Bitter Fame: A Life of Sylvia Plath* (1989)—a "veneration for work"; together, they raised an obedient, overachieving daughter who found security (or, at least, a semblance thereof) in the structures and schedules of the classroom and whose sense of self-definition appears to have depended from an early age upon her ability not only to meet but to exceed the expectations of her parents and teachers. Otto's death when Sylvia was eight years old (she insisted, the next day, on going to school) led to a lifetime of largely suppressed rage at him, both for being a tyrant—which he may or may not have been, depending upon how one defines the word—and for abandoning her, and led also to a lifetime of tireless effort to surpass the goals set for her by the authority figures she erected in his place.

To be sure, as long as she was a student, Sylvia functioned splendidly—or seemed to. At twenty, invoking an image that later provided the title for her autobiographical novel, she would write to a friend that "I've gone around for most of my life as in the rarefied atmosphere under a bell-jar, all according to schedule, four college years neatly quartered out in seasons." But the daughter of Otto Plath needed that bell-jar, needed the structure provided by school and college, needed her mother and teachers to set goals for her. If, as she admitted, she suffered from a "terrifying fear of mediocrity," it was because anything less than first-rate work might shatter her fragile sense of self; and if, furthermore, she referred to a college boyfriend as her "major man," one suspects that it was because she was unable to understand anything in life—whether it was dating, marriage, or the making of a literary career—except by analogy with schoolwork, choosing friends as if they were honors courses and competing for beaux as if they were class prizes.

Peter Davison, who met Plath when she was a star undergraduate at Smith, wrote later that she was "always trying to create an effect, to make an impression," and that she talked about her own life "as though she were describing a stranger to herself, a highly trained circus horse." Which, in a way, she was: for she would jump through almost any hoop to please those in authority. The vapid prototypes established by others formed the foundation of her identity: she embraced the role of All-Around Coed, for instance, with an inane fervor astonishing in one so intelligent ("I still can't believe I'm a SMITH GIRL!" she wrote her mother soon after entering college). She would stop at little to win academic distinction: friends complained of her manipulativeness, of how she used people to get ahead and discarded them callously when they were no longer needed.

Even in literature, image ruled. Plath writes her mother about course possibilities at Smith: "Imagine saying, 'Oh, yes, I studied writing under Auden!' ... Honestly, Mum, I could just cry with happiness." If many a bard before and since has longed to forge the uncreated conscience of his race, Plath, in journal entries about her poetic aspirations, takes the tone of a high-school climber angling for a graduation medal, noting that "I must get philosophy in [i.e., into her poetry]. Until I do so I shall lag behind A[drienne] C[ecile] R[ich]." Her willingness to bow to both literary and subliterary totems is exemplified by her habit (as noted by Stevenson) "of talking of Wallace Stevens in one breath and *Mademoiselle* in the next." Just as she deliberately wrote insipid stories at Smith to win approval from the editors of *Seventeen*, in later years she was equally desperate for the approbation of *The New Yorker*, whose first acceptance of a Plath poem occasioned an almost frighteningly rhapsodic journal entry.

Writing was always important to Plath. Her father had been an author— of, among other things, a textbook on bumblebees—and had used the family supper table as a writing desk. Stevenson, who has a sensitivity to the motives behind Plath's writing that seems to have eluded earlier biographers, highlights a memory of Mrs. Plath's. During Sylvia's early childhood, at times when her mother was attending to Sylvia's infant brother, Warren, and wanted to prevent her daughter from trying to draw attention away from the boy, she encouraged the little girl to read letters in newspapers. Stevenson's savvy comment: "even at two and a half her daughter was being urged to treat negative emotion (jealousy of her brother) with words." This was something that Plath would do throughout her life. For her, writing became a way of asserting herself, of combating her deficient sense of identity. "Haunted by a fear of her own disintegration," Stevenson notes, Plath "kept herself together by defining herself, writing constantly about herself, so that everyone could see her there, fighting and conquering an outside world that forever threatened her frail being." No wonder, then, that, as Edward Butscher observes in his 1976 biography *Sylvia Plath: Method and Madness*, "getting published was not merely important [for Sylvia], it was everything": for her, seeing one's name in print was the ultimate proof not merely of acceptance but of existence.

The literary life, however, proved to differ so drastically from life at home, school, and college that Sylvia's first excursion from familiar territory into the *terra incognita* of publishing was almost her last. During the summer of 1953, she went to New York as an undergraduate editorial intern for *Mademoiselle*—an experience that exposed her for the first time to a chaotic, equivocal adult world in which the first thing authority figures demanded of her was simply that she be herself. And being herself, alas, was one thing that Sylvia was not good at. Butscher quotes Plath's editor at *Mademoiselle* as saying that she had "never found anyone so unspontaneous so consistently ... [Sylvia was] all façade, too polite, too well-brought-up and well-disciplined." In any event, removed from the closed system of accomplishment and approval within which she had operated for so long, Plath became unstrung. Soon after returning home, she attempted suicide, and spent the next several months undergoing psychiatric treatment at McLean Hospital, which over the years would gain fame as the treatment center of choice for Plath's fellow confessionalists Robert Lowell and Anne Sexton. (The whole experience, of course, is retold in fictional form in her 1963 novel *The Bell Jar.*)

What is one to make of this suicide attempt? Though they differ considerably in tone and emphasis, the interpretations of Plath's biographers are not as inconsistent as one might expect. Butscher's centers on the notion that Sylvia

> was three persons, three Sylvias in constant struggle with one another for domination: Sylvia the modest, bright, dutiful, hard-working, terribly efficient child of middle-class parents and strict Calvinist values who was grateful for the smallest favor; Sylvia the poet, the golden girl on campus who was destined for great things in the arts and glittered when she walked and talked; and Sylvia the bitch goddess, aching to go on a rampage of destruction against all those who possessed what she did not and who made her cater to their whims.

To complicate matters, Butscher speaks of additional, if secondary-level, Sylvias, whom he describes as "fitful shadows of the three main configurations." One was "Sylvia the sad little girl still hurting from the profound wound of her father's rejection and abandonment of her and wanting to crawl back into her mother's cave-safe womb"; another was "Sylvia the ordinary teenager who yearned for a kind husband, children, and a house like her grandmother's by the seashore."

Stevenson, for her part, settles for two Sylvias—a false outer self and a real inner self—and argues that the poet's self-destructiveness sprang from the yearning of her real self to kill her false self "so that her real one might burn free of it." This picture seems much simpler than Butscher's, but Stevenson also chooses to complicate things a bit by maintaining that

> Sylvia had long been confusing two very different battles within herself. One was with an artificial Sylvia, modeled on her mother, driven by ambitions she believed Aurelia harbored for her and ideas she thought Aurelia projected. This battle was occurring on a comparatively superficial level. Beneath it, so to speak, raged an altogether more serious war, where the "real" Sylvia—violent, subversive, moon-struck, terribly angry—fought for her existence against a nice, bright, gifted American girl. This "real" self may have been created, and gone underground, at the time of her father's death in November 1940. It had emerged in August 1953, before her suicide attempt, and it remained in charge during the months of her slow recovery at McLean. It would be too simple to say that the nice girl wanted to live while the vengeful, deserted daughter wanted to die. But it was probably the case that Sylvia's powerful buried self was deadly in its determination to emerge at any cost.

To a considerable extent, of course, there is no need to choose between Butscher's and Stevenson's formulations: they are largely two ways of looking at the same thing. Stevenson's "real' self," for instance, despite the drastic difference in tone, is essentially equivalent to Butscher's "bitch goddess."

At McLean, Plath underwent shock treatments and was told by her doctor that it was all right (a) to hate her parents and (b) to have sex. She claimed to have found all this liberating, and returned to Smith supposedly cured. (Certainly her success-oriented approach to literature returned, strong as ever. "Must get out SNAKE PIT," she confided to her journal in 1959, referring to Mary Jane Ward's bestseller. "There is an increasing market for mental hospital stuff. I am a fool if I don't relive it, recreate it.") But Butscher and Stevenson both believe that McLean did her more harm than good. Butscher's view is that Plath's doctor "resurrected the mask [i.e., her good-girl façade] and gave it a firmer fit by letting Sylvia participate in the unearthing of the classic Electra complex." Stevenson focuses her attack not on the psychoanalysis but on the shock treatments, arguing that they critically weakened Plath's façade (which she, unlike Butscher, sees as protective and necessary). "It may be that she never really recovered" from the shock treatments, writes Stevenson, suggesting that they

> changed her personality permanently, stripping her of a psychological "skin" she could ill afford to lose. Attributable to her ECT is the unseen menace that haunts nearly everything she wrote, her conviction that the world, however benign in appearance, conceals dangerous animosity, directed particularly toward herself. Sylvia's psychotherapy almost certainly opened up the dimensions of her Freudian psychodrama, revealing the figure of her lost, "drowned" father ... whose death she could neither forgive nor allow herself to forget; psychotherapy also intensified the presence of her much-loved yet ultimately resented mother, whose double she had to be, for reasons of guilt or ego weakness, and to whom she was tied by a psychic umbilicus too nourishing to sever.

Though the "Freudian psychodrama" is at the center of both interpretations, Butscher places more emphasis on Otto Plath, stating on his first page that Sylvia's "central obsession from the beginning to the end of her life and career was her father," and interpreting that life in terms of a "frustrated will to power." Stevenson, by contrast, insists that "[i]t is not clear how much of Sylvia Plath's existential anxiety can be traced to her social isolation as a girl and how much to her father's death." But it seems to me that both factors are important: if Plath hadn't been sequestered from other children, her father might not have been such a god to her and his death might therefore not have affected her so catastrophically.

Though their interpretations can be seen as largely consistent in their essentials, Plath's biographers differ dramatically in style, method, and perspective. Butscher's book is a mixed—and rather overstuffed—bag. Though he offers a number of perceptive observations and sensitive close readings, he includes countless extraneous details (providing, among much else, the dates on which the Bradford High School honor roll was released). As he demonstrated in his recent biography of Conrad Aiken, moreover, Butscher has an inordinate faith in the ultimate power of psychiatric nomenclature to illuminate anything and everything in the realm of human behavior; to his mind, one gathers, understanding an individual is almost entirely a matter of attaching labels like "neurotic" and "schizophrenic" to that individual's behavior. Butscher assigns these labels with an alarming alarcity and a well-nigh palpable relish, and, quite often, on what would appear to be the slightest of evidence. (A sentence about the mother of one of Plath's boyfriends begins: "Sylvia's dislike of Mrs. Willard, which she of course repressed. ..." And: "Sylvia's attitude toward Davison himself remained distant, perhaps because of repressed guilt.") One comes away from Butscher's book thinking that there should be a psychological label to describe someone overly devoted to psychological labels. Linda Wagner-Martin, in *Sylvia Plath: A Biography* (1987), has the opposite problem: she performs too little analysis, whether literary or psychological. She treats Plath's suicidal depression almost as if it were a phenomenon unrelated to the poet's day-to-day psychology, and occasionally leaves the impression that she considers Plath to have been, most of the time, as sound of mind as anyone else—at least, that is, until Ted Hughes entered the picture in February 1956, barely more than two years after her suicide attempt.

It was Plath, then an exchange student in Cambridge, who engineered their meeting: one day she read some of his poems in a magazine—poems as intense and dark as she wanted hers to be, and *real* in a way hers were not—and decided immediately that she had to meet him. That same night, she introduced herself to him at a party, where (as she wrote in her journal) the tall, brooding, Lawrentian young Yorkshireman "kissed me bang smash on the mouth and ripped my hair-band. ... And when he kissed my neck I bit him long and hard on the cheek, and when we came out of the room, blood was running down his face." And so they were married. Hughes was the first man Plath had ever known to whom she could imagine subordinating herself without difficulty—as both poet *and* woman—in the way that her mother had subordinated herself to her father. Months later, she would write that Hughes "fills somehow that huge, sad hole I felt in having no father"; for the meantime, however, in letters divulging her new love to her kith and kin, Plath described him as "a violent Adam," "the only man in the world who is my match," "the strongest man in the world ... with a voice like the thunder of God," "a breaker of things and of people." What more could a girl want?

It was after her marriage to Hughes that Plath began to write the poems that eventually appeared in her first collection, *The Colossus and Other Poems* (1960). In their intellectual and stylistic sophistication, they represent a significant advance over the unremarkable verse of earlier years (fifty examples of which are relegated to the appendix of her 1981 *Collected Poems*). Like their predecessors, however, all but a few of these *Colossus* poems read like descriptive exercises—and with good reason, for many of them *were* exercises, written to order for Hughes, who when Plath could not come up with anything to write about, would arbitrarily select some object, animal, or setting that was near at hand and assign her the task of composing a poem about it. Plath did her job competently, employing all the resources about which she had learned during her years of study. The metaphors and similes in these poems are often quite vivid (the cadavers in a dissecting room are "black as burnt turkey"), and her language frequently betrays the influence of some of the major poets of the day, notably Dylan Thomas. ("No doubt now in dream-propertied fall some moon-eyed, / Star-lucky sleight-of-hand man watched / My jilting lady squander coin, gold leaf stock ditches, / And the opulent air go studded with seed.") And an especially important influence is that of the early poems of Hughes himself, whose lean, grave, and austerely symbolic evocations of nature red in tooth and claw were in turn influenced both by his moor country upbringing and by his extensive reading in anthropology. To be sure, many of the harsh natural phenomena Plath observed in Devon and described in the *Colossus* poems did apparently move her deeply; Hughes, in an essay published after her death, notes that "[h]er reactions to hurts in other people and animals, and even tiny desecrations of plant-life, were extremely violent."

As a rule, however, Plath's *Colossus* poems seem more skillful than inspired. They are, as Anne Sexton commented, "all in a cage (and not even her own cage at that)." Though Hughes presumably tried to suggest topics that would tap Plath's profoundest emotions, almost everything in these verses strikes one as forced, from the intensifying adjectives and adverbs to the patterns of alliteration and assonance. Stevenson notes that as a student Plath, copying words from a thesaurus onto flash cards, had built poems "word by word, like novel, intricate structures"; reading the *Colossus* poems one can almost see her poring over her Roget's. The irony, of course, is that while the bleak, often violent depictions of nature in many of these poems sincerely reflect Plath's own brittle sense of security in a brutal world—and though some of them plainly seek to draw on her complex, powerful emotions about her father's death—almost all of them have a labored quality, a manufactured intensity, their savage images striking one as over-wrought and self-conscious, their ire and loathing coming across as false. Unlike Hughes's poems, moreover, the *Colossus* poems almost invariably fail to convey a personality, a point of view, let alone a passionate attachment to or understanding of the people, places, and things that they take as their subjects. Time and again, one feels that Plath is attempting to force greater significance upon scenes and situations than they really hold for her—to force it upon them, that is, rather than to discover it within them. While these poems, then, contain vivid images, striking lines, and pleasing configurations of sound, the poems don't work *qua* poems.

Not until 1960 did Plath begin to write the poems that would appear in *Ariel* (1965). The contrast with the most typical *Colossus* verses is remarkable: her new poems are colloquial, muscular, unafraid of repeated words or odd line lengths or the first person singular pronoun. In the best of them, such as "Tulips," she breathes some life into her descriptive skills, and yokes wit to feeling. The poems that are almost universally acknowledged as her strongest, however, and that more faithfully represent the characteristic style and tone of the book, are those like "Lady Lazarus" and "Daddy," in which, rather than try to turn homely objects and settings into objective correlatives for her emotions, she embraces wholeheartedly the idea of poem as subjective (and often highly surrealistic) effusion. So frequently praised and ubiquitously quoted are these two poems that it almost seems at times as if Plath's entire reputation rests upon them. There is, to be sure, good reason why these two perverse and passionate poems should receive special attention, because nowhere else in her verse does Plath more bluntly address her most fundamental psychological conflicts. In both poems, Otto Plath and Hughes figure prominently, as does Plath's suicide attempt at twenty. The speaker of "Lady Lazarus," indeed, brags darkly about her prowess at such attempts ("I do it so it feels real"), marvels at her survival of her attempt at age twenty (and of a near-fatal "accident" a decade earlier), and addresses an unnamed tormentor as "Herr Doktor" and "Herr Enemy." She compares herself to an extermination-camp inmate, suggests that her victory over death makes her a "sort of walking miracle, my skin / Bright as a Nazi lampshade," and perceives that victory as securing for her a grotesque vengeance upon the opposite sex: "Beware / Beware. / Out of the ash / I rise with my red hair / And I eat men like air." Manifestly, we are meant to understand here that the speaker's experience with men (or with a certain man) was responsible in some way for her suicide attempt, and that her survival of it represents a miraculous triumph over them. "Daddy" draws on the same preoccupations and takes the same tone. Here the speaker refers to her father as a "black shoe" in which she has lived for thirty years and attributes her suicide attempt to a desire to "get back, back, back" to him. Spared death, she "made a model" of her father, a man with "a love of the rack and the screw," said "I do, I do," and lived with him for some time; but now she's murdered one man, in some sense, and by so doing has killed both: "Daddy, daddy, you bastard, I'm through."

These poems, along with the other most ferocious and famous poems in *Ariel*, flowed from Plath's pen in October and November of 1962, sometimes at the rate of more than one a day, soon after Hughes became involved with one Assia Wevill (who would become his second wife) and separated from Sylvia. Anne Sexton referred to these as "hate poems," and that they most certainly are, expressing time and again, in very similar terms, the most extreme and blatant of emotions, invariably aimed in the same direction. "Lady Lazarus" and "Daddy" are the most arresting of Plath's verses, and it is their hate, really, that makes them so—a hate communicated, often quite effectively, by way of natural language and rhythms, manically insistent repetitions and multiple rhymes, and sensational, often surrealistic images, all of which are designed to grab the attention of the most impassive reader. And grab the reader they do—on a first reading, anyway. In fact, this ability to capture the attention of readers—and even, at times, to shock them—helps explain why the *Ariel* poems, nearly three decades after Plath's death, remain a force to be reckoned with. And yet, what ultimately makes the poems memorable is less the hate that they express, or the blunt language that they employ, or even the inexcusable, hyperbolic metaphors that equate the poet's suffering with that of prisoners in Nazi concentration camps, than it is the fact that all these elements combine to convey, with vigor and directness, the extreme emotional state of a highly unbalanced, self-destructive woman.

It might be argued that there is a degree of aesthetic value in such an accomplishment. But the more one reads these poems, the more one realizes that beneath the thoroughly convincing representation of psychological disturbance—behind, that is, Plath's shrill, deranged voice—there is precious little human dimension. It has been argued that the *Ariel* poems are saved by their irony, but Plath's irony is facile and, moreover, always directed at others—never at the poet herself. She is capable of quipping sardonically, in "Lady Lazarus," "Do not think I underestimate your great concern"; but it doesn't occur to her, in her utter self-absorption, that her own dearth of concern for others might itself be a worthwhile target for irony. It is hardly an exaggeration, I think, to say that the chief problem with these poems is their constricting, claustrophobic solipsism. Compared to Plath, even Lowell— himself no tower of sanity or selflessness—seems quite actively involved with mankind, what with his numerous *Life Studies* poems about relatives, fellow poets, Czar Lepke, and the like; alongside Plath, even Berryman, with his often puerile attitude toward romantic relationships, comes off in the *The Dream Songs* as painting a nuanced, mature picture of love, sex, and marriage, and as providing, in his Henry persona, a model of proper authorial distance.

This is not to say that poems of self-scrutiny, as such, are necessarily bad, but rather to say that in the *Ariel* poems the self is so engrossed in itself that there appears to be little possibility of enlightenment, of discovery; to read them is to feel that their goal is not self-knowledge but self-display, a morbid absorption in and superficial celebration of the poet's own sensitivity and imagined victimhood. Throughout the poems, the world beyond the poet is seen consistently as despotic, destructive; yet she seems not to realize to what degree she is in fact her own destroyer, her own victim. The biographies of Plath make it clear that these poems are the work of a psychologically complicated and fascinating woman; but the poems themselves are, by comparison to the woman, woefully simple and—after the first reading—progressively less interesting.

In virtually every regard, then—in range of theme and invention, in complexity of feeling and structure, and in sophistication of style and technique—the *Ariel* poems are less impressive than the best so-called confessional poems of Lowell and Berryman. Certainly they are smaller in vision. Butscher quotes Irving Howe as complaining that "in none of the essays devoted to praising Sylvia Plath have I found a coherent statement as to the nature, let alone the value, of her vision." Butscher's reply is that "Sylvia did indeed have a vision: it was to plunge into the depths of self, the dark side of the mind's moon, and hope to touch the bottom of degradation and sorrow." Putting aside for the moment Butscher's mixed metaphor, what can one say about this defense? It can hardly be denied, of course, that the *Ariel* poems take such a plunge as Butscher describes. But is it correct, really, to say that they evince a "vision," in the sense that Howe plainly means? Yes, poems like "Daddy" and "Lady Lazarus" pierce the poet's surface as sharply as a surgeon's knife; but the incisions are narrow, the innards unilluminated, the result (for the reader) not a laying bare of the intricate workings of a self and soul but a raw, lurid exhibition of private agony and blood-letting. To put it a bit differently, the *Ariel* poems provide a startlingly naked glimpse into the mind of a deeply disturbed woman; but a glimpse, however naked, is not necessarily the same as an insight, nor revelation necessarily the same as art.

Wagner-Martin would have us believe that the *Ariel* poems were a triumphant apotheosis—the inevitable consequence of Plath's rejection of Hughes's artificial little assignments and of her "com[ing] into her own as a woman"—and that Plath's suicide, which came soon after the completion of the poems, was essentially the result of Hughes's betrayal and withdrawal from her life. There is, however, nothing triumphant about the *Ariel* poems; far from reflecting a newly proud and independent womanhood, these poems, with their mad, unbridled hostility, plainly express the poet's sudden helplessness at the withdrawal of the protective canopy underneath which she had erected her entire life as wife, mother, and author. In Hughes, Plath had found a father-substitute, and his departure from her life served to release, after decades of suppression, an eight-year-old's exorbitant fear and fury at her father's death. Plath's sudden outpouring of thoroughly unfettered *Ariel* poems, in other words, represents less a breakthrough than a breakdown; for the poems show little sign of control over or understanding of her rage, let alone mature perception into the human complexities that produced it.

Nor can one blame Plath's suicide on Hughes. Her original attraction to him, after all, had much to do with his status as a "breaker of things and of people"; plainly, the self-destructive part of her had craved such a consort, and if he had never existed, she would have had to invent him. While in some sense, moreover, Hughes may indeed have failed Plath, in her mind the failure was doubtless her own: their marriage was, so to speak, a postgraduate honors course that she could not pass. For just as she had aimed for excellence in school and college, she had also set herself the goal of being an A-plus wife and mother; what she could not accept was that one cannot conduct one's personal life as if they gave prizes for it, any more than one can write serious fiction or poetry while aiming, above all, to please some editor, whether at *Mademoiselle* or *The New Yorker.*

If Wagner-Martin renders Plath's marriage as something of a feminist domestic tragedy—with Hughes as the villain—Stevenson seems eager to prove that, in W. S. Merwin's words, "there was something in Sylvia of a cat suspended over water, but it was not Ted who had put her there or kept her there." The sharp contrast between the views of Wagner-Martin and Stevenson in this matter is reflected in their respective prefaces: whereas Wagner-Martin claims, in her preface, that her unwillingness to alter her manuscript in accordance with demands by Olwyn Hughes (Ted Hughes's sister and Plath's literary executor) led to a denial of permission to quote at length from Plath's works, Stevenson thanks both Ted and Olwyn for all sorts of assistance (and, by the way, quotes extensively from the poems). Stevenson appears to go out of her way to catalogue Plath's offenses, especially against her husband (for instance, her rudeness to his humble Yorkshire mother), and to point out the various ways in which she considers him to have been a positive force in Plath's life. Some of the latter observations—for example, the argument that Hughes made the *Ariel* poems possible by persuading Plath "to be true to her gift rather than to her ambition"—seem valid. But Stevenson's tone is too often prosecutorial, and sometimes one feels as if she is doing little more than proffering a list of the Hughes camp's long-nursed grievances. Plath's *Ariel* poems, we are reminded, have caused great pain "to the innocent victims of her pen"; after Plath's separation from Hughes, her frequent reference to her lawyer's instructions "helped to make negotiations ... difficult." To hear Stevenson tell it, Plath was always the one making things "difficult": time and again, the biographer leaves the impression that Hughes was a perfectly balanced and responsible man dealing as honorably as he could with a demented woman. Perhaps most astonishing of all is Stevenson's implication that the attraction between Hughes and Assia might never have developed into an affair had Plath reacted less hysterically upon noticing it—that, in short, Plath, not Hughes, was responsible for his adultery. All this is most unfortunate, for, such matters aside, Stevenson's is by far the most intelligent and sensitive of the Plath biographies; until Hughes steps onstage, Stevenson's picture of Plath rings truer, on the whole, than anyone else's.

What did the poet herself make of *Ariel*? It is interesting to note that Plath—presumably sensing that the *Ariel* poems' crude, superficial confessionalism was a deficiency, while not knowing precisely how to mitigate it in presenting her verses to an audience—described "Daddy" and "Lady Lazarus" to A. Alvarez as "some light verse." Likewise, in an apparent attempt to put over the idea that the voice in these poems was not hers but rather that of an imaginary persona, she told an interviewer that "Daddy" had as its speaker a girl whose father was actually a Nazi and whose mother "very possibly [was] part Jewish." Such addenda, of course, if seriously accepted by a reader, rob a poem like "Daddy" of what force it has, a force that derives precisely from the speaker's mad, unreasoning hate; yet the fact that Plath felt compelled to describe the poem in this fashion suggests that, even though she was incapable of eliminating the poem's weakness, she was astute enough to recognize where that weakness lay. It is only to be hoped that, in the next century, such astuteness in regard to Plath's work will be less rare than it is today among poetry readers, and that future generations will be less inclined to confuse questions of aesthetic significance with those of political serviceability or personal idolatry.

JACQUELINE ROSE

'Daddy'

Who will forgive me for the things I do ...
I think it would be better to be a Jew.
   (Anne Sexton, 'My Friend, My Friend', 1959)

I am lame in the memory.
   (Sylvia Plath, 'Little Fugue', 1962)

For a writer who has so consistently produced outrage in her critics, nothing has produced the outrage generated by Sylvia Plath's allusions to the Holocaust in her poetry, and nothing the outrage occasioned by 'Daddy', which is just one of the poems in which those allusions appear. Here is one such critic, important only for the clarity with which he lays out the terms of such a critique. Leon Wieseltier is reviewing Dorothy Rabinowicz's *New Lives: Survivors of the Holocaust* in an article entitled 'In a Universe of Ghosts', published in *The New York Review of Books*:

> Auschwitz bequeathed to all subsequent art perhaps the most arresting of all possible metaphors for extremity, but its availability has been abused. For many it was Sylvia Plath who broke the ice ... In perhaps her most famous poem, 'Daddy,' she was explicit ... There can be no disputing the genuineness of the pain here.

From *The Haunting of Sylvia Plath*: pp. 205–238. © 1991 by Jacqueline Rose.

But the Jews with whom she identifies were victims of something worse than 'weird luck'. Whatever her father did to her, it could not have been what the Germans did to the Jews. The metaphor is inappropriate ... I do not mean to lift the Holocaust out of the reach of art. Adorno was wrong—poetry can be made after Auschwitz and out of it ... But it cannot be done without hard work and rare resources of the spirit. Familiarity with the hellish subject must be earned, not presupposed. My own feeling is that Sylvia Plath did not earn it, that she did not respect the real incommensurability to her own experience of what took place.[1]

It is worth looking at the central terms on which this passage turns—the objection to Plath's identification with the Jew: 'the Jews with whom she identifies'; to the terms of that identification for introducing chance into Jewish history (into history): 'victims of something worse than "weird luck"'; above all, to Plath's failure to recognise the 'incommensurability to her experience of what took place'. Wieseltier is not alone in this criticism. Similarly, Joyce Carol Oates objects to Plath 'snatching [her word] metaphors for her predicament from newspaper headlines'; Seamus Heaney argues that in poems like 'Lady Lazarus', Plath harnesses the wider cultural reference to a 'vehemently self-justifying purpose'; Irving Howe describes the link as 'monstrous, utterly disproportionate'; and Marjorie Perloff describes Plath's references to the Nazis as 'empty' and 'histrionic', 'cheap shots', 'topical trappings', 'devices' which 'camouflage' the true personal meaning of the poems in which they appear.[2] On a separate occasion, Perloff compares Plath unfavourably to Lowell for the absence of any sense of personal or social history in her work.[3] The two objections seem to cancel and mirror each other—history is either dearth or surplus, either something missing from Plath's writing or something which shouldn't be there.

In all these criticisms, the key concept appears to be metaphor—either Plath trivialises the Holocaust through that essentially personal (it is argued) reference, or she aggrandises her experience by stealing the historical event. The Wieseltier passage makes it clear, however, that if the issue is that of metaphor ('Auschwitz bequeathed to all subsequent art perhaps the most arresting of all possible metaphors for extremity') what is at stake finally is a repudiation of metaphor itself—that is, of the necessary difference or distance between its two terms: 'Whatever her father did to her it cannot be what the Germans did to the Jews.' Plath's abuse (his word) of the Holocaust as metaphor (allowing for a moment that this is what it is) rests on the demand for commensurability, not to say identity, between image and experience, between language and event. In aesthetic terms, what Plath is being criticised for is a lack of 'objective correlative' (Perloff specifically uses the term[4]). But behind Wieseltier's objection, there is another demand—that only those who directly experienced the Holocaust have the right to speak of it—speak of it in what must be, by implication, non-metaphorical speech. The allusion to Plath in his article is there finally only to make this distinction—between the testimony of the survivors represented in Rabinowicz's book and the poetic metaphorisation (unearned, indirect, incommensurate) of Plath.

Turn the opening proposition of this quotation around, therefore, and we can read in it, not that 'Auschwitz bequeathed the most *arresting* of all possible metaphors for extremity', but that in relation to literary representation—or at least this conception of it—Auschwitz is the place where metaphor is *arrested*, where metaphor is brought to a halt. In this context, the critique of Plath merely underlines the fact that the Holocaust is the historical event which puts under greatest pressure—or is most readily available to put under such pressure—the concept of linguistic figuration. For it can be argued (it has recently been argued in relation to the critic Paul de Man) that, faced with the reality of the Holocaust, the idea that there is an irreducibly figurative dimension to all language is an evasion, or denial, of the reality of history itself.[5] But we should immediately add here that in the case of Plath, the question of metaphor brings with it—is inextricable from—that of fantasy and identification in so far as the image most fiercely objected to is the one which projects the speaker of the poem into the place of a Jew. The problem would seem to be, therefore, not the *slippage* of meaning, but its *fixing*—not just the idea of an inherent instability, or metaphoricity, of language, but the very specific fantasy positions which language can be used to move into place. Criticism of 'Daddy' shows the question of fantasy, which has appeared repeatedly as a difficulty in the responses to Plath's writing, in its fullest historical and political dimension.

In this final chapter, I want to address these objections by asking what the representation of the Holocaust might tell us about this relationship between metaphor, fantasy and identification, and then ask whether Sylvia Plath's 'Daddy' might not mobilise something about that relationship itself. The issue then becomes not whether Plath has the right to represent the Holocaust, but what the presence of the Holocaust in her poetry unleashes, or obliges us to focus, about, representation as such.

To pursue this question, I want first to take a detour through psychoanalysis, as the discourse which makes language and fantasy the direct object of its concern—specifically through the 1985 Hamburg Congress of the International Association of Psycho-Analysis, as the psychoanalytic event which illustrated most acutely the shared difficulty of language and fantasy in relation to the Holocaust itself.[6] To say that the Congress was 'about' Nazism and the Holocaust would, however, be a simplification given the conditions and difficulties in which it took place. It was the first Congress of the Association to be held in Germany since the Congress of Wiesbaden in 1932, and it was held in Hamburg only because an original invitation to Berlin had caused such an outcry that it had to be withdrawn. Hamburg, then, was the result of a compromise, the first of a series of compromises which continued with the organisational committee's decision that Nazism would not be referred to directly—not as history—but only in terms of clinical practice; that is, in terms of what patients who were survivors, the children of survivors or the children of Nazis brought to the psychoanalytic couch.[7] From the very beginning, therefore, and at every level of organisation, it was the problem of direct address, of direct representation, in relation to this historical moment, that was at stake.

Despite that decision to avoid direct historical reference, history and politics erupted on the fringes of the Congress in the inaugural meeting of 'International Psychoanalysts against Nuclear Weapons'. There is of course a direct connection to the Holocaust in the shared terminology: the term 'holocaust' was used to refer to the nuclear threat in 1949 before being projected back on to the camps. There is also a connection at the level of fantasy, made clearest by Hanna Segal's opening address on nuclear rhetoric, which she analysed in terms of the psychotic mechanisms of splitting and denial—the same mechanisms which were being negotiated and renegotiated in the cases described in the papers of the main event.[8] If all this was a sign of compromise, therefore, like all compromise-formations, it spoke as much as it concealed. Specifically, it spoke the fact that experience is no guarantee of memory since the Congress itself, like the cases it transcribed and in transcribing repeated, was so clearly operating under the dual imperative to remember and to forget. The very title of Hanna Segal's paper, 'Silence is the Real Crime', with all that it implied by way of an injunction, a historical urgency, to speak, was matched by the recognition, endlessly rehearsed in the main Congress, that speech itself is the problem, caught up as it is in the very fantasies she was describing, and nowhere more so than in relation to the Holocaust itself.

To say that the Congress was not addressing Nazism directly is, therefore, misleading inasmuch as the Congress found itself acting out, or repeating, the problem—or impossibility—of direct address in relation to Nazism and the Holocaust as such. At the opening session, Janine Chasseguet-Smirgel quoted these famous words from Freud: 'what has been abolished internally returns from the outside in the form of a delusion'.[9] In the memories of the patients, the Holocaust endlessly recurred in the form of such a delusion, demonstrating with painful clarity the detours which lie, of necessity, between memory and this (any) historical event.

No simple memory, therefore, especially for a second generation shown by analysis as in need of remembering to the precise extent that they did not participate concretely in the event. And no simple identification—not for this second generation but, equally and more crucially perhaps, not for the first generation. For if the experience of this generation was, historically, so unequivocal, their identifications at the level of fantasy constantly dislocated that certainty of historical place. I am referring here not only to what one writer described as the 'sacrilege' or 'disjunct parallelism' involved in juxtaposing the cases of the children of survivors to the children of Nazis (and the reverse)[10] but also, and even more, to the internal vicissitudes of identification revealed in the individual case-histories (two papers had the title 'Identification and its Vicissitudes in the Context of the Nazi Phenomenon').[11] Over and over again these patients found themselves in fantasy occupying either side of the victim/aggressor divide. Like the daughter of a German military family caught in a double role as victor and vanquished, and who thus mirrored, her analyst commented, the children of Jewish survivors who identify with the aggressor and victim alike;[12] or the two sons of the Third Reich fathers oscillating between the 'polar extremes of submission and exertion of power' as the 'defence of experiencing oneself as a victim' gradually met up with the 'repressed experience of harbouring the intentions of the perpetrator';[13] or the daughter of a member of the SS whose analyst comments—and not only in relation to her—on the conflict between the 'partial identities of the shame of the victim and the guilt of the culprit'.[14]

Suspended between these partial identities, these patients lived in a world of fantasy where actuality and memory both did and did not correspond (it would be ridiculous to suggest—even in cases of quasi-psychotic denial—that there was no connection between these fantasies and what they had concretely and historically experienced in the past). But what did emerge from these case-histories was that the question of historical participation in no sense exhausted that of identification and of fantasy—it did not settle the question of from where, and in what form, memory takes place. For being a victim does not stop you from identifying with the aggressor; being an aggressor does not stop you from identifying with the victim. To which we can add a formula only deceptively tautological—that being a victim (or aggressor) does not stop you from identifying with the victim (or aggressor). Identification is something that always has to be constructed. Wherever it is that subjects find themselves historically, this will not produce any one, unequivocal, identification as its logical effect.[15]

Look again at the term 'holocaust' and the ambivalence of identification can be seen to reside inside the very term. What special relationship—Zev Garber and Bruce Zuckerman have asked—does the concept of 'holocaust' set up between Nazi and Jew, what idea of supreme or chosen purpose, carrying as it does the biblical meaning of a sacrifice that is divinely inspired?[16] Track the term through Plath's poetry and the word appears first in this earlier biblical sense: 'Then hurl the bare world like a bluegreen ball / back into the holocaust' ('Song For a Revolutionary Love'), 'till the Announcer's voice is lost / in heresies of holocaust'! ('Insolent Storm Strikes at the Skull').[17] This meaning persists throughout Plath's writing—it could be said to be the meaning of *Ariel* itself: 'The meaning of Isaiah 29:1–2 seems to be that Jerusalem,' here (prophetically?) called Ariel, is to become like an altar, i.e., 'a scene of holocaust' ... 'The altar of holocausts is called the "ariel of God".'[18] This also suggests another interpretation of the passage: 'hoping for houses in a holocaust ...' discussed in Chapter 2 above.

This is not to deny that the oscillations revealed by these patients can be analysed partly in terms of a logic of the event—the perpetrators experience themselves as victims in order both to deny and to legitimate their role (to be a perpetrator you *have* first to 'be' a victim); the victim identifies with the aggressor out of retaliation in a situation where not only psychic but concrete survival is at stake. Primo Levi made this logic central to what he describes as 'ambiguity fatally provoked by oppression' in his last book, *The Drowned and the Saved*, in which he insists that there must be no historical confusion between the two roles ('precious service rendered (intentionally or not) to the negators of truth').[19]

There is no disagreement with this analysis, therefore, even if one suggests that it leaves a residue unexplained. And that is the very process of alternation—what it is that these partial and transferable identities reveal about the workings of fantasy itself. They show subjects taking up positions in the unconscious which are the opposite of the ones they occupy at the level of their conscious life. The one-sidedness of that conscious identity, even where it corresponds to the concretely lived experience (especially where it does so), is what causes the difficulty. The problem for Mrs B, for example, was not just the violence to which she had been subjected in the camps, but the fact that the extremity of it had made it impossible for her to accept those violent and extreme elements in herself.[20] Her need then was to recognise her own participation in the psychic positions she most desired to exclude. For it is the psychic exclusion or repudiation of those positions which, for psychoanalysis, is most likely to precipitate their projection or acting out. Exclusion turns into unconscious repetition.

For Hanna Segal at least, it is this mechanism which constitutes the political as much as the psychic threat. Thus nuclear rhetoric endlessly reproduces and legitimates a violence which it always locates outside itself, whose cause always, and by definition, belongs somewhere else—a rhetoric of violence which mobilises, not aggression (it denies, projects, splits off aggression) but defence. It is these mechanisms which, it can be argued, were at work in Nazism itself, and were rediscovered here in the fantasies of Nazis and their children, and then (risking that 'sacrilege' of 'disjunct parallelism') in those of the survivors and their children in turn. In *Night and Hope*, one of his collections of short stories about the camps, the Czech author Arnost Lustig writes: 'fear was merely the transformation of one's own thoughts into those of the enemy'.[21]

Projection is not, therefore, something that we can safely locate in the world of the psychotic alone. In his discussion of Schreber, Freud wrote:

> ... [projection] has a regular share assigned to it in our attitude towards the external world. For when we refer the causes of certain sensations to the external world, instead of looking for them (as we do in the case of others) inside ourselves, this normal proceeding, too, deserves to be called projection.[22]

As if he was suggesting that the way we distribute causality—the way we distinguish—between ourselves and others is something of a paranoid mechanism in itself. Think back to that analysis of Plath as answerable for everything in her life, to the battle that has constantly taken place around her over the location (inner or outer) of the cause, and her story can then be read as a saga of projection, whose fullest historical ramifications can be traced out beneath the surface of responses to, as well as inside, her late texts. Against the entire logic that has so often been brought to bear on Plath as woman and as writer, these cases suggest that psychological innocence is not guaranteed by the historical attribution of guilt (nor the reverse).

Is it going too far to suggest that what is being asked for in the cases described at the Hamburg Congress is a further act of identification, or rather a recognition on the part of these subjects that such an identification has *already* taken place? In the field of sexuality, such a demand has become fairly well known. As Freud puts it with reference to homosexual object-choice: 'By studying sexual excitations other than those that are manifestly displayed, [psychoanalytic research] has found that all human beings are capable of making a homosexual object-choice and *have in fact made one* in their unconscious' (my emphasis).[23] 'Recognise that unconscious desire' has become a commonplace of a recent sexual political version of Freud, meaning:

'Beyond that apparently assumed heterosexual identity in which you think you know yourself so well, know your unconscious participation in its other side.' For it is the homophobic who is most deeply and compulsively involved in the repudiation of homosexuality in him/herself (the social implications of such a general recognition would clearly be vast).

But what happens if we extend that demand beyond the world of neurosis and repression to that of psychosis and projection, where it is not a socially outlawed object of desire but a psychically and ethically unmanageable identification which is at stake? Could it be that the very different encounter between psychoanalysis and politics precipitated here (partially and tardily of necessity) by the Holocaust cannot help but produce this demand as its effect? Note just how far this takes us from those who criticise Plath for putting herself in the wrong place in 'Daddy', for putting herself—the two are, as we will see, inseparable in her poem—in the place of the Nazi as well as in the place of the Jew.

Go back once again to that criticism of Plath, specifically on the issue of metaphor, and it then appears that such a demand, such an identification, relies on the possibility of metaphor: the problem is not the presence of metaphor, but the risk that metaphor, along with the possibility of language itself, may be lost. Loss of metaphor is in itself a form of defence which threatens memory and identification alike. This is the central point of a paper by Ilse Grubrich-Simitis; 'From Concretism to Metaphor: Thoughts on Some Theoretical and Technical Aspects of the Psychoanalytic Work with Children of Holocaust Survivors', a paper not given at the Congress but one to which several of the other papers referred.[24] According to Grubrich-Simitis, the problem for these children of survivors is that the metaphoric function is *impaired*. They reify language into an object world whose blunt and repetitious literality, whose loss of figurality, signals the impossibility for these patients of grasping the nature of the event. They regard what they say as 'thinglike', unable to see it as 'something imagined or remembered', as something having the character of a sign.[25] As one analyst at the Congress put it, with direct reference to the paper: losing metaphor, they have lost that function 'without which the origins of language are unthinkable'.[26] Take metaphor out of language and there is no memory, no history, left.

In the analytic setting, this requires a return to the event, to what Grubrich-Simitis calls a 'non-metaphorical' recognition that it took place (a reversal, as she acknowledges, of that famous and infamous move from actuality to fantasy made by Freud).[27] But this return is made in order to *restore* the function of metaphor, to release the essentially metaphorical work of analysis itself: 'alongside poetry perhaps the metaphorical enterprise *par excellence*'.[28] Only in this way will these patients be freed from the literalness of a language which makes memory impossible—which, paradoxically, is the sign that they have no real knowledge that the Holocaust even took place. Only in this way, too, will they be able to acknowledge the aggressive side of fantasy which the loss of metaphor allows them simultaneously to erase. For metaphor is the recognition and suspension of aggression (the second as the condition of the first), allowing the subject to take up any one of these propositions in turn:

I want X but I do not intend to do it
I want X but I am not doing it
I do X (in fantasy) but I do not (actually) do it
I want X but I do not want to want it

—all mutations of an unspeakable desire, or rather one that can be spoken only to the extent that, as in analysis, as in poetry (the poetry of Plath, for example), it remains within the bounds of speech.

There is a sense here, therefore, in which we can truly say that metaphor was arrested in Auschwitz, in so far as the figural possibilities of language, without which 'the origins of language are unthinkable', are one of the things that the Holocaust put at risk. We can turn that criticism of Plath around again and ask: not whether the Holocaust is 'abused' by metaphor, but rather under what conditions of representation can the fantasies underpinning metaphor itself be spoken?

There is of course an inverse position on the representation of the Holocaust which situates it on the other side of representation itself, and can sometimes take the form of a privileging of poetry. According to Hannah Arendt, the judges at the trial of Eichmann rested their right to judge him on the distinction between 'deeds and motives' that belonged in the courtroom, and 'sufferings on so gigantic a scale' as to be '"beyond human understanding"', a matter for the '"great authors and poets"' of the world.[29] When George Steiner praises 'Daddy' as the 'Guernica of modern poetry', he makes the same point: 'perhaps it is only those who had no part in the events who can focus on them rationally and imaginatively' (Wieseltier takes issue with Steiner specifically on this).[30] Steiner underlines the metaphoric status of Plath's writing in the poem: 'committing the whole of her poetic and formal authority to metaphor, to the mask of language'; but in doing so he seems to attribute the fact of metaphor to poetic language alone. For the Holocaust theologian Emil Fackenheim; the Holocaust is a 'more than poetic truth', a truth that can be measured only by its failure to represent itself: 'each and every explanation is false, if not downright obscene, unless it is accompanied by a sense of utter inadequacy'.[31]

In this case, literature has become the repository for the non-representability of the event. For both positions, however—the rejection of metaphor, the demand for poetic representation alone—the Holocaust seems to be placed outside the domain of language proper, either in the before or beyond of language itself. The question of uniqueness and particularity is latent to the debate about language. The Holocaust can only represent itself, the Holocaust can only fail to be represented. The singularity of the Holocaust is that it is proper only to itself. Without taking sides in the dispute over the uniqueness of the Holocaust, we can notice its implications for—or rather, the extent of its implication *in*—the problem of what can and cannot, what should and should not, be represented in speech. Compare these lines from Karl Kraus, cited in one of the papers at the Hamburg Congress:

> Don't ask me why all this time I never spoke.
> Worldless am I,
> and won't say why ...
> The word expired when that world awoke.[32]

With these lines from the epigraph to Primo Levi's *If This Is A Man*:

> I commend these words to you ...
> Repeat them to your children,
>   Or may your house fall apart,
>   May illness impede you,
>   May your children turn their faces from you.[33]

An end to language that can be figured only in words, and an injunction to speech, to bear a witness whose impossibility Levi himself has described: 'I must repeat—we, the survivors, are not the true witnesses'.[34] Compare Paul Celan: 'Niemand / zeugt für den / Zeugen' ('Aschenglorie': 'No one / bears witness / for the witness').[35] How can one argue that certain writers do, or do not, have the right to represent the Holocaust, unless one has settled in advance, or suspended, these most fundamental paradoxes that the Holocaust opens up at the heart of language?

One more term, finally, from the criticism of Plath with which this chapter began—the concept of luck ('The Jews with whom she identifies were victims of something worse than "weird luck"'). It can be set against a moment from another representation of the Holocaust by the Ukrainian writer Piotr Rawicz, a survivor of the camps. At the end of his 1961 novel *Le sang du ciel* (translated in 1964 as *Blood From the Sky*), he adds this postscript:

> This book is not a historical record. If the notion of chance (like most other notions) did not strike the author as absurd, he would gladly say that any reference to a particular period, territory or race is purely coincidental. The events that he describes could crop up in any place, at any time, in the minds of any man, planet, mineral ...[36]

By introducing the element of chance back into the story, Rawicz opens up the issue of who should be able—who should be required—to recognise themselves in what took place. As he himself has argued in debate with Fackenheim, the experience of the Holocaust exceeds concrete participation in the event: 'those who physically lived through the Holocaust are not the only ones who experienced it'.[37] This observation is merely the other side of the recognition that experience and memory do not simply coincide. Note too the date of Rawicz's novel (1961), the historical gap which it signals between event and memory, between memory and writing. Add to this book a list of the other novels of the Holocaust that appeared in the early 1960s—Josef Bor's *Terezín Requiem* (1963), Elie Wiesel's *Night* (1960), Ilse Aichinger's *Herod's Children* (1963)—and we start to get a sense of the general, collective nature of that delay.[38] All these books are discussed in Alvarez's article 'Literature of the Holocaust', first published in *Commentary* in 1964, and reprinted in *Beyond All This Fiddle*, the collection which also includes the article he wrote on Plath at the time of her death.[39] If, therefore, the Holocaust appears as historical reference only in the last years of Plath's writing, the delay is coincident with the memory of the survivors themselves. Her tardiness mimics, or chimes in with, their own.

Forget in order to remember. Somewhere in the trials of this process, Plath's writing—at the most basic level—finds its place. Remember Hughes's statement on his destruction of Plath's last journals: that forgetting, the destruction of memory, was essential in order to survive: 'Two more notebooks *survived* for a while' ... 'in those days I regarded forgetfulness as essential to *survival*' (my emphasis).[40] The repetition is eloquent of the internal contradiction of this statement (its self-abolition?), which Hughes partly seems to recognise himself: 'in those days'. Annotating T.S. Eliot's *Four Quartets*, Plath writes: 'We live by memory of the past (the dead).'[41]

To all of this must be added another point of instability, and that is the instability of Jewishness itself. In his essay on Paul Celan, Jacques Derrida links this hesitancy of identity, of self-situating in relation to the Jew, to the question of holding, naming, remembering a moment by dating it in time. On 'Conversation in the Mountains'—the line 'July is not July'—he comments:

> This is in the course of a meditation on the Jew, son of a Jew, whose name is 'unpronounceable,' and who has nothing of his own, nothing that is not borrowed, so that, like a date, what is proper to the Jew is to have no property or essence. Jewish is not Jewish.[42]

But that very instability—of Jewishness and of the date—establishes the conditions of a general recognition: 'The Jew is also the other, myself and the other; I am Jewish in saying: the Jew is the other who has no essence, who has nothing of his own or whose essence is not to have one.'[43] Hence both the 'alleged universality of Jewish witness ("All the poets are Jews," says Marina Tsvetayeva, cited in epigraph to "Und mit dem Buch aus Tarussa") and the incommunicable secret of the Judaic idiom, the singularity of its "unpronounceable name"'.[44] What I am focusing on here, however, what I read in Plath, is a related but distinct form of uncertainty—the point at which the abyss at the centre of Jewish identity, for the one who is Jewish and not Jewish, appears in the form of a drama about psychic aggression and guilt.

Most obviously, this is the subject of Anne Sexton's poem 'My Friend, My Friend', on which, it has been argued, Plath's 'Daddy' was based.[45] The poem was written in the year Sexton and Plath attended Lowell's poetry class in Boston together. In this poem, Jewish is an enviable state. It confers origin and divine paternity—the conditions of forgiveness for a crime that is never named:

> Who will forgive me for the things I do?
> With no special legend or God to refer to,
> With my calm white pedigree, my yankee kin.
> I think it would be better to be a Jew.

Victim, without agency, the Jew escapes the burden of historic (of any) guilt:

> I forgive you for what you did not do.
> I am impossibly guilty. Unlike you,
> My friend, I cannot blame my origin
> With no special legend or God to refer to.

For the speaker of this poem, Jewishness offers the possibility of a symbolic deferral of guilt. Blaming one's origin—the poem makes its own diagnosis—is nothing less than the ultimate, divinely sanctioned, attribution, or projection, of the cause. Victimisation becomes an advantage of which its bearer can then be *accused*: 'I forgive you for what you did not do'. The total innocence of the Jew, for the one who is not Jewish, turns into a form of guilt. According to the strictest logic of projection, the Jew becomes culpable for the fact that she cannot be blamed.

As the poem progresses, the guilt comes to centre on the death of the mother, a death experienced as the 'first release' of the speaker of the poem:

> Watching my mother slowly die I knew
> My first release. I wish some ancient bugaboo
> Followed me. But my sin is always my sin.

This is the only content attributed, albeit indirectly, to that impossible burden of guilt, other than the guilt, collective, of simply not being a Jew: 'my calm white pedigree, my yankee kin'. At another level, guilt can remain without content, precisely in so far as it takes the form of a relentless self-accusation, one that the speaker of the poem makes over and again of herself: the repeated refrain 'Who will forgive me for the things I do?', to which the line 'I think it would be better to be a Jew' comes as the repeated reply. In this little-known poem by Anne Sexton, only recently unearthed from the *Antioch Review* of 1959 and published in a selection of her work, Jewishness is offered unequivocally, if not unapologetically, as an object of desire. It is as if Sexton is answering in advance those who criticise Plath on the grounds that her identification with the Jew serves some personal purpose. For what could be an identification *without* purpose? In Sexton's poem, the desire to be Jewish reveals the tendentiousness (and guilt) of identification as such.

In Sexton's poem, the guilt centres on the mother. By transposing the dilemma on to the father, Plath shifts this drama into the realm of symbolic as well as personal law. The father carries the weight, not only of guilt, but of historic memory. In 'Little Fugue', one of the less well known poems from *Ariel* and forerunner of 'Daddy', Plath presents the relation to the father most directly in terms of a language or communication that fails:

> The yew's black fingers wag;
> Cold clouds go over.
> So the deaf and dumb
> Signal the blind, and are ignored.[46]

In fact the poem does not start with failed communication, but with the complete loss of the physical conditions that make communication possible. Deaf and dumb signalling to blind—there are no words here, and what there is in the place of words still goes astray. Likewise, the memory of the speaker's father takes the form of a confusion in the register of signs:

> Deafness is something else.
> Such a dark funnel, my father!
> I see your voice
> Black and leafy, as in my childhood.
>
> A yew hedge of orders,
> Gothic and barbarous, pure German.
> Dead men cry from it.
> I am guilty of nothing.

What does it mean here to 'see a voice'? To be deaf to it?—not in the sense of hearing nothing, but of hearing, of seeing too much. That voice is pure German, a surfeit of orders that is full of the cries of dead men. The poem proposes an impossible alternative at the level of language: signs that are empty because they cannot be heard, either by those who utter or by those who fail to see them, and a language pure only in its powers of destruction, which can speak finally only from the place of the dead. Before the first of these two stanzas, the original draft has: 'The yew is many-footed. / Each foot stops a mouth. / So the yew is a go-between: talks for the dead.' According to Robert Graves, there is a belief in Brittany that churchyard yews spread a root to the mouth of each corpse.[47]

In all this, guilt is not located. Isolated at the end of the verse, the line 'I am guilty of nothing' can be read back retroactively into the cries of the dead men heard in the voice of the father, into—as a consequence—the father's own voice, or into the voice of the speaker herself. The line works at once as denial and as plaint. Doubling over or disappearing into itself as utterance— dead men inside the voice of the father inside the voice of the poet who speaks—it stages a crisis in the historical location of guilt. Plath removes from the first draft at the start of the stanza: 'This dominates me', which offers a more exact, more precisely and directly oppressive, distribution of roles.

In fact, 'Little Fugue' repeatedly unsettles the subjective positions on which such a distribution depends. In the second stanza of the poem, the yew's 'black fingers' meet the 'featurelessness' of a cloud that is 'white as an eye all over! / The eye of the blind pianist'. Black and white, yew and eye, you and I—in the finger alphabet described by Graves, the letter of the yew tree is the 'I' which is also the death vowel. Death belongs on either side of the binaries—yew/eye: you/I—on which the poem repeatedly puns. It slides from the yew tree to the father, but then, since 'yew' equals 'I', on to the speaker herself. The slippage of the pronouns produces an identity between the speaker and the father she accuses. In 'Little Fugue', therefore, the relationship to the father belongs on the axis of identification, as much as—in this poem to the exclusion of—that of desire (this point will be crucial for 'Daddy').

But if the poem produces such a radical destabilisation, such an unsettling of its enunciative place, it equally offers a more direct sequence, something in the order of a transmission or inheritance passed from the father to the child. The speaker takes on, finds herself forced to utter, words silenced by her father's refusal to speak:

> And you, during the Great War
> In the California delicatessen
>
> Lopping the sausages!
> They color my sleep,
> Red, mottled like cut necks.
> There was a silence!
>
> Great silence of another order.
> I was seven, I knew nothing.
> The world occurred.
> You had one leg, and a Prussian mind.
>
> Now similar clouds
> Are spreading their vacuous sheets.
> Do you say nothing?
> I am lame in the memory.

The sequence seems to offer a narrative of silence. This silence ensures that the war can be known only in the sleep of the child who did not live through it, the same child for whom it also represents the coming into being of the world: 'I was seven, I knew nothing. / The world occurred.' It cripples the speaker's memory, maims her like her one-legged father. The identification between them is only one part of a repetition already guaranteed by the fact that what happened has still not been spoken in words. As the poem shifts from the general 'There was a silence!' to the particular 'Do you say nothing?', the father's silence becomes accountable for the speaker's inability to write her own history—'I am lame in the memory'—as well as for the destiny of the world: 'Now similar clouds / Are spreading their vacuous sheets'. In an article published in *Encounter* in September 1963, 'In Search of a Lost Language', Hans Magnus Enzensberger describes Germany as 'mute', a 'speechless country'—hence the linguistic paralysis which afflicted German poets after the war.[48] The silence figured in this poem thus mimics, as Judith Kroll has pointed out, a more general postwar silence that was laid on the German tongue. This silence can therefore be called historical in two senses—accountable for the future, a product of the trauma of the past. The tense of 'Little Fugue' then becomes the psychoanalytic tense of the future perfect: 'What I shall have been for what I am in the process of becoming'.[49] Remembering for the future—the very formula that has been chosen for returning to the Holocaust today.[50]

To argue that the personal accusation against the father is part of a more collective dilemma about memory is not, however, to substitute a historical for the more common, personal and psychological reading of Plath's work (the alternative that Perloff seems to propose) but to suggest that Plath is writing from a place where they are precisely inseparable. As a title, 'Little Fugue' condenses these different levels in itself—fugue as (historic) flight, fugue as a technical term for psychological amnesia, a temporary flight from reality, according to Webster (cause and/or effect of the first), as well as the music of the blind pianist (a little, not gross, fugue). The last lines of the poem are particularly apposite here:

I survive the while
Arranging my morning.
These are my fingers, this my baby.
The clouds are a marriage dress, of that pallor.

They move the poem into the speaker's personal present—temporary survivor: 'I survive the while'. So easily reduced, after the fact, to the level of personal, biographical premonition (only a while to survive), the line can equally be read as 'this transitional time is the medium in which—or what—I have to survive'. Note too the allusion to the line 'I sing the while' from Blake's 'Infant Joy', an allusion which evokes a poetic and linguistic tradition in which the speaker cannot take her place: she does not sing to her child, she only survives (like the Holocaust survivor who, until approximately this moment, survives but does not speak). The dilemma is thus both more and less than the dilemma of the woman writer oppressed by a male tradition in which she cannot find her voice. Likewise, 'Arranging my morning'—the speaker prepares her death (arranging her own mourning), or the speaker completes a mourning that has been historically denied: 'The second generation mourns the denied mourning of their parents' (Hillel Klein and Ilany Kogan, 'Identification Processes and Denial in the Shadow of Nazism').[51]

In 'Little Fugue', the personal present is engendered in its possibility—provisional, precarious—by the drama of a fully historical past. To say, in this context, that Plath uses history as metaphor is to establish a hierarchy of levels—the historic simply signifies the personal drama—and by implication a hierarchy of values between the two levels, which overlooks something presented here more as a sequence, more in the nature of a logic of the event. Inside that sequence, the form of determination between the historic and the psychic instance is impossible to pin down in any easy way. What the poem seems to narrate is at once the historical engendering of personal time and the psychic engendering of history.

'Daddy' is a much more difficult poem to write about.[52] It is of course the poem of the murder of the father which at the very least raises the psychic stakes. It is, quite simply, the more aggressive poem. Hence, no doubt, its founding status in the mythology of Sylvia Plath. Reviewing the American publication of *Ariel* in 1966, *Time* magazine wrote:

> Within a week of her death, intellectual London was hunched over copies of a strange and terrible poem she had written during her last sick slide toward suicide. 'Daddy' was its title; its subject was her morbid love-hatred of her father; its style was as brutal as a truncheon. What is more, 'Daddy' was merely the first jet of flame from a literary dragon who in the last months of her life breathed a burning river of bale across the literary landscape.[53]

Writing on the Holocaust, Jean-François Lyotard suggests that two motifs tend to operate in tension, or to the mutual exclusion of each other—the preservation of memory against forgetfulness and the accomplishment of vengeance.[54] Do 'Little Fugue' and 'Daddy' take up the two motifs one after the other, or do they present something of their mutual relation, the psychic economy that ties them even as it forces them apart? There is a much clearer narrative in 'Daddy'—from victimisation to revenge. In this case it is the form of that sequence which has allowed the poem to be read purely personally as Plath's vindictive assault on Otto Plath and Ted Hughes (the transition from the first to the second mirroring the biographical pattern of her life). Once again, however, it is only that preliminary privileging of the personal which allows the reproach for her evocation of history—more strongly this time, because this is the poem in which Plath identifies with the Jew.

The first thing to notice is the trouble in the time sequence of this poem in relation to the father, the technically impossible temporality which lies at the centre of the story it tells, which echoes that earlier impossibility of language in 'Little Fugue':

DADDY

You do not do, you do not do
Any more, black shoe
In which I have lived like a foot
For thirty years, poor and white,
Barely daring to breathe, or Achoo.

Daddy, I have had to kill you.
You died before I had time—
Marble-heavy, a bag full of God,
Ghastly statue, with one gray toe
Big as a Frisco seal

And a head in the freakish Atlantic
Where it pours bean green over blue
In the waters off beautiful Nauset.
I used to pray to recover you.
Ach, du.

What is the time sequence of these verses? On the one hand, a time of unequivocal resolution, the end of the line, a story that once and for all will be brought to a close: 'You do not do, you do not do / Any more'. This story is legendary. It is the great emancipatory narrative of liberation which brings, some would argue, all history to an end. In this case, it assimilates, combines into one entity, more than one form of oppression—daughter and father, poor and rich—licensing a reading which makes of the first the meta-narrative of all forms of inequality (patriarchy the cause of all other types of oppression, which it then subordinates to itself). The poem thus presents itself as protest and emancipation from a condition which reduces the one oppressed to the barest minimum of human, but inarticulate, life: 'Barely daring to breathe or Achoo' (it is hard not to read here a reference to Plath's sinusitis). Blocked, hardly daring to breathe or to sneeze, this body suffers because the father has for too long oppressed.

If the poem stopped here then it could fairly be read, as it has often been read, in triumphalist terms—instead of which it suggests that such an ending is only a beginning, or repetition, which immediately finds itself up against a wholly other order of time: 'Daddy, I have had to kill you. / You died before I had time.' In Freudian terms, this is the time of '*Nachtraglichkeit*' or after-effect: a murder which has taken place, but after the fact, because the father who is killed is already dead; a father who was once mourned ('I used to pray to recover you') but whose recovery has already been signalled, by what precedes it in the poem, as the precondition for his death to be repeated. Narrative as repetition—it is a familiar drama in which the father must be killed in so far as he is already dead. This at the very least suggests that, if this is the personal father, it is also what psychoanalysis terms the father of individual prehistory, the father who establishes the very possibility (or impossibility) of history as such.[55] It is through this father that the subject discovers—or fails to discover—her own history, as at once personal and part of a wider symbolic place. The time of historical emancipation immediately finds itself up against the problem of a no less historical, but less certain, psychic time.

This is the father as godhead, as origin of the nation and the word graphically figured in the image of the paternal body in bits and pieces spreading across the American nation state: bag full of God, head in the Atlantic, big as a Frisco seal. Julia Kristeva terms this father '*Père imaginaire*', which she then abbreviates 'PI'.[56] Say those initials out loud in French and what you get is 'pays' (country or nation)—the concept of the exile. Much has been made of Plath as an exile, as she goes back and forth between England and the United States. But there is another history of migration, another prehistory, which this one overlays—of her father, born in Grabow, the Polish Corridor, and her mother's Austrian descent: 'you are talking to me as a general American. In particular, my background is, may I say, German and Austrian.'[57]

If this poem is in some sense about the death of the father, a death both willed and premature, it is no less about the death of language. Returning to the roots of language, it discovers a personal and political history (the one as indistinguishable from the other) which once again fails to enter into words:

In the German tongue, in the Polish town
Scraped flat by the roller
Of wars, wars, wars.
But the name of the town is common.
My Polack friend

Says there are a dozen or two.
So I never could tell where you
Put your foot, your root,
I never could talk to you.
The tongue stuck in my jaw.

It stuck in a barb wire snare.
Ich, ich, ich, ich,
I could hardly speak.
I thought every German was you.
And the language obscene

Twice over, the origins of the father, physically and in language, are lost—
through the wars which scrape flat German tongue and Polish town, and
then through the name of the town itself, which is so common that it fails
in its function to identify, fails in fact to name. Compare Claude Lanzmann,
the film-maker of *Shoah*, on the Holocaust as 'a crime to forget the name',
or Lyotard: 'the destruction of whole worlds of names'.[58] Wars wipe out
names, the father cannot be spoken to, and the child cannot talk, except
to repeat endlessly, in a destroyed obscene language, the most basic or
minimal unit of self-identity in speech: 'ich, ich, ich, ich' (the first draft
has 'incestuous' for 'obscene'). The notorious difficulty of the first-person
pronoun in relation to identity its status as shifter, the division or splitting
of the subject which it both carries and denies—is merely compounded by
its repetition here. In a passage taken out of her journals, Plath comments
on this 'I':

> I wouldn't be I. But I am I now; and so many other millions are
> so irretrievably their own special variety of 'I' that I can hardly
> bear to think of it. I: how firm a letter; how reassuring the three
> strokes: one vertical, proud and assertive, and then the two short
> horizontal lines in quick, smug, succession. The pen scratches on
> the paper I ... I ... I .. I .. I ... I.[59]

The effect, of course, if you read it aloud, is not one of assertion but, as with
'ich, ich, ich, ich', of the word sticking in the throat. Pass from that trauma of
the 'I' back to the father as a 'bag full of God', and 'Daddy' becomes strikingly
resonant of the case of a woman patient described at Hamburg, suspended
between two utterances: 'I am God's daughter' and 'I do not know what I am'
(she was the daughter of a member of Himmler's SS).[60]

In the poem, the 'I' moves backwards and forwards between German and English, as does the 'you' ('Ach, du'). The dispersal of identity in language follows the lines of a division or confusion between nations and tongues. In fact language in this part of the poem moves in two directions at once. It appears in the form of translation, and as a series of repetitions and overlappings—'ich', 'Ach', 'Achoo'—which dissolve the pronoun back into infantile, patterns of sound. Note too how the rhyming pattern of the poem sends us back to the first line. 'You do not do, you do not do', and allows us to read it as both English and German: 'You du not du', 'You you not you'—'you' as 'not you' because 'you' do not exist inside a space where linguistic address would be possible.

I am not suggesting, however, that we apply to Plath's poem the idea of poetry as *écriture* (women's writing as essentially multiple, the other side of normal discourse, fragmented by the passage of the unconscious and the body into words). Instead the poem seems to be outlining the conditions under which that celebrated loss of the symbolic function takes place. Identity and language lose themselves in the place of the father whose absence gives him unlimited powers. Far from presenting this as a form of liberation—language into pure body and play—Plath's poem lays out the high price, at the level of fantasy, that such a psychic process entails. Irruption of the semiotic (Kristeva's term for that other side of normal language), which immediately transposes itself into an alien, paternal tongue.

Plath's passionate desire to learn German and her constant failure to do so, is one of the refrains of both her journals and her letters home: 'Wickedly didn't do German for the last two days, in a spell of perversity and paralysis' ... 'do German (that I *can* do)' 'German and French would give me self-respect, why don't I act on this?' ... 'Am very painstakingly studying German two hours a day'... 'At least I have begun my German. Painful, as if "part were cut out of my brain"' ... 'Worked on German for two days, then let up' ... 'Take hold. Study German today.'[61] In *The Bell Jar*, Esther Greenwood says: 'every time I picked up a German dictionary or a German book, the very sight of those dense, black, barbed wire letters made my mind shut like a clam'.[62]

If we go back to the poem, then I think it becomes clear that it is this crisis of representation in the place of the father which is presented by Plath as engendering—forcing, even—her identification with the Jew. Looking for the father, failing to find him anywhere, the speaker finds him everywhere instead. Above all, she finds him everywhere in the language which she can neither address to him nor barely speak. It is this hallucinatory transference which turns every German into the image of the father, makes for the obscenity of the German tongue, and leads directly to the first reference to the Holocaust:

> And the language obscene
>
> An engine, an engine
> Chuffing me off like a Jew.
> A Jew to Dachau, Auschwitz, Belsen.
> I began to talk like a Jew.
>
> I think I may well be a Jew.
> The snows of the Tyrol, the clear beer of Vienna
> Are not very pure or true.
> With my gypsy ancestress and my weird luck
> And my Taroc pack and my Taroc pack
> I may be a bit of a Jew.

The only metaphor here is that first one that cuts across the stanza break—'the language obscene // An engine, an engine'—one of whose halves is language. The metaphor therefore turns on itself, becomes a comment on the (obscene) language which generates the metaphor as such. More important still, metaphor is by no means the dominant trope when the speaker starts to allude to herself as a Jew:

> Chuffing me off *like* a Jew.
> I began to talk *like* a Jew.
> I *think* I may well be a Jew.
> I may be a *bit* of a Jew.

Plath's use of simile and metonymy keeps her at a distance, opening up the space of what is clearly presented as a partial, hesitant, and speculative identification between herself and the Jew. The trope of identification is not substitution but displacement, with all that it implies by way of instability in any identity thereby produced. Only in metaphor proper does the second, substituting term wholly oust the first; in simile, the two terms are co-present, with something more like a slide from one to the next; while metonymy is, in its very definition, only ever partial (the part stands in for the whole).

If the speaker claims to be a Jew, then, this is clearly not a simple claim ('claim' is probably wrong here). For this speaker, Jewishness is the position of the one without history or roots: 'So I never could tell where you / Put your foot, your root'. Above all, it is for her a question, each time suspended or tentatively put, of her participation and implication in the event. What the poem presents us with, therefore, is precisely the problem of trying to claim a relationship to an event in which—the poem makes it quite clear—the speaker did not participate. Given the way Plath stages this as a problem in the poem, presenting it as part of a crisis of language and identity, the argument that she simply uses the Holocaust to aggrandise her personal difficulties seems completely beside the point. Who can say that these were not difficulties which she experienced in her very person?[63]

If this claim is not metaphorical, then, we should perhaps also add that neither is it literal. The point is surely not to try and establish whether Plath was part Jewish or not. The fact of her being Jewish could not *legitimate* the identification—it is, after all, precisely offered as an identification—any more than the image of her father as a Nazi which now follows can be *invalidated* by reference to Otto Plath. One old friend wrote to Plath's mother on publication of the poem in the review of *Ariel* in *Time* in 1966 to insist that Plath's father had been nothing like the image in the poem (the famous accusation of distortion constantly brought to bear on Plath).[64] Once again these forms of identification are not exclusive to Plath. Something of the same structure appears at the heart of Jean Stafford's most famous novel, *A Boston Adventure*, published in 1946.[65] The novel's heroine, Sonie Marburg, is the daughter of immigrants, a Russian mother and a German father who eventually abandons his wife and child. As a young woman, Sonie finds herself adopted by Boston society in the 1930s. Standing in a drawing-room, listening to the expressions of anti-Semitism, she speculates:

> I did not share Miss Pride's prejudice and while neither did I feel strongly partisan towards Jews, the subject always embarrassed me because, not being able to detect Hebraic blood at once except in a most obvious face, I was afraid that someone's toes were being trod on.[66]

It is only one step from this uncertainty, this ubiquity and invisibility of the Jew, to the idea that she too might be Jewish: 'And even here in Miss Pride's sitting-room where there was no one to be offended (unless I myself were partly Jewish, a not unlikely possibility) ...'.[67] Parenthetically and partially, therefore, Sonie Marburg sees herself as a Jew. Like Plath, the obverse of this is to see the lost father as a Nazi: 'what occurred to me as [Mrs. Hornblower] was swallowed up by a crowd of people in the doorway was that perhaps my father, if he had gone back to Wurzburg, had become a Nazi'[68]—a more concrete possibility in Stafford's novel, but one which turns on the same binary, father/daughter, Nazi/Jew, that we see in Plath.

In Plath's poem, it is clear that these identities are fantasies, not for the banal and obvious reason that they occur inside a text, but because the poem addresses the production of fantasy as such. In this sense, I read 'Daddy' as a poem about its own conditions of linguistic and phantasmic production. Rather than casually produce an identification, it asks a question about identification, laying out one set of intolerable psychic conditions under which such an identification with the Jew might take place.

Furthermore—and this is crucial to the next stage of the poem— these intolerable psychic conditions are also somewhere the condition, or grounding, of paternal law. For there is a trauma or paradox internal to identification in relation to the father, one which is particularly focused by the Holocaust itself. At the Congress, David Rosenfeld described the 'logical-pragmatic paradox' facing the children of survivors: 'to be like me you must go away and not be like me; to be like your father, you must not be like your father'.[69] Lyotard puts the dilemma of the witness in very similar terms: 'if death is there [at Auschwitz], you are not there; if you are there, death is not there. Either way it is impossible to prove that death is there'[70] (compare Levi on the failure of witness). For Freud, such a paradox is structural, Oedipal, an inseparable part of that identification with the father of individual prehistory which is required of the child: '[The relation of the superego] to the ego is not exhausted by the precept: "You *ought to be* like this (like your father)." It also comprises the prohibition: "You *may not be* like this (like your father)".'[71] Paternal law is therefore grounded on an injunction which it is impossible to obey. Its cruelty, and its force, reside in the form of the enunciation itself.

'You stand at the blackboard, Daddy / In the picture I have of you'—it is not the character of Otto Plath, but his symbolic position which is at stake. In her story 'Among the Bumblebees', Plath writes of the—father: 'Alice's father feared nothing. Power was good because it was power.'[72] Commenting on what he calls the 'père-version' of the father, the French psychoanalyst Jacques Lacan writes: 'nothing worse than a father who proffers the law on everything. Above all, spare us any father educators, rather let them be in retreat on any position as master.'[73] The reference is to the father of Schreber, eminent educationalist in pre-Nazi Germany, whose gymnasia have been seen as part of the institutional and ideological prehistory of what was to come.[74] It might then be worth quoting the following lines from Otto Plath's 'Insect Societies' (he was a professor of entomology, famous for his work *Bumblebees and their Ways*).[75] Whether or not they tell us anything about what he was like as a person, they can be cited as one version of such paternal 'perversion', of such an impossible paternal ideal: 'When we see these intelligent insects dwelling together in orderly communities of many thousands of individuals, their social instincts developed to a high degree of perfection, making their marches with the regularity of disciplined troops ...', or this citation from another professor, with which he concludes:

> Social instincts need no machinery of control over antisocial instincts. They simply have no antisocial tendencies. These were thoroughly eliminated many millions of years ago and the insects have progressed along a path of perfect social coordination. They have no need for policemen, lawyers, government officials, preachers or teachers because they are innately social. They have no need of learning the correct social responses. These are predetermined by their social constitution at the time of birth.[76]

Loss or absence of the father, but equally symbolic overpresence of the father (only the first is normally emphasised in relation to Plath)—it is the father as master who encapsulates the paradox at the heart of the paternal function, who most forcefully demands an identification which he also has to withhold or refuse. On more than one occasion, Plath relates the celebrated violence of her writing to the violence of that function. In 'Among the Bumblebees', the father sits marking scripts: 'the vicious little red marks he made on the papers were the color of the blood that oozed out in a thin line the day she cut her finger with the bread knife'.[77] And if we go back for a moment to 'Little Fugue', the same image can be traced out underneath the repeated 'blackness' of that text. On the back of the first draft is the passage from *The Bell Jar* in which Esther Greenwood is almost raped. The typescript has this line—'In that light, the blood looked black'—crossed out and replaced with this one written by hand: 'Blackness, like ink, spread over the handkerchief'.[78] Underneath the poem to the father, a violence of writing—the poem's writing (the ink on the page), but equally his own. For those who would insist that what mattered most for Plath was the loss of her father, we might add that the only other father who can stand in for this overmastery of the paternal function is the father who is dead.

One could then argue that it is this paradox of paternal identification that Nazism most visibly inflates and exploits. For doesn't Nazism itself also turn on the image of the father, a father enshrined in the place of the symbolic, all-powerful to the extent that he is so utterly out of reach? (and not only Nazism—Ceausescu preferred orphans to make up his secret police). By rooting the speaker's identification with the Jew in the issue of paternity, Plath's poem enters into one of the key phantasmic scenarios of Nazism itself. As the poem progresses, the father becomes more and more of a Nazi (note precisely that this identity is not given, but is something which emerges).

Instead of being found in every German, what is most frighteningly German is discovered retrospectively in him:

> I have always been scared of you
> With your Luftwaffe, your gobbledygoo.
> And your neat moustache,
> And your Aryan eye, bright blue.
> Panzer-man, panzer-man, O You—
>
> Not God but a swastika
> So black no sky could squeak through.

The father turns into the image of the Nazi, a string of clichés and childish nonsense ('your gobbledygoo'), of attributes and symbols (again the dominant trope is metonymy) which accumulate, and cover the sky. This is of course a parody—the Nazi as a set of empty signs. The image could be compared with Virginia Woolf's account of the trappings of fascism in *Three Guineas*.[79]

Not that this makes him any the less effective, any the less frightening, any the less desired. In its most notorious statement, the poem suggests that victimisation by this feared and desired father is one of the fantasies at the heart of fascism, one of the universal attractions for women of fascism itself. As much as predicament, victimisation is also *pull*:

> Every woman adores a fascist,
> The boot in the face, the brute
> Brute heart of a brute like you.

For feminism, these are the most problematic lines of the poem—the mark of a desire that should not speak its name, or the shameful insignia of a new license for women in the field of sexuality which has precisely gone too far: 'In acknowledging that the politically correct positions of the Seventies were oversimplified, we are in danger of simply saying once more that sex is a dark mystery, over which we have no control. "Take me—I'm yours", or "Every woman adores a fascist".'[80] The problem is only compounded by the ambiguity of the lines which follow that general declaration. Who is putting the boot in the face? The fascist certainly (woman as the recipient of a sexual violence she desires). But, since the agency of these lines is not specified, don't they also allow that it might be the woman herself (identification *with* the fascist being what every woman desires)?

There is no question, therefore, of denying the problem of these lines. Indeed, if you allow that second reading, they pose the question of women's implication in the ideology of Nazism more fundamentally than has normally been supposed.[81] But notice how easy it is to start dividing up and sharing out the psychic space of the text, Either Plath's identification with the Jew is the problem, or her desire for/identification with the fascist. Either her total innocence or her total guilt. But if we put these two objections or difficulties together? Then what we can read in the poem is a set of reversals which have meaning only in relation to each other: reversals not unlike those discovered in the fantasies of the patients described at Hamburg, survivors, children of survivors, children of Nazis—disjunct and sacrilegious parallelism which Plath's poem anticipates and repeats.

If the rest of the poem then appears to give a narrative of resolution to this drama, it does so in terms which are no less ambiguous than what has gone before. The more obviously personal narrative of the next stanzas—death of the father, attempted suicide at twenty, recovery of the father in the image of the husband—is represented as return or repetition: 'At twenty I tried to die / And get back, back, back to you' ... 'I made a model of you', followed by emancipation: 'So Daddy I'm finally through', and finally 'Daddy, daddy, you bastard, I'm through'. They thus seem to turn into a final, triumphant sequence the two forms of temporality which were offered at the beginning of the poem. Plath only added the last stanza—'There's a stake in your fat black heart', etc.—in the second draft to drive the point home, as it were (although even 'stake' can be read as signalling a continuing investment).

But for all that triumphalism, the end of the poem is ambiguous. For that 'through' on which the poem ends is given only two stanzas previously as meaning both ending: 'So daddy, I'm finally through' and the condition, even if failed in this instance, for communication to be possible: 'The voices just can't worm through'. How then should we read that last line—'Daddy, daddy, you bastard, I'm through'? Communication *as* ending, or dialogue *without end*? Note too how the final vengeance in itself turns on an identification—'you bastard'—that is, 'you father without father', 'you, whose father, like my own, is in the wrong place'.[82]

A point about the more personal narrative offered in these last stanzas, for it is the reference to the death of the father, the attempted suicide, and the marriage which calls up the more straightforward biographical reading of this text. Note, however, that the general does not conceal—'camouflage'—the particular or personal meaning. It is, again, the relationship of the two levels—which is important (it is that relationship, part sequence, part overdetermination, which the poem transcribes). But even at the most personal level of this poem, there is something more general at stake. For the link that 'Daddy' represents between suicide and a paternity, at once personal and symbolic, is again not exclusive to Plath.

At the end of William Styron's *Lie Down in Darkness*, Peyton, with whose suicide the book opened, is allowed to tell her story; the book has worked backwards from her death to its repetition through her eyes. In one of her last moments, she thinks—encapsulating in her thoughts the title of the book—'I've sinned only in order to lie down in darkness and find, somewhere in the net of dreams, a new father, a new home.'[83] And then, as if in response to that impossible dream—impossible amongst other things because of the collapse of the myth of America on Nagasaki day, the day Peyton dies—the book ends with a 'Negro' revival baptism, as the servants of the family converge on the mass congregation of 'Daddy Faith'. As if the book was suggesting that the only way forward after the death of Peyton was into a grossly inflated symbolic paternity definitively lost to middle America, available only to those whom that same America exploits.[84] 'Daddy' is not far from this—if it is a suicide poem, it is so only to the extent that it locates a historically actualised vacancy, and excess, at the heart of symbolic, paternal law.

*   *   *

I have said relatively little about the sexual politics of the poem. Although there is nothing to mark its gender identity until fairly late, the poem can none the less be read as offering—after Sherry Ortner—the equation 'as father to daughter' so 'Nazi to Jew' (Ortner's formula was 'as nature to culture' so 'woman to man').[85] According to this interpretation, the representation of the father as Nazi would reveal something about the violence of patriarchy (patriarchy as violence). The speaker's own violence would then be a legitimate and triumphant retaliation—one feminist reading of the text. Clearly this is one way in which the poem can be read, but, taken on its own, the celebration of this narrative seems as problematic as that other feminist celebration of the breakdown or fragmentation of language to which I have already referred.

Assertion of the ego versus a body and language without identity or form—these are two positions on the poetic language of women which correspond respectively to the political demand for equality and to the demand for difference in the most fundamental psychic sense of the term. But perhaps more than any other poem by Plath, 'Daddy' seems to offer a type of corrective in advance to them both. It demonstrates the psychic and political cost of that desire for fragmentation (both in terms of origin and effects); but it also insists on the speaker's (and reader's) full participation in the most awkward of fantasies, fantasies which the feminist assertion of selfhood can read only as a type of psychic false consciousness, as the internalisation of patriarchy and mimicry of the eternal behaviour of men. It is particularly awkward for this second reading that the father oppresses to the precise extent that he is not there. Once again it is the category of fantasy that these readings have to play down—which also means, perhaps paradoxically, that they have to play down the concrete history in which the poem is set. For fascism must surely be distinguished from patriarchy, even if in some sense it can be seen as its effect. Fantasy and history are both lost in these two readings—in the eternal sameness of patriarchy and of women's singular relationship to it, in the eternal sameness of the femininity which erupts against its law.

Writing on Nazism in their famous book *The Inability to Mourn*, Alexander and Margarete Mitscherlich describe how vengeance as an alternative to failed mourning constitutes one of the unconscious sub-texts of what they call 'a particular German way of loving'.[86] If we add the mourning to the vengeance, then we cannot read 'Daddy' simply in terms of revenge against the oppressor. If we take the revenge and the mourning together, as the poem seems to do, we can reintroduce the concept of fantasy as that which links the motifs of memory and revenge, whose separation in responses to the Holocaust is discussed by Lyotard. More important, if we take their co-presence as a counter-narrative or caution against any straightforward narrative reading of the poem as a whole, then 'Daddy' appears as a poem that represents a set of fantasies which, at a precise historical moment and with devastating consequences, found themselves at the heart of our collective political life. In this context, there seems no point in trying to establish a one-way relation between the personal and the wider political history the poem evokes. The poem offers the implication of the one in the other—implication, rather than determination, precisely because one cannot establish a single, one-track relation between the two.

Whether the poem reproduces these fantasies or exposes them, whether it offers them to the reader for a further identification or critique, is not a question which I think can be answered. Saul Friedlander makes the difficulty of this distinction central to his book *Reflections of Nazism*, which describes the preoccupation with Nazi fantasies in our contemporary cultural life.[87] But the question is not yet historically settled as to whether knowledge of our implication in these fantasies, or the idea that we can and should separate ourselves from them completely, is most likely to prevent their repetition in the world today. Somewhere in the space between the inside and outside of the Hamburg Congress, between the Holocaust and nuclear rhetoric, it was this question that was being posed. In this context, what is most striking about 'Daddy' is its mobility of fantasy, the extent to which it takes up psychic positions which, it is often argued, if they cannot be clearly distinguished, lead to the collapse of morality itself. Plath, on the other hand, moves from one position to the other, implicating them, in each other, forcing the reader to enter into something which she or he is often willing to consider only on condition of seeing it as something in which, psychically no less than historically, she or he plays absolutely no part.

Plath was a pacifist. The question then arises of the relation between her politics and these fantasies—between her pacifism and the psychic violence she represents in this poem, and of course not only here. In a much earlier psychoanalytic conference on the psychology of peace and war, held in London in 1934, two years after Wiesbaden, Edward Glover discusses the different relationships between violence in the inner and outer worlds.[88] Pacifism, he suggests, can be as much a repetition of, as a solution to, the problem of inner war. The militarist, on the other hand, is too desperately in search of inner peace to forgo war. But normality, or equilibrium, far from being the ideal scenario, is in many ways the most risky state of all:

> The drawbacks to this state of equilibrium are threefold. First, having no urgent inner problem to solve, the man in the street is likely to ignore the real external urgency of war problems; secondly, the equilibrium will not withstand the panic and excitement of a war crisis; thirdly, it prevents the man in the street ever realising that the problem of war is his own unconscious problem.[89]

I offer Glover's remarks not as an analysis of Plath, nor indeed of pacifism, but in order to suggest something of the reversibility that might hold between pacifism and the commitment to (inner) war. (As Plath puts it in the *Journals*: 'I know it is too simple to wish for war, for open battle.'[90]) In order to suggest too—although Glover does not say it—something of the possible link between knowing the war is in fact one's own unconscious war, and working for peace. More simply, to note how little concepts such as antagonism, illegitimate appropriation, or theft (the terms of that critique of Plath with which this chapter began) can help us to understand the relation of these two concerns, the coexistence of external and inner urgency, in Plath's work.

Finally, I would suggest that 'Daddy' does allow us to ask whether the woman might not have a special relationship to fantasy—the only generalisation in the poem regarding women is, after all, that most awkward of lines: 'Every woman adores a fascist.' It is invariably taken out of context, taken out of the ghastly drama which shows where such a proposition might come from— what, for the woman who makes it, and in the worse sense, it might *mean*. Turning the criticism of Plath around once more, could we not read in that line a suggestion, or even a demonstration, that it is a woman who is most likely to articulate the power—perverse, recalcitrant, persistent—of fantasy as such? Nor would such an insight be in any way incompatible with women's legitimate protest against a patriarchal world. This is for me, finally, the wager of Plath's work.

Marguerite Duras's *La douleur* is her wartime diary. It describes the time when she was waiting for her husband to return from the camps, and her resistance during the war. At the end of this narrative, she introduces two stories:

> Thérèse is me. The person who tortures the informer is me. So also is the one who feels like making love to Ter, the member of the Militia. Me. I give you the torturer along with the rest of the texts. Learn to read them properly: they are sacred.[91]

The psychic terrain that Duras is covering here seems to be not unconnected to that represented in 'Daddy' by Plath—as if the story of the victim (concretely and historically in this instance) had to be followed by the story of herself as torturer, as well as by the story of desire. The last word, however, goes to Sylvia Plath. It is her first outline for the story 'The Shadow', a passage from the unedited journals at Smith, not included in the published text:

> My present theme seems to be the awareness of a complicated guilt system whereby Germans in a Jewish and Catholic community are made to feel, in scapegoat fashion, the pain, psychically, the Jews are made to feel in Germany by the Germans without religion. The child can't understand the wider framework. How does her father come into this? How is she guilty for her father's deportation to a detention camp? [As (*sic*)] this is how I think the story will end. Joanna will come in on her own with the trapeze, Uncle Frank and the fiction of perfect goodness.[92]

NOTES

1. Leon Wieseltier, 'In a Universe of Ghosts', *New York Review of Books*, 25 November 1976, pp. 20–23 (p. 20).

2. Joyce Carol Oates, 'The Death Throes of Romanticism', op. cit., p. 39; Seamus Heaney, 'The indefatigable hoof-taps', *Times Literary Supplement*, 5–11 February 1988, pp. 134–44 (p. 144); Irving Howe, 'The Plath Celebration: A Partial Dissent', in Butscher, *Sylvia Plath: The Woman and the Work*, op. cit., pp. 224–35 (p. 233); Marjorie Perloff, 'The Two Ariels', op. cit., pp. 14–15. For a discussion of similar objections to Marianne Moore's poem 'In Distrust of Merits' and more generally to women's war poetry see Sue Schweik, 'Writing War Poetry Like a Woman,' *Critical Inquiry*, 13, 3, Spring 1987, pp. 532–56, part

of her forthcoming study, *A Word No Man Can Say For Us: American Women Poets and the Second World War*.

3. 'The sense of history, both personal and social, found in a poem like "For the Union Dead" is conspicuously absent from the *Ariel* poems. This is not mere coincidence: for the oracular poet, past and future are meaningless abstractions ... For Sylvia Plath, there is only the given moment, only *now*.' Marjorie Perloff, '*Angst* and Animism in the Poetry of Sylvia Plath', op. cit., p. 121. For a much more positive assessment of Plath's relationship to history, see Stan Smith, *Inviolable Voice: History and Twentieth-Century Poetry*, Dublin: Gill & Macmillan, 1982, Chapter 9, 'Waist-Deep in History: Sylvia Plath', pp. 200–25.

4. Perloff, 'The Two Ariels', op. cit., p. 15.

5. The criticism was first directed at Ferdinand de Saussure's *Course in General Linguistics* (1915), London: Fontana, 1974, for what has been seen as an emphasis on the synchronic, at the expense of the diachronic, dimension of language, and on the arbitrary nature of the linguistic sign which, it was argued, made it impossible to theorise the relationship between language and reference. It has become a commonplace to reproach post-Saussurian literary theory with ahistoricism. For discussion of some of these debates, see Derek Attridge, Geoff Bennington and Robert Young, eds., *Post-Structuralism and the Question of History*, Cambridge: Cambridge University Press, 1987, especially Geoff Bennington and Robert Young, 'Introduction: posing the question', pp. 1–11. More specifically, I am referring here to the controversy which has followed the discovery of Paul de Man's wartime writings for the Belgian collaborationist newspaper *Le Soir*. See Werner Hamacher, Neil Hertz and Thomas Keenan, eds, *Responses*, Lincoln, NB/London: University of Nebraska Press, 1989.

6. The conference took place in Hamburg in 1985. The papers were published in a special issue of the *International Journal of Psycho-Analysis*, vol. 67, 1986.

7. I take this account from Janine Chasseguet-Smirgel, '"Time's White Hair We Ruffle", Reflections on the Hamburg Conference', *International Review of Psycho-Analysis*, 14, 1987, pp. 433–44.

8. Hanna Segal, 'Silence is the Real Crime', *International Review of Psycho-Analysis*, 14, 1987, pp. 3–12. For the main Congress, see F.-W. Eickhoff, 'Identification and its Vicissitudes in the Context of the Nazi Phenomenon', *International Journal of Psycho-Analysis*, 67, 1986, pp. 33–44; Hillel Klein and Ilany Kogan, 'Identification Processes and Denial in the Shadow of Nazism', pp. 45–52; David Rosenfeld, 'Identification and its Vicissitudes in Relation to the Nazi Phenomenon', pp. 53–64; Mortimer Ostow, 'The Psychodynamics of Apocalyptic: Discussion of Papers on Identification and the Nazi Phenomenon', pp. 277–85; Dinora Pines, 'Working with Women Survivors of the Holocaust: Affective Experiences in Transference and Counter-Transference', pp. 295–307; Ira Brenner and Judith S. Kestenberg, 'Children who Survived the Holocaust: The Role of Rules and Routines in the Development of the Superego', pp. 309–16; Anita Eckstaedt, 'Two Complementary Cases of Identification Involving Third Reich Fathers', pp. 317–27. See also Steven A. Luel and Paul Marcus, *Psychoanalytic Reflections on the Holocaust: Selected Essays*, Denver: Holocaust Awareness Institute and Center for Judaic Studies/New York: Ktav Publishing, 1984. I am grateful to Nina Farhi and Rachel Sievers for bringing my attention to this book, and to the article by Chasseguet-Smirgel cited above.

9. Freud, 'Psycho-Analytic Notes on an Autobiographical Account of a Case of Paranoia (Schreber)', op. cit., *Standard Edition*, p. 71; Pelican Freud, p. 210, cited by Janine Chasseguet-Smirgel, opening comments, *International Journal of Psycho-Analysis*,

vol. 67, 1986, p. 7. Compare also the opening address of Adam Limentani, President of the International Association of Psycho-Analysis: '... we also hope that it will facilitate the mending of old wounds in typically psychoanalytic fashion—through remembering and understanding, rather than denial, rationalisation and forgetting' (p. 5); and of Deiter Olmeier, President of the German Psycho-Analytic Association: 'It is only possible to work through things which are accessible to the conscious, which can again and again and ever more clearly become conscious, which can and must be remembered' (p. 6).

10. Eickhoff, 'Identification and its Vicissitudes in the Context of the Nazi Phenomenon', op. cit., p. 34.

11. ibid., and Rosenfeld, op. cit.

12. The reference here is to an earlier paper by Anita Eckstaedt, one of the contributors to the Hamburg Conference, cited by Henry Krystal in a review of Martin S. Bergmann and Milton E. Jucovy, *Generations of the Holocaust*, New York: Basic Books, 1982, in the *Psycho-Analytic Quarterly*, 53, pp. 466–73 (p. 469).

13. Eckstaedt, op. cit., p. 326.

14. Eickhoff (citing L. Wurmser), op. cit., p. 37.

15. I am aware of the danger of reducing the complexities of these individual case-histories to a formula. Each of them showed a particular set of vicissitudes, not only in relation to the historical position of the patient's parents and their own history in relation to Nazism, but also as regards other details of the patient's personal history (whether or not the parents chose to speak, the death of one or other parent, exile, reinstatement, etc.). Readers are encouraged to refer to the papers, which make an extraordinary historical document in themselves.

16. Zev Garber and Bruce Zuckerman, 'Why Do We Call the Holocaust "The Holocaust"? An Inquiry into the Psychology of Labels', in *Remembering For the Future*, Oxford: Oxford University Press, 1988, vol. 2, *The Impact of the Holocaust on the Contemporary World*, pp. 189–92.

17. Both poems are included in the 'Juvenilia' section of the *Collected Poems*, pp. 320, 325.

18. *Encyclopedia Judaica and Catholic Encyclopedia*, both cited by Judith Kroll, *Chapters in a Mythology*, op. cit., p. 181.

19. Primo Levi, *The Drowned and the Saved*, London: Michael Joseph, 1988, pp. 43, 33. See this whole chapter, Chapter 2, 'The Grey Zone', pp. 22–51.

20. Pines, 'Working with Women Survivors of the Holocaust', op. cit., p. 300.

21. Arnost Lustig, 'Rose Street', in *Night and Hope*, New York: Dutton, 1962, p. 78.

22. Freud, 'Psycho-Analytic Notes on an Autobiographical Account of a Case of Paranoia (Schreber)', op. cit., *Standard Edition*, p. 66; Pelican Freud, p. 204.

23. Freud, *Three Essays on the Theory of Sexuality*, 1905, *Standard Edition*, vol. VII, pp. 123–245 (p. 145n); Pelican Freud, 7 pp. 31–169 (p. 56n).

24. Ilse Grubrich-Simitis, 'From Concretism to Metaphor: Thoughts on Some Theoretical and Technical Aspects of the Psychoanalytic Work with Children of Holocaust Survivors', *Psychoanalytic Study of the Child*, 39, 1984, pp. 301–29.

25. ibid., p. 302.

26. Eickhoff, op. cit., p. 34.

27. Grubrich-Simitis, op. cit., pp. 313, 309n.

28. ibid., p. 316.

29. Hannah Arendt, *Eichmann in Jerusalem: A Report on the Banality of Evil*, New York: Viking, 1963, revised and enlarged edition 1965; Harmondsworth: Penguin, 1977, p. 211.

30. Steiner, 'Dying is an art', op. cit., p. 217.

31. Emil L. Fackenheim, 'From Bergen-Belsen to Jerusalem: Contemporary Implications of the Holocaust', The Cultural Department World Jewish Congress, Jerusalem, Institute of Contemporary Jewry, The Hebrew University of Jerusalem, 1975, pp. 17, 12.

32. Karl Kraus, *Das Karl Kraus Lesebuch*, Zurich: Diogenes, 1980, cited Eickhoff, op. cit., p. 40; Eickhoff discusses these lines in relation to lines from a poem by Brecht— quoted as epigraph to his paper (p. 33)—who had attacked Kraus for raising his voice 'only in complaint that it was insufficient'.

33. Levi, *If This Is A Man*, Oxford; The Bodley Head, 1960, first published in Italian in 1947; Harmondsworth: Penguin, 1979 (with *The Truce*), p. 17.

34. Levi, *The Drowned and the Saved*, op. cit., p. 63.

35. Paul Celan, 'Aschenglorie', *Atemwende*, 1967; *Gedichte*, Frankfurt: Suhrkamp Verlag, 1975, p. 72. The line is discussed by Jacques Derrida, 'Shibboleth' (for Paul Celan), G.H. Hartman and S. Budick, eds, *Midrash and Literature*, New Haven: Yale University Press, 1986, pp. 307–47 (p. 326).

36. Piotr Rawicz, *Le sang du ciel*, Paris: Gallimard, 1961; *Blood From the Sky*, London: Secker & Warburg, 1964. These lines are quoted at the end of Alvarez, 'Literature of the Holocaust', op. cit., p. 33.

37. Fackenheim, op. cit. 'Discussion', p. 26.

38. Josef Bor, *Terezin Requiem*, New York: Knopf, 1963 (original date not given, in translation); Elie Wiesel, *Night*, New York: Hill & Wang, 1960, first published in Yiddish in 1956; Ilse Aichinger, *Herod's Children*, New York: Atheneum, 1963 (Alvarez refers to this work as a recent novel); Arnost Lustig, *Night and Hope*, op. cit., was first published in Prague in 1962.

39. Alvarez, 'Literature of the Holocaust', op. cit. Alvarez comments that the Polish writer, Tadeusz Borowski is one of the few to have written about the camps close to the time. See 'This Way for the Gas—A Story', *Commentary*, vol. 1, no. 34, July 1962, pp. 39–47. See also the Hungarian poet and camp survivor Janos Pilinsky's *Selected Poems*, translated by Ted Hughes, Manchester: Carcanet Press, 1976 (his first collection of poems appeared in 1946); and Levi, *If This Is A Man*, op. cit. The history of the publication of Levi's book is interesting in itself. Levi wrote it as soon as he returned from the camps. It was rejected by several large publishers and then published by a small publishing house run by Franco Antonicelli in 1947; 2500 copies were published. Antonicelli then collapsed and the book was not republished until 1958 by Enaudi. Levi comments: 'in that harsh post-war world, people didn't have much desire to go back in their memories to the painful years that had just finished.' Levi, *Se questo è un uomo*, Turin: Enaudi, 1982, Author's Note, p. 231.

40. Hughes, Foreword, *J*, p. xv.

41. Kroll, p. 243n.

42. Derrida, op. cit., p. 329.

43. ibid., p. 338.

44. ibid., and Paul Celan, op. cit., vol. 1, pp. 287–9.

45. Diane Wood Middlebrook and Diana Hume George, eds, *Selected Poems of Anne Sexton*, Boston: Houghton Mifflin, 1988, p. 5; originally published in *The Antioch Review*, 19, 1959; see Heather Cam, '"Daddy": Sylvia Plath's Debt to Anne Sexton', in Diana Hume George, ed., *Sexton: Selected Criticism*, Urbana/Chicago: University of Illinois Press, 1988, pp. 223–6. I am grateful to Diane Middlebrook for drawing my attention to this poem.

46. *CP*, 2 April 1962, pp. 187–9, first published in *Encounter*, 21 October 1963, and in *Ariel*. The poem was not included in Plath's own list for *Ariel*.

47. Graves, *The White Goddess*, op. cit., p. 194.

48. Hans Magnus Enzensberger, 'In Search of a Lost Language', *Encounter*, September 1963, pp. 44–51. The article is discussed by Judith Kroll in relation to 'Little Fugue'. She compares Plath's poem to a poem by Gunter Eich cited by Enzensberger, but the historical allusion is finally synthesised into the overall mythological schema. Kroll, op. cit., pp. 114–15, 246–7n.

49. The concept comes from Jacques Lacan, who formulates it thus: 'What is realised in my history is not the past definite of what was, since it is no more, or even the present perfect of what has been in what I am, but the future anterior of what I shall have been for what I am in the process of becoming', 'The function and field of speech and language in psychoanalysis', 1953, in *Ecrits: A Selection*, London: Tavistock, 1977, pp. 30–113 (p. 86). See also D.W. Winnicott: 'This search [for a past detail which is not yet experienced] takes the form of looking for this detail in the future', 'Fear of Breakdown', in Gregorio Kohon, ed., *The British School of Psychoanalysis: The Independent Tradition*, London: Free Association Books, 1986, pp. 173–82 (p. 178).

50. *Remembering for the Future*, op. cit.

51. Klein and Kogan, op. cit., p. 48.

52. *CP*, 12 October 1962, pp. 222–4 (strangely, the poem is omitted from the Index), first published in *Encounter*, 21 October 1963, and in *Ariel*.

53. 'The Blood jet is Poetry', review of *Ariel*, *Time*, 10 June 1966, pp. 118–20 (p. 118). The review is copiously illustrated with photographs from Aurelia Plath's personal collection. A letter from her to Ted Hughes suggests that she felt she had been tricked by the reviewer and that this, plus the cover of the issue of *The Atlantic* which published 'Johnny Panic and the Bible of Dreams' ('Sylvia Plath on Going Mad'), had contributed to her reluctance to see *The Bell Jar* published in the United States. Letter from Aurelia Plath to Ted Hughes, 11 April 1970, Correspondence, Lilly, op. cit.

54. Jean-François Lyotard, *The Differend: Phrases in Dispute*, Manchester: Manchester University Press, 1988, p. 27. Lyotard is discussing the issue of Holocaust denial or the Faurisson debate, see p. 3 ff. See also Gill Seidal, *The Holocaust Denial: Antisemitism, Racism and the New Right*, Brighton: Beyond the Pale Collective, 1986.

55. The concept comes from Freud, *The Ego and the Id*, op. cit. *Standard Edition*, pp. 31–2; Pelican Freud, 11, pp. 370–71, and *Group Psychology and the Analysis of the Ego*, 1921, *Standard Edition*, vol. XVIII, pp. 105–6; Pelican Freud, 12, pp. 134–5. It has been most fully theorised recently by Julia Kristeva in *Tales of Love*, New York: Columbia University Press, 1987, pp. 24–9.

56. For Kristeva this father founds the possibility of identification for the subject and is critically linked to—enables the subject to symbolise—the orality, and hence the abjection, which was the focus of discussion of 'Poem for a Birthday', in Chapter 2.

57. 'Sylvia Plath', in Peter Orr, ed., *The Poet Speaks*, London: Routledge & Kegan Paul, 1966, pp. 167–72 (p. 169).

58. Claude Lanzmann in discussion of the film *Shoah*, Channel 4 Television, 27 October 1987; see also Lanzmann, *Shoah, An Oral History of the Holocaust: The Complete Text of the Film*, New York: Pantheon, 1985; Lyotard, 'Judiciousness in Dispute, or Kant after Marx', in Murray Krieger, ed., *The Aims of Representation: Subject, Text, History*, New York: Columbia University Press, 1987, pp. 24–67 (p. 64).

59. *Journals*, Smith, July 1950–July 1953, op. cit., September 1950, p. 60 (*J*, p. 20).

60. Eickhoff, op. cit., p. 38.

61. 4 July 1958, 7 July 1958, 11 October 1959, *J*, pp. 244, 246, 319; 13 October 1959, *LH*, p. 356; 13 October 1959, 19 October 1959, *J*, pp. 319, p. 321; *Journals*, Smith, 12 December 1958–15 November 1959, op. cit., 7 November 1959, p. 94 (*J*, p. 327).

62. *The Bell Jar*, p. 35.

63. 'On one side I am a first generation American, on one side I'm a second generation American, and so my concern with concentration camps and so on is uniquely intense', Orr, op. cit., p. 169.

64. Letter from Thomas J. Clohesy to Aurelia Plath, 4 September 1966, Smith, Section 5, Biography.

65. Jean Stafford, *A Boston Adventure*, op. cit.

66. ibid., p. 335.

67. ibid.

68. ibid., p. 482.

69. Rosenfeld, op. cit., p. 62.

70. Lyotard, 'Judiciousness in Dispute', op. cit., p. 59. In a reply to Lyotard, Stephen Greenblatt takes issue with him on this specific question: Greenblatt, 'Capitalist Culture and the Circulatory System', in Krieger, op. cit., pp. 257–73 (pp. 260–61).

71. Freud, *The Ego and the Id*, op. cit., *Standard Edition*, p. 34; Pelican Freud, p. 374.

72. 'Among the Bumblebees' (early 1950s), *Johnny Panic*, pp. 259–66 (p. 263).

73. Lacan, 'Seminar of 21 January 1975', in Juliet Mitchell and Jacqueline Rose, eds, *Feminine Sexuality: Jacques Lacan and the École freudienne*, London: Macmillan, 1982, pp. 162–71 (p. 167).

74. Freud, 'Psycho-Analytic Notes on an Autobiographical Account of a Case of Paranoia (Schreber)', op. cit.; see also Samuel Weber, Introduction to Daniel Paul Schreber, *Memoirs of My Nervous Illness*, edited by Ida Macalpine and Richard Hunter, 1955, new edition, Cambridge, MA/London: Harvard University Press, 1988, pp. vii–liv.

75. Otto Plath, *Bumblebees and their Ways*, New York: Macmillan, 1934.

76. Otto E. Plath, 'Insect Societies', in Carl Murchison, ed., *A Handbook of Social Psychology*, Massachusetts: Clark University Press; London: Oxford University Press, 1935, pp. 83–141 (p. 83, 136–7). The first quote comes from the epigraph to the chapter and is part of a quotation from Thomas Belt, *The Naturalist in Nicaragua*, 1874; its account of the perfect regiment belongs to a more generally utopian image of community which ends with a quotation from Thomas More.

77. 'Among the Bumblebees', op. cit., p. 262.

78. 'Little Fugue', Draft 1, page 2, verso, Smith, *Ariel* Poems.

79. Virginia Woolf, *Three Guineas*, London: Hogarth, 1938; Harmondsworth: Penguin, 1977, p. 162.

80. Elizabeth Wilson, 'Coming out for a brand new age', the Guardian, 14 March 1989. The same line has also been taken as a slogan to explain German women's involvement in Nazism; see Murray Sayle, 'Adolf and the Women', *The Independent Magazine*, 9 November 1988: '"Every woman adores a Fascist," wrote Sylvia Plath. Is this why so many German women voted for Hitler, despite the male emphasis of the Nazi regime?' (caption under title).

81. For a study of this difficult question, see Claudia Koonz, *Mothers in the Fatherland: Women, the Family and Nazi Politics*, London; Jonathan Cape, 1987.

82. Thanks to Natasha Korda for pointing this out to me.

83. Styron, *Lie Down in Darkness*, op. cit., p. 379.

84. On the question of racism, see John Henrik Clarke, ed., *William Styron's Nat Turner: Ten Black Writers Respond*, Boston: Beacon Press, 1968; and Richard Ohmann,

Politics of Letters, Chapter 5, 'The Shaping of a Canon: US Fiction, 1960–1975', Middletown: Wesleyan University Press, 1987, p. 68.

85. Sherry Ortner, 'Is Female to Male as Nature Is to Culture?', in Michelle Zimbalist Rosaldo and Louise Lamphere, eds, *Woman, Culture and Society*, California: Stanford University Press, 1974, pp. 67–87. For a critique of this article, see Carol P. MacCormack, 'Nature, culture and gender: a critique', in Carol P. MacCormack and Marilyn Strathern, *Nature, Culture and Gender*, Cambridge: Cambridge University Press, 1980, pp. 1–24.

86. Alexander and Margarete Mitscherlich, *The Inability to Mourn*, London: Grove Press, 1975, Chapter 1 'The Inability to Mourn—With Which Is Associated A German Way of Loving', pp. 3–68.

87. Saul Friedlander, *Reflections of Nazism*, New York: Harper & Row, 1984.

88. Edward Glover and Morris Ginsberg, 'A Symposium on the Psychology of Peace and War', *British Journal of Medical Psychology*, 14, 1934, pp. 274–93.

89. ibid., p. 277.

90. Excerpt from a letter to Richard Sassoon, 15 January 1956, *J*, p. 97.

91. Marguerite Duras, *La douleur*, Paris: POL, 1985; London: Fontana, 1987, introductory statement to 'Albert of the Capitals' and 'Ter of the Militias', p. 115.

92. *Journals*, Smith, 12 December 1958–15 November, 1959, op. cit., 28 December 1958, p. 28 (*J*, p. 283).

NANCY D. HARGROVE

The Poems of 1957

1957 was largely a year of drudgery, hard work, and frustration for Plath. From January to June, she toiled at her studies, finishing her coursework and preparing for and taking her final exams for the M.A. degree at Cambridge. Although she wrote to her mother that she had "three jobs— writing; cooking and housekeeping, and studying for tough exams" (342), most of her energies were devoted to the latter: "I am living at the University library from morning to night ... steadily reading tragedy now, the Greeks, then on through 2000 years up to Eliot" (LH 355). She was frustrated at having so little time to write; indeed, only five poems can definitely be attributed to this period. However, a cause for joy was the notification in late February that Hughes's *Hawk in the Rain* had won the New York Poetry Center competition and would be published by Harper.

The summer, while a time of comparative freedom and leisure, was not much more productive for Plath. The two spent most of the month of June in Heptonstall, visiting his parents before their departure for the United States on June 20. After a brief period in Wellesley, they lived during July and August at Eastham, Cape Cod, where Plath wrote some fiction and poetry and prepared for the courses she would teach at Smith College in Northampton, Massachusetts in the fall. In addition to suffering from a severe case of writer's block, she was depressed by the news in August that

From *The Journey Toward Ariel: Sylvia Plath's Poems of 1956–1959*, pp. 99–133. © 1994 by Nancy D. Hargrove.

Two Lovers and a Beachcomber had been rejected by the Yale Series of Younger Poets.

The months of September through December were extremely difficult ones. Understandably, Plath felt, as she herself said, "a little awed" (LH 345) and, more honestly, "scared blue" (LH 349) about being an instructor at her alma mater. Desiring even more than usual to excel, she worked very hard on her lectures and paper grading, often feeling exhausted as a result of the demands she placed on herself, and she confided to her brother that she was "always deathly nervous" (LH 376) about lecturing itself. Further, she was disappointed not to be given the glorious reception which she had imagined and expected from Smith. Finally, she was frustrated at having neither time nor energy for her own writing: "this life is not the life for a writer" (LH 377). Thus by late November she made the decision to leave teaching permanently at the end of the academic year in order to become a full-time writer.

The poems for 1957 are the most problematical of the four years in question, for hard evidence of times of composition exists for only a few; placing the others then is largely a matter of speculation. Of the twenty-one poems that Hughes has included in the 1957 section of *The Collected Poems*, only five can definitely be attributed to that year: "The Snowman on the Moor," "Sow," "Mayflower," "The Lady and the Earthenware Head," and "All the Dead Dears." Five were without question composed in other years ("On the Plethora of Dryads" and "Natural History" in 1956 and "The Disquieting Muses," "On the Decline of Oracles," and "Snakecharmer" in 1958), and four others almost certainly were ("On the Difficulty of Conjuring Up a Dryad" in 1956, "Night Shift" in 1958, "The Other Two" in 1958 or 1959, and "Words for a Nursery" in 1959 or 1960). Of those remaining, there are few clues about whether they are in fact the products of 1957 and, if so, when exactly during the year they were written. At any rate, it is clear that she wrote a very small number of poems, approximately twelve in all. The reason seems to have been the heavy demands on her time as a student studying for examinations in the spring and as a new teacher at Smith preparing class lectures and grading papers in the fall; in the summer when she did have some leisure time, she experienced writer's block much of the time.

That she had little time to devote to poetry is also reflected in the paucity of comments on her poetic goals during this year in journal entries and letters; in one of the few notes on this subject, a journal entry for February 25, she remarks, "I am splitting the seams of my fancy terza rima" (151), no doubt a reference to the use of that form in "The Snow Man on the Moor" and "Sow," and indeed she avoids it entirely in the remainder of 1957. Only during July and August does she allude to her goals, before again lapsing into silence on this subject in the autumn under the pressures of her teaching position at Smith. In the summer comments, she indicates a desire to write in "quite elaborate rhymed and alliterative forms without sounding like self-conscious poetry, but rather like conversation" (LH 373). She speaks of avoiding abstractions and "brittle, stilted artificial stuff" (J 164; see also 170, 172) and aiming for the natural and conversational. To this end she advises herself to concentrate on descriptive poems and concrete details: "[Try] little exercise poems in description that don't demand philosophic bear traps of logical development. Like small poems about the skate, the cow by moonlight, à la the Sow. Very physical" (J 163; see also J 170). Other comments focus on the difficulty of finding adequate subjects, always a problem for her in the early work: "The main problem is breaking open rich, real subjects to myself" (J 170).

Concerning subjects, Plath took her own advice cited above to concentrate on descriptive poems with abundant concrete details, relying largely on scenes, creatures, and events which she has observed or been involved in currently or in the recent past—various episodes on the moorland of West Yorkshire ("The Snowman on the Moor," "Two Views of Withens," "Hardcastle Crags," and "The Great Carbuncle"), a huge sow that she and Hughes had seen in the fall of 1956 on a farm near Heptonstall, a model head that the two had placed in a tree in Grantchester Meadows, a display that fascinated her in the Archaeological Museum on Downing Street in Cambridge. In almost every case, she distances herself by describing object or event accurately but dispassionately, and, when material is highly personal, as in the stanzas on the father in an early version of "All the Dead Dears," she deletes it. In general, she seems deliberately to concentrate on material that is historical, philosophical, or social in nature: "Mayflower" focuses on American history, "All the Dead Dears," "A Lesson in Vengeance," and "The Great Carbuncle" on various philosophical or metaphysical concerns, and "The Thin People" on the social injustice of poverty.

The poems of 1957 reveal a greater variety in theme than those of 1956, which were dominated by the relationship of men and women and the conflict between flesh and intellect or reality and the imagination. Plath explores the relationship of the individual to some aspect of his/her world, usually a menacing one as in "The Thin People" and "All the Dead Dears" or a coldly indifferent one as in "Hardcastle Crags"; however, in two instances the aspect is a positive one ("Sow" and "The Great Carbuncle"). Only "The Snowman on the Moor" treats the relationship of men and women. Other themes include the valor of the pilgrims on the Mayflower ("Mayflower") and the inability to escape one's less admirable traits ("The Lady and the Earthenware Head").

In terms of style, Plath continues here the types of experiments begun in the 1956 poems. Although, as indicated in the comments from her letters and journals cited earlier, she desires to create a more natural style, her diction is still a mixture of the archaic or artificial and the conversational (as in "The Lady and the Earthenware Head"), but poems such as "All the Dead Dears," "Hardcastle Crags," and "The Thin People" show an encouraging move to the latter. Her experiments with stanza form, rhyme, and meter are as wide-ranging in this year as in the previous one, within the more limited scope of poems produced. She continues to prefer a set stanza form but to experiment with numerous lengths and types of stanzas, and all but three poems ("All the Dead Dears," "The Great Carbuncle," and "Ouija") have set rhyme schemes usually of imperfect rhymes. Again she works with various patterns of different degrees of difficulty; in "A Lesson in Vengeance," for example, the last word of every line ends in "s," while "Sow" and "The Snowman on the Moor" employ the demanding interlocking terza rima. The meter is highly irregular in most poems with a decrease in the percentage of stressed syllables reflecting Plath's movement away from her imitation of Thomas's and Hopkins's practices of omitting articles, prepositions, and the like. However, "Ouija," while abandoning rhyme, is written in iambic pentameter, and "The Great Carbuncle" employs syllabics (perhaps an indication that it was written in the summer of 1958 when she undertook extensive experiments with them).

The influences of other poets are less marked in this year's poems. The two dominant ones are Wallace Stevens and Ted Hughes; echoes of Yeats and Eliot are still apparent, but only occasionally. Most striking is that Plath's own voice is heard in "Hardcastle Crags," "The Thin People," and "All the Dead Dears." Yet, because of the paucity of poems produced, 1957 does not figure as a stellar year in Plath's development as a poet.

In an unpublished passage of a letter of January 14, 1957, Plath tells her mother that she has just written two long poems of approximately fifty lines each and feels much better for having broken the dry spell of the previous few months, occasioned by her numerous practical problems (Lilly Library); the two referred to are "The Snowman on the Moor" and "Sow." An unpublished letter of April 1, 1957, which announces the acceptance of the two (along with "Ella Mason and Her Eleven Cats" and "On the Difficulty of Conjuring Up a Dryad") by Poetry, describes "The Snowman on the Moor" as "a 50-line one about a man and woman fighting in the winter and she running out on to the moors and having a vision" and "Sow" as "the long one about a gigantic pig"; she then adds a parenthetical comment that she considers them "2 of my best poems" (Lilly Library). Further, in an unpublished letter of January 21, 1957 to Mrs. Plath and Warren, Hughes notes that Plath has recently completed one or two very good poems; although he does not name them, he is surely referring to these two (Lilly Library). Both were inspired by earlier experiences in Heptonstall, the former by an argument apparently during their Christmas visit (see J 149) and the latter by a huge pig that the two had seen on a neighbor's farm on September 7, 1956, described in the Cambridge Pocket Diary for 1955–6 (Lilly Library).

Hughes's Chronology		Reordered Chronology
"The Snowman on the Moor"	by Jan 14	"The Snowman on the Moor"
"Mayflower"		"Sow"
"Sow"	21	"Mayflower"
"The Everlasting Monday"	by Feb 3	"The Lady and the Earthenware
"Hardcastle Crags"		Head"
"The Thin People"	Apr 7	"All the Dead Dears"
"On the Difficulty of Conjuring Up	Aug?	"Ouija"
a Dryad"	Summer?	"Two Views of Withens"
"On the Plethora of Dryads"		"The Great Carbuncle"
"The Other Two"		"Hardcastle Crags"
"The Lady and the Earthenware		"The Thin People"
Head"	late 57/	"A Lesson in Vengeance"
"All the Dead Dears"	early 58?	"The Everlasting Monday"
"Natural History"		
"Two Views of Withens"		
"The Great Carbuncle"		
"Words for a Nursery"		
"The Disquieting Muses"		
"Night Shift"		
"Ouija"		
"On the Decline of Oracles"		
"Snakecharmer"		
"A Lesson in Vengeance"		

"The Snowman on the Moor" was no doubt inspired by the argument between Plath and Hughes recorded in the journals as "Poem," one of several entries describing experiences and scenes in West Yorkshire placed between those of the summer at Benidorm in 1956 and those of February 1957 at Cambridge; the original journal pages at the Smith College Library give no clue as to the exact date of this entry. However, its references to snow suggest that it was written in late December or early January during Plath and Hughes's Christmas visit to Heptonstall. Many of its details appear in the poem:

> Wild hot fury—*cold snow: thick white moor mist*— ... walk in *white blank world*—symbol of shutting off from normal clear vision— *futile outburst*. human limits versus grand marmoreal vast *power of cold, snow*, stars and blackness—vanished *daisies: white in head*, remembered from summer—she imposes them on dry barren broken stalks— ... *black stone fences,—stark wild landscape*— ... *red coal fires ... frosted hedge*—pose vast impersonal white world of nature against small violent spark of will.
>
> (149; italics added)

Its title ironically evoking a figure associated with pleasure, the poem recounts the experience of a young woman who has a violent argument with a man, perhaps her husband. Determined to "win / Him to his knees," she storms out into a snowy landscape where she encounters a giant symbolizing male dominance over proud, upstart women. Suddenly chastened, the young woman turns toward home, "brimful of gentle talk / And mild obeying." The poem's double theme reflects two of the major concerns of the 1956 poems: the pain involved in love relationships between women and men and the conflict between woman as an intellectual and independent entity and as submissive, inferior wife; as in most of the early poems, the former loses out.

Set on the moors surrounding Heptonstall, the poem has a third-person speaker who reflects the woman's point of view. While Broe contends that the woman is a comic persona (21), I would argue that she, as well as the situation portrayed, is entirely serious; there is nothing amusing about her or her experience.

The opening section (stanzas 1–3) describes the argument itself, with military imagery quite literally reflecting the battle between the sexes: "stalemated," "armies," "tottering banners," "grim battlement." Its violence is further conveyed by "flung," "ringing," and "glowering." Indeed, Plath wrote to her mother on January 9, 1957, perhaps with this actual argument in mind, "Ted and I sometimes have violent disagreements, to be sure" (331).

In the next section (stanzas 4–9), the young woman stalks across the moors, in her fury calling "hell to subdue an unruly man." The concrete details of the setting are not only precise, echoing those of the journal entry, but also symbolic, suggesting the hostility of the natural world toward the protagonist. It is "a landscape / Of stark wind-harrowed hills and weltering mist," of "moor snows / Pocked by rook-claw and rabbit-track," of "bare whistling heather [and] stiles of black stone." The "world's white edge" accurately describes the abrupt, sheer edge of the Heptonstall moors as they overlook the valley of Hardcastle Crags far below.

In part three (stanzas 10–16), a terrifying giant[1] from the world of nightmare and horror stories appears to subdue, not the "unruly man," but the unruly wife: "to ride that woman / With spur and knout / Down from pride's size." His strength is suggested by his "iron thighs" and grisly sinews and his violent nature by his spurs, "spike-studded belt," stone hatchet, and knout, a whip for flogging criminals. A symbol of male dominance, he has beheaded some intelligent, proud women as punishment for their daring. Hanging as trophies from his belt, their skulls admit "their guilt" of being superior to men:

'Our wit made fools
Of kings, unmanned kings' sons: our masteries
Amused court halls:

For that brag, we barnacle these iron thighs.'

In the last stanza, even though the giant dissolves into smoke as he attacks the protagonist, she is chastened: "Humbled then, and crying, / The girl bent homeward, brimful of gentle talk / And mild obeying." Plath indicates her submission through the shift from "that woman" in stanza nine to "girl" in stanza seventeen and through the word "bent," which implies not only that she turns toward home but that she is bent over in humility as well. This submission, too easily and quickly won considering the fury and intensity of the protagonist, seems contrived and unconvincing.

Plath works with a number of difficult technical tasks in the poem. In terms of stanzaic form and rhyme, she reveals a mastery of terza rima, employing an interlocking rhyme scheme of imperfect rhymes. In addition, she alternates line lengths in a strict pattern so that all odd-numbered stanzas contain long first and third lines and short second lines, while all even-numbered stanzas contain the reverse. Although not used to reinforce the content, this difficult pattern is an amazing technical feat. Further, the feminine rhymes that end some lines reflect the "proper" role of women as weak, especially in the last stanza ("crying," "obeying"). Finally, the repetition of the harsh consonant sounds of "k," "r," and "t" conveys the violence of the landscape and of the giant ("brunt of axe-crack").

The poem also contains weaknesses typical of Plath's early style. Some word choices are stilted or archaic ("bruit," "weltering"), rhyme-forced ("taunt," "battlement," "gaunt"), imprecise ("*Crumbled* to smoke"), or excessive (fourteen hyphenated compounds), while the alliteration of "Ambushed birds by / Dozens dropped dead in the hedges" and the attempt at assonance in "She shied sideways: a white fizz!" are overdone.

"The Snowman on the Moor" is valuable for its treatment of the relationship between men and women, particularly in light of the female's submission at the end, as well as for its effective description of the wintertime West Yorkshire landscape, its fusion of realism and fantasy, and its mastery of a demanding technical form. The conventional stance that women must ultimately submit to their more powerful mates accepted, though not advocated, in this early work may be shocking to those who know only the more aggressively feminist late poems; it is, therefore, all the more important to see where Plath began in order to appreciate fully the point at which she finally arrived.

"Sow" is quite different from "The Snowman on the Moor" in subject matter, tone, and theme, although it shares the terza rima form. On February 3, Plath wrote her mother that she was "very happy and alive and writing better poems—a big one about a sow, about 45 lines" (335). She and Hughes had visited a farm near Heptonstall on September 7, 1956 and, as a result of their expression of great interest, the farmer had allowed them to see "His great sow" which was ordinarily kept from public view. The sheer size and weight of the animal so impressed them that each wrote a poem based upon it; however, beyond the "Brobdingnag bulk" of their subject, their poems have nothing in common, for Hughes's "View of a Pig" conveys the speaker's feelings of depression over the hard, heavy reality of an enormous dead pig, while Plath's "Sow" describes the feelings of awe and amazement felt by two people upon observing an enormous living pig.

"Sow" has received two opposing interpretations from critics. Guttenberg (146), Rosenblatt (61), and Butscher (212) suggest that the sow represents the evil and hostile forces of nature, the latter going so far as to say that it is a central figure in a Satanic myth that Plath was creating. Aird, on the other hand, feels that the poem is frivolous, a "light-hearted extravaganza" with "affirmative vigor" (*Sylvia* 16). A careful reading of the text supports Aird's view, for it is a "light-hearted" and straightforward description of the sow and of the awe evoked by its size (the couple "gape" and "marvel"). This positive view is reinforced by Hughes's comment that the poem "*commemorates* a great sow" ("Notes" 189; italics added), indicating that she both memorializes and celebrates it.

In the first three stanzas, the narrative voice, which speaks in the first-person plural as a couple, explains that they were given a rare tour of the barns and "gaped"—in wonder, not in horror—at the size of the pig they saw. In the next four stanzas, they assert that it was not a painted, china piggy bank, a pig for roasting, or a typical barnyard mother pig with a litter of piglets, but rather a quite extraordinary pig:

> This vast
>
> Brobdingnag bulk
>
> Of a sow lounged belly-bedded on that black compost,
> Fat-rutted eyes
> Dream-filmed.

Plath makes effective use of heavy "b" and "d" sounds ("Brobdingnag bulk," "belly-bedded"), numerous modifiers ("fat-rutted"), and the literary allusion to the land in *Gulliver's Travels* where all was of enormous size. The visitors, who respond by marvelling (not quaking in horror or revulsion) at the sow, then imagine that she must be dreaming of an equally extraordinary boar, one magnificent enough to be her mate, in an enchanted chivalric past:

> our marvel blazoned a knight,
> Helmed, in cuirass,
>
> Unhorsed and shredded in the grove of combat
> By a grisly-bristled
> Boar, fabulous enough to straddle that sow's heat.

Plath's diction in the early poems is often justly criticized for being archaic or stilted, but in this case "blazoned," "Helmed," "cuirass," "grove of combat," and "fabulous" are entirely appropriate to the imagined age of chivalry.

The couple's reverie is short-lived, however, as the farmer's whistle abruptly brings them back to the present. "Thwack[ing]" the sow's nape, he causes her to awaken and rise from the dirt; as she heaves herself up, the romantic past of which she was dreaming, at least in the imaginations of the on-lookers, disappears. Plath experiments somewhat successfully with various technical devices here. She uses the hyphenated compound "green-copse-castled," a Hopkinsian device, to indicate that the dreaming pig was, for the length of her dream, living in the green grove of combat; while romantic, the phrase aptly evokes the world of knighthood and fabulous beasts. The simile "letting legend like dried mud drop" effectively compares the dropping away of the dream world to the dropping away of mud as the sow rises. In this construction parallel to "Pig hove ... up," Plath separates the second word of the verb unit from the first to emphasize the animal's movement, in the first case down and in the second up. Further, by separating "up" from "hove" by ten words and an entire intervening line, she suggests the slowness with which the heavy sow rises. Once on her feet, she seems to the onlookers

> A monument
> Prodigious in gluttonies as that hog whose want
> Made lean Lent
>
> Of kitchen slops and, stomaching no constraint,
> Proceeded to swill
> The seven troughed seas and every earthquaking continent.

The two hyperboles convey the sow's enormity and gluttony; "monument" suggests that her size makes her worthy of record and her comparison to the mythical hog which, finding kitchen slops insufficient, gulped down the seven seas and all the continents to satisfy his hunger and thirst describes her great appetite. Most early critics misread the hog simile, assuming that the sow herself swallows oceans and continents, thus seeing her as a symbol of nature's destructiveness or of evil incarnate, a far cry from the speaker's playful, awed description. Guttenberg asserts that the hog embodies the "destructiveness of the natural cycle" (140): "The horror of 'Sow' is that the hog consumes the 'seven troughed seas' as well as the land" (146). Rosenblatt, while admitting the light tone, sees beneath it the menace of a threatening and hostile nature (61). Butscher goes even further, describing the pig as a "gigantic villain," a Satan on the scale of Milton's and Dante's Satans (211–12).

Aird rightly praises Plath for her "virtuoso performance as a deft craftsman" in "Sow" (*Sylvia* 16–17). As in "The Snowman on the Moor," she employs terza rima and line lengths alternating in a regular pattern: lines one and three are long and line two is short in all odd stanzas with the reverse in all even stanzas, the opposite of the pattern in "Snowman." However, despite Rosenblatt's assertion that its "syllabics ... restrain emotional material" (61), she does not employ syllabics, but rather an entirely irregular meter. Further, she experiments with various sound values: hyphenated compounds that echo similar sounds ("mire-smirched," "grisly-bristled") and onomatopoeia both in existing words ("thwacking") and her own coinages ("maunching"). Finally, she works hard to attain her goal of being more realistic by including numerous concrete details ("belly-bedded on that black compost").

"Sow" is important in tracing Plath's development, for in it she attempts to move away from the subjects and approaches of the previous year to new ones, in this case trying a straightforward description of an animal. While she cannot yet free herself of reliance on highly structured forms and rhyme schemes and while the style is still ornate and heavily loaded with adjectives and hyphenated compounds, she clearly intends to attain greater realism by employing concrete details and accurate diction.

In the unpublished letter of January 21, 1957 to Plath's mother and brother, Hughes notes that she wrote "Mayflower" that day for a poetry competition sponsored by one of the Oxford colleges (Lilly Library). A typescript of the poem in the Smith College Library Rare Book Room bears a notation at the top in pen referring to the Hamilton Prize of Oriel College. Responding to the set topic with a conventional sonnet, Plath considers the source and significance of the name of the pilgrims' ship: "Remembering the white, triumphant spray / On hawthorn boughs, with goodwill to endure / They named their ship after the flower of May." As in the previous poem, she works to produce a descriptive poem filled with concrete details; indeed, the only significance of this slight piece is its testimony to Plath's poetic aims at this point in her career.

Plath must also have produced "The Lady and the Earthenware Head" during mid to late January, for she mentions it to her mother in a letter of February 3, commenting that it has "the best verse I've ever written" (335); further, she considered *The Earthenware Head* as "the right title, the only title" (J 193) for her book of poems from February to April 1958, when she replaced it first with *The Everlasting Monday* and then two weeks later with *Full Fathom Five* (CP 13). However, by July 3, 1958 she has reevaluated it, writing in her journal that it was "once, in England, my 'best poem': too fancy, glassy, patchy and rigid—it embarrasses me now—with its ten elaborate epithets for head in 5 verses" (244). Her second judgment seems the more accurate one.

The title refers to a clay model of Plath's head made by her roommate during her junior year at Smith. Because Hughes found it unattractive and unlike Plath's actual face,[2] they had taken it out of their flat on Eltisley Avenue and placed it in a willow tree in Grantchester Meadows. On February 8, Plath sent her mother a copy of the poem along with an explanation:

> Remember the model head M.B. Durr made of me? ... Ted suggested we walk out into the meadows and climb up into a tree and ensconce it there so it could look over the cow pastures and river. I returned there for the first time today, and there it was, high up on a branch-platform in a gnarled willow, gazing out over the lovely green meadows with the peace that passes understanding.... I even wrote a rather longish poem about it (only ending differently), which I'll type out in an adjoining letter and send you. (336)

A comparison of the original with the final version published in *The Collected Poems* reveals numerous changes, made perhaps as a result of Hughes's criticism of it recorded in a journal entry for February 26: "He criticized my Earthenware Head poem. Bad time for criticism. Me with no new poem to fight on yet" (155). His criticism was probably valid, for it is not among the best of the early works, even in its revised form. Awkward and loose, with stilted and excessive diction, it is nevertheless of interest psychologically because of its theme that one's negative side (symbolized by the head) can never successfully be destroyed.

The third-person speaker first describes the protagonist's decision to get rid of the "outrageous" head with its "spite-set / Ape ... look." Although she is reluctant (and, in the original, "Scared" and "unhappy" as well) to "junk it," she considers and rejects various options. Should she throw it on a garbage dump, it might be mistreated by vicious boys, and her superstitious side fears that she, as the original, could suffer as a result. (In the original version, she worries specifically that it would afflict her sleep.) Should she drop it into a dark pool, it might leer at her, "Lewdly beckoning" her to join it by drowning herself. Finally, she decides, as did Plath, to "lodge / The mimic head—in a crotched willow, green— / Vaulted by foliage," where it will disintegrate "to simple sod again." However, she is unable to carry out her plan and leaves it on the bookshelf where it continues to haunt and torment her with "its basilisk-look of love." This final comparison suggests that the protagonist will ultimately be destroyed by the head since she is unable to destroy it; in psychological terms, Plath suggests that, if left unchecked, one's dark or evil aspect will overcome one's positive nature.

Uninspired and weak from a technical point of view, the poem employs a regular rhyme scheme of abacbbc with one variation. Its word choices are poor: "brickdust-complected" is not only awkward in sound but is also dialectal; the slang term "junk it" is a jarring contrast to the archaic expression "in shocking wise"; and "out of the watery aspic, laureled by fins, / The simulacrum leers" is perhaps the most excessive two-line collection of ornate, poetic diction in all the early poems.

Plath is exaggerating only slightly when she tells her mother in a letter of August 6, 1957 that she is "writing my first poem for about six months" (372), for she seems to have produced little from late January through July under the various pressures of studying for her exams ("I am living at the University library from morning to night," she says in late April, LH 355), cooking and keeping house, and preparing to return to the United States in late June; during the long vacation at Cape Cod, she seemed to concentrate on short stories rather than poetry, noting in an unpublished journal entry for July 27 that she is working on five stories at once (Smith College Library).

Only one poem can definitely be attributed to this period; in a letter of April 8, Plath tells her mother, "I just finished yesterday one of my best, about 56 lines, called 'All the Dead Dears'" (352). While she typically tends to label the poem that she has most recently completed as her best yet or among her best, in this instance her evaluation is sound, for it is among the strongest of the early poems in content, imagery, and style.

Presenting death as a sinister, hovering presence in the form of one's own dead relatives who wait greedily and impatiently to drag the living into the grave with them, it was inspired by an exhibit that she saw at the Archaeological Museum on Downing Street in Cambridge, to which she refers in the poem's headnote. Discovered in 1952 at the Roman ruins in Cambridge and designated the Arbury Roman Burial, the stone coffin containing the skeletons of a woman and two small rodents was displayed with an explanatory card which read: "Apart from some fragments of textiles remaining from the shroud in which the body had been wrapped, and the skeletons of a shrew and a mouse, no objects were found with the bones of the woman buried in this double coffin of stone and lead. A.D. 400." The viewer was then instructed to "note distal end (near foot) of left tibia, which had been gnawed" (Butscher 204). The exhibit is no longer on display in the museum but is stored in the museum's warehouse on the outskirts of Cambridge. Still in its coffin, the human skeleton is protected by foam rubber with the tiny bones of both mouse and shrew glued to a card which reads, "Remains of a shrew and mouse which were found in this coffin" along with the same final line reported by Butscher, who apparently viewed the exhibit while it was still in the museum.

At first glance, "All the Dead Dears" seems to present the rather conventional view of death as the grim reaper, as the inevitable terrifying experience which awaits everyone at the end of life. Yet Plath has added some grotesque twists to this conventional view, combining childhood ghost stories with fairy tales of witches, ghouls, and monsters; its most ironic and frightening aspect is the revelation that one's own dead loved ones are the death figures waiting to drag one into the horror of the grave "to lie deadlocked with them." The images, metaphors, and diction are brilliant in their concreteness and aptness, and the harsh grating consonant sounds, the combinations of the hard "g," "k," and "r," reinforce the harshness of the theme.

Plath opens the poem with the concrete image of death which she had observed in the Archaeological Museum, developing from it the metaphor of eating as the two rodents had gnawed the woman's ankle before dying themselves. The rigidity and hardness of death are conveyed by "poker-stiff" and "granite" as well as by the repeated "g," "k," and "r" sounds:

> Rigged poker-stiff on her back
> With a granite grin
> This antique museum-cased lady
> Lies, companioned by the gimcrack
> Relics of a mouse and a shrew
> That battened for a day on her ankle-bone.

The light, casual description of the animals as companions, fanciful ornaments, and souvenirs gives way to the gruesome revelation that they became bloated after eating her flesh.

In the second stanza, this image becomes a symbol for time's devouring the living, aptly portrayed as a grist mill grinding not grain but flesh and bones, the word "grist" suggesting gristle or cartilage; the grating consonant sounds chillingly reproduce the grinding sounds of the mill:

> These three, unmasked now, bear
> Dry witness
> To the gross eating game
> We'd wink at if we didn't hear
> Stars grinding, crumb by crumb,
> Our own grist down to its bony face.

The third stanza introduces two new but equally gruesome and appropriate metaphors, the dead who await the living as barnacles clinging tightly to them and this particular dead woman as a relative of the speaker, in the sense that all must die. With a grisly play on the expression "blood relatives," the speaker describes the latter as a cross between a vampire and a scavenging animal: "she'll suck / Blood and whistle my marrow clean / To prove it."

The poem now moves from the general to the specific as the speaker sees herself and her own relatives caught in this cycle of decay and death; indeed, the next three stanzas develop the idea implied by the title—that all her dear dead ancestors wait to drag her into death with them. Looking at her face in a mirror, she sees the features she has inherited from them as one by one their faces blend with hers. They are described as witches, more frightening than those in fairy tales for they reach out "hag hands to haul [her]" into death. She also sees in the mirror a grotesque reflection of her insane father's drowned body floating up from the pond, the first of many images in the early poems to portray the dead father: "And an image looms under the fishpond surface / Where the daft father went down / With orange duck-feet winnowing his hair."[3]

An early version of the poem located in the Smith College Library
Rare Book Room contains two additional stanzas on the father in which the
speaker describes him as skillful and fearless and laments his early death:

> A man who used to clench
> Bees in his fist
> And out-rant the thundercrack,
> That one: not known enough: death's trench
> Digs him into my quick:
> At each move I confront his ready ghost
>
> Glaring sunflower-eyed
> From the glade of hives,
> Antlered by a bramble-hat,
> Berry-juice purpling his thumbs: o I'd
> Run time aground before I met
> His match. Luck's hard which falls to love
>
> Such long gone darlings.

Plath draws on two specific memories of her father. His feat of catching a
bee in his hand and holding it to her ear so that she could hear its buzzing
is described in the short story "Among the Bumblebees" (JP 311) and is
confirmed by Mrs. Plath in the Plath video in the series "Visions and Voices,"
while his defiance of thunder and lightning appears in the former (JP 310). At
this point in her development, Plath must have felt that these stanzas were too
personal and deleted them from the final version. Two years later, however,
she would use the first, albeit somewhat obliquely, in both "The Beekeeper's
Daughter" and "Poem for a Birthday."

With the final two stanzas, the speaker moves back to the universal
and general, first commenting on how the dead use every family occasion to
haunt their living descendants:

> All the long gone darlings: they
> Get back, though, soon,
> Soon: be it by wakes, weddings,
> Childbirths, or a family barbecue:
> Any touch, taste, tang's
> Fit for those outlaws to ride home on....

An early version in the Smith College Library reveals that Plath had an additional stanza at this point, which she later omitted:

And to sanctuary:
Like the footless woman
Keening out of the blizzard
Who flies against the wind when snow
Hisses, to vamp for bed and board
In the guise of my sister. Still they'll swarm in

Willynilly, usurping the armchair....

While the "footless woman" may refer to the museum skeleton, it is ambiguous, and the stanza as a whole appears extraneous, simply reiterating that the dead woman, with whom the speaker shares a kinship, continues to haunt her. Its omission suggests that Plath was beginning to be more judicious in editing her work.

The inescapability of death dominates the final stanza, in which the harsh consonant sounds resemble the ticking of the clock as well as a hammer pounding nails into a coffin. The dead relatives usurp the familiar, domestic world, pushing the living out of life with every "tick / And tack of the clock, until we go / Each skulled-and-cross boned Gulliver" to join them. The final devastating image projects into the near future in which the living are now in the grave, "Deadlocked with them, taking root as cradles rock." "Deadlocked" is a brilliant word choice, suggesting that they are locked in the embrace of the dead darlings and, as a result, are in a state of inaction which cannot be escaped. However, the last words are the most macabre and spine-chilling of all, for, as the recently dead bodies begin to decompose and "take root" in the earth, the cycle of life to death continues as newly-born babies rock in their cradles. The rhythm of the rocking cradles recalls the "tick / And tack of the clock" as time moves them toward death, while the word "rock" echoes the "granite grin" of the skeleton with which the poem began and thus foreshadows the deaths of these infants. Ironically, the recently dead will now become the "dead dears" who will haunt these babies, their descendants, as they pass through the cycle of decay and death. The wheel has come full circle with a bitter reversal of roles, for the haunted in life become the haunters in death.

"All the Dead Dears" is noteworthy not only for the originality of its bizarre concept of death but also for the high level of its craftsmanship as Plath successfully fuses manner and matter, using startling but appropriate images, metaphors, and vocabulary and effective sound patterns that underscore her theme. It is also important in revealing her unwillingness at this point to include highly personal subject matter and her growing ability to edit herself more skillfully.

With the exception of "Mayflower," these poems from early 1957 are included in the Cambridge Manuscript, indicating that Plath felt them to be among her strongest.

The remaining poems cannot be placed with any certainty, although the fact that none appear in the Cambridge Manuscript suggests that they were written after the spring of 1957; some may have been produced in the late summer before her job as instructor of English at Smith College absorbed most of her attention, leaving her little time or energy for creative writing in the fall, while others may have come during the next year.

In a letter of August 6, 1957, she tells her mother that she is "writing my first poem for about six months," describing it as "a short verse dialogue ... over a Ouija board, which is both dramatic and philosophical" (372–3). Although she does not identify the poem by title, it must be "Dialogue Over a Ouija Board," which grew to be much longer than she had originally planned. Perhaps because of its length, Hughes put it in the notes for the 1957 section of *The Collected Poems* (276–86) rather than in the section itself. However, he does place the short poem "Ouija" in the section proper. While the latter was perhaps written earlier in the year since Hughes and Plath had been consulting a spirit in the Ouija board since February (see LH 337), it seems more plausible that it emerged in August as an off-shoot of the longer work; indeed, a journal entry for August 9 indicates that Plath may have tired of the "long lumbering dialogue verse poem" (170) and abandoned it for this shorter non-dialogue version on the same subject.

"Ouija" is highly ambiguous, breaking down after the first stanza; as Pollitt accurately remarks, it "opens with eerie splendor," but then bogs down in the rhetoric of Stevens (69) and in an almost indecipherable train of thought. Perhaps because the poem as a whole fails to come off, it has attracted little critical comment. Rosenblatt and Broe, the only two who give it more than a sentence, present widely differing interpretations. The former sees it as a description of "the father-god [who] is in love with the 'bawdy queen of death' and wants only to write florid poetic praises of death's beauty. 'Ouija' thus states the daughter's unhappy realization that the father is married not to her but to his own deathly queen" (121–22). Broe, who mistakenly assumes that it is a later transition poem since it first appeared in *Crossing the Water*, asserts that it is "a casebook study of ingredients necessary to the new poetry" and "a cynical comment on the foppish limitations of Plath's academic style" (102–3). Since the poem is, in fact, an early one, Broe's theory is unconvincing, and, at any rate, while one might agree that it does describe an outworn style, it is hardly a "casebook study" of a new style.

The best sources for help in reading "Ouija" come from Plath and Hughes themselves. Both were interested in astrology, the occult, and fortune-telling; Hughes gave her a pack of Tarot cards for her birthday in 1956 (LH 322), she had written "Crystal Gazer" in 1956, and the two were consulting a spirit in the Ouija board by February 1957. Plath wrote her mother that "Pan (our Ouija imp) has been getting better and better about [predicting the soccer pools].... We keep telling Pan we want [the prize money] so we can have leisure to write and have lots of children, both" (337). Hughes's own note to the poem refers to this episode after informing us that "SP occasionally amused herself, with one or two others, by holding her finger on an upturned glass, in a ring of letters laid out on a smooth table, and questioning the spirits" (CP 276). Further, Hughes specifically describes Plath's dealings with the Ouija Board as attempts to communicate with her dead father:

> She would describe her suicide attempt as a bid to get back to her father.... Her father's name was Otto, and "spirits" [of the Ouija Board] would regularly arrive with instructions for her from one Prince Otto, who was said to be a great power in the underworld. When she pressed for a more personal communication, she would be told that Prince Otto could not speak to her directly, because he was under orders from The Colossus. And when she pressed for an audience with The Colossus, they would say he was inaccessible. ("Sylvia" 155)

Plath herself describes "Dialogue Over a Ouija Board" as "a more ambitious topic: a short verse dialogue which is supposed to sound just like conversation but is written in strict 7-line stanzas, rhyming ababcbc. It ... is at last a good subject—a dialogue over a Ouija board, which is both dramatic and philosophical" (LH 372–3; see also J 170). Based rather obviously on Plath and Hughes's own dealings with the Ouija Board, it concerns Sybil and Leroy, a couple who call up the spirit of their Ouija board, named Pan, and question him about the afterlife and her dead father; then they attempt to determine whether he is ill fact a god or only a reflection of their own psyches. While his first two responses imply the former, the third implies the latter, so that the conclusion is ambiguous. Because this poem contains numerous similarities to "Ouija" not only in situation but also in concrete details, images, and phrases, it seems to me the best commentary on it.

The poem's primary concern, I would suggest, is to describe Pan, the spirit of the Ouija board, as a worn-out, ineffective, and basically powerless god associated with death more than life, with evil more than good, with weakness more than strength. He may well, as Rosenblatt argues, represent the dead father who has "chosen" death, portrayed as a decayed queen, over his living daughter; Plath refers in a journal entry for December 27, 1958 to her "fear of my father's relation with my mother and Lady Death" (280). It reflects also the disappointment of Sybil in "Dialogue" who desperately wants to believe that Pan is the voice of a real god; in this context, it might well be subtitled "On the Decline of Gods."

The dramatic opening stanza sets the situation, as the speaker calls up the spirit of the board by placing her finger on an upturned glass; attracted by the heat of living flesh, the "chilly god ... / Rises to the glass from his black fathoms" (an echo of the father beneath the water in "All the Dead Dears" and an anticipation of a similar image in "Full Fathom Five"), while other spirits, "those unborn, those undone," gather at the window, longing to reassume warm bodies: "Imagine their deep hunger, deep as the dark / For the blood-heat that would ruddle [redden] or reclaim." The brilliant play of cold versus warmth and blackness versus "vermilions, bronzes, colors of the sun" skillfully reinforces the contrast between the world of the living and that of the spirits. Responding to the warmth from the speaker's finger, the old god begins to speak slowly, making the glass move from letter to letter on the board to spell out his message.

After this spectacular opening, the poem deteriorates into an ornate and heavily loaded description first of the old god's loss of power and his inability to communicate effectively and then of his amorous relationship with the queen of death. Using stilted and archaic diction such as "aureate," "maundering," and "Fair chronicler," the speaker suggests in stanza two that Pan's communicative powers have greatly diminished as a result both of "Age, and ages of prose" so that his "talking whirlwind" and "excessive temper," both operative in the past, have been reduced to the bare minimum, like the corncobs in the simile; indeed, echoing the argument of Stevens's "Sunday Morning," the speaker suggests that the power of the gods in general has descended to the level of mankind: "Skies once wearing a blue, divine hauteur / Ravel above us, mistily descend, / Thickening with motes, to a marriage with the mire."

In the third stanza, the focus of the poem shifts yet again to an ambiguous description of the old god's worship of "the rotten queen with saffron hair," identified as "the queen of death." Even though he himself is about to die ("Her wormy couriers are at his bones"), he still adores her and sings her praises:

> Still he hymns juice of her, hot nectarine.
> . . . .

He, godly, doddering, spells
No succinct Gabriel from the letters here
But floridly, his amorous nostalgias.

Like Sybil in the verse dialogue, the speaker seems to regret that Pan is not (or does not represent) an actual powerful god and/or that the father prefers death to her. In both works the absence of the archangel Gabriel, the herald of the coming of the Messiah and a bringer of comfort to humanity, suggests that a benign and omnipotent god / father no longer exists.[4]

Stylistically, this poem illustrates one of the major weaknesses of Plath's early work, for it is ornate, clogged, and precious. The diction in particular is artificial and stilted: nouns ("chronicler," "hauteur"), verbs ("ravels," "hymns"), adjectives ("aureate," "saffron"), and adverbs ("floridly"). However, the almost entirely regular iambic pentameter is uncharacteristic of Plath as are the lack of any rhyme and the varied stanzaic pattern of eleven lines in the first and third stanzas and ten lines in the second.

Despite the overall failure of the poem, its sinister opening stanza is a provocative preview of some of the striking successes to come, and its (ambiguous to be sure) evocation of the dead father is one of Plath's most constant themes.

"Two Views of Withens," "The Great Carbuncle," and "Hardcastle Crags," all based on the scenery of West Yorkshire and revealing Plath's reliance on landscape as a subject and as a symbol by which to convey but also to distance personal emotion, may have been inspired by the Hugheses' June 1957 visit there before setting sail for the States and written later in the summer, but their times of composition cannot be ascertained.

"Two Views of Withens" recounts the differing responses of two people to Top Withens, "a ruinous farmhouse under the moor's edge above Haworth, West Yorkshire—allegedly the model for Emily Brontë's *Wuthering Heights*. Sylvia Plath approached it from the south, over some miles of moorland, on her first visit" (CP 276); although Plath first saw it in September 1956 (LH 306), she may well have returned during the June stay in Heptonstall. In a subdued tone and pared-down style, the first-person speaker accurately describes the scenery on her way to Top Withens: "Above whorled, spindling gorse, / Sheepfoot-flattened grasses, / Stone wall and ridgepole rise" out of the fog. She then contrasts her bleak and melancholy perceptions of "bare moor, / A colorless weather" and of the house itself, "no palace," with the more positive ones of an unidentified "you": "You, luckier, / Report white pillars, a blue sky, / The ghosts, kindly." While a slight piece, it is a perceptive comment on how profoundly one's view of the world is influenced by one's nature. And, although it is somewhat freer in style, it nevertheless employs a regular rhyme scheme (abbacc) and contains awkward word choice and alliteration in "Where second wind, hip boot / Help over hill / And hill."

"The Great Carbuncle," an Eliotean meditation on a moment out of time caused by "an odd phenomenon sometimes observed on high moorland for half an hour or so at evening, when the hands and faces of people seem to become luminous" (CP 276), is perhaps based on an actual occasion, recorded in an unpublished portion of a letter written by Plath on September 11, 1956, when the horizontal light of the setting sun turned Hughes and Plath a glowing pink as they hiked on the moors (Lilly Library). Plath's choice of title is extremely accurate, not only reflecting literally the brilliant setting sun on the West Yorkshire moors, but also alluding to the red precious stone, like a ruby, which has the marvellous, even mystical ability to free one of bodily substance and weight and inspire him/her to accomplish exalted things.

As described in the poem, this Eliotean moment out of time is a sudden and unexpected occurrence, happening abruptly as the speaker and seven companions come up "over the moor-top" in the strange greenish light "neither of dawn / Nor nightfall." It not only makes their hands and faces "Lucent as porcelain," but also gives them a sense of weightlessness so that they seem to be floating free of the earth: "the earth's / Claim and weight gone out of them." She then describes the source of this transfiguring light as the "great jewel" of the title, defining it in terms of opposites which evoke Eliot's "Burnt Norton":

> shown often,
> Never given; hidden, yet
> Simultaneously seen
> On moor-top, at sea-bottom....

The speaker points out in a quasi-mystical fashion echoing "Little Gidding" ("The once-known way becoming / Wholly other") that both place and people are transformed, the latter becoming

> Estranged, changed, suspended where
> Angels are rumored, clearly
>
> Floating, among the floating
> Tables and chairs.

The image of floating tables and chairs on the moors seems to me a flaw in the poem's logic and creates an unfortunately humorous visual image in a work meant to be entirely serious.

The emotional/spiritual effects of this ecstatic moment out of time give the participants a sense of being able to accomplish great or exalted deeds: "and there is nothing / So fine we cannot do it," an echo of Yeats's "Adam's Curse." The moment out of time, however, is brief, as in *Four Quartets*; the light abruptly disappears, and everything returns to the weight and monotony of ordinary existence: "At the common homecoming / Light withdraws. Chairs, tables drop / Down: the body weighs like stone." The alliteration of the "d" and the traditional simile of the stone effectively contrast the heavy downward return to reality with the ecstatic sensation of lightness and floating upward.

"The Great Carbuncle" cannot at this time with certainty be considered a product of the summer of 1957; indeed, its heavy indebtedness to Eliot and its meditative cast link it with the poems of 1956, while its use of syllabics (seven per line with two exceptions) allies it with those of the summer of 1958. Thus, until a definitive composition date can be established, it is difficult to draw conclusions concerning its place in Plath's development. Nevertheless, its treatment, though awkward, of a mystical natural experience, a topic which Plath rarely explores, makes it worth perusal.

"Hardcastle Crags," whose earlier titles include "Night Walk," "A Walk in the Night," and "Nocturne" (Lilly Library), may have been composed in the summer of 1957, but another possibility is the period of May 22 to June 13 of 1958 (see the following chapter). Between a recording of her poems made on April 18, 1958 and another made on June 13, 1958, Plath deleted three poems from the group she read earlier and added five: "Maudlin" (then titled "Mad Maudlin"), "Mussel Hunter at Rock Harbor," "Child's Park Stones," "Hardcastle Crags" (then titled "Nocturne"), and "The Thin People" (then titled "The Moon Was a Fat Woman Once") (Tabor 140). Although "Maudlin" was an earlier work, having been included in the Cambridge Manuscript, that both "Mussel Hunter" and "Child's Park Stones" had been written in the three weeks prior to the June recording date suggests that "Hardcastle Crags" and "The Thin People" may also have been products of the same period; further, "Hardcastle Crags" and "Mussel Hunter" were accepted for publication in *The New Yorker* on June 25, indicating that they may well have been sent out together soon after being composed. However, since neither "Hardcastle Crags" nor "The Thin People" is written in the syllabics typical of the spring and summer of 1958, the evidence is not conclusive, and I will discuss both in this chapter.

"Hardcastle Crags" is the most complex of this group of West Yorkshire poems, making symbolic use of the landscape in the manner of Eliot. Its female protagonist flees the town hoping to find solace on the moors, but discovers a sinister indifference so frightening and overwhelming that she turns back at the poem's end; as Rosenthal and Gall note, "her senses [are] almost neurotically alert to her changing surroundings" (37). Plath's final choice of title seems to have been made only for its harsh sound effects, since the valley of Hardcastle Crags lies far below the village and moors where her protagonist walks; Perloff's assertion that she is in Hardcastle Crags itself is thus mistaken (*"Angst"* 62).

Plath accurately recreates Heptonstall, whose buildings of black stone closely line the steep main street, creating a stone corridor in which sounds are magnified and multiplied as described in the opening lines. At night, the village appears dark, hard, and foreboding. The surrounding moorland is vast and empty, its pastures where sheep and cattle graze bordered by walls made of the same black stone. In a letter written in September 1956, Plath describes the "incredible, wild, green landscape of bare hills, crisscrossed by innumerable black stone walls like a spider's web in which gray, woolly sheep graze, along with chickens and dappled brown-and-white cows" (305). And in her short story "All the Dead Dears" (1957–8), she creates a nighttime moorland scene quite similar to that in the poem: "Outside, in the clear, windy night, the moon shone high and full; a blue, luminous mist was rising from the bottom of the valley where the mountain stream flowed black and deep" (JP 197).

This literal landscape functions as a symbol both of nature's hostility and of its indifference to the human being, represented by the vulnerable, frail, and solitary protagonist. The distant moon sheds a chill, blue light; the "long wind" threatens to annihilate her, "paring her person down / To a pinch of flame"; the hills of iron and stone may crush her to "quartz grit"; its sleeping animals, described in terms of stones, boulders, and granite, are oblivious to her. The landscape is self-sufficient, powerful, and enormous in contrast to the weak individual, characterized by "pinch," "paltry," and "small."

The town offers no comfort either, although it is not actively menacing as are parts of the moor. It too is dark and hard, being made entirely of black stone, and its inhabitants, asleep like the moorland animals, are as inaccessible to the protagonist. Aird perceptively suggests that the town "represents the security of a human community which *should* provide some refuge against the blind, crushing indifference of nature but it is itself presented with some ambivalence. References to the 'steely street,' 'The stone-built town' [sic] and 'the dark dwarfed cottages [sic] suggest that the village itself is contaminated by the threat of the stony land beyond' (*Sylvia* 19). The protagonist thus represents the total isolation of the human being, and her turning back at the end of the poem is frighteningly ambiguous; she turns from the terror of the moor, but the town offers no consolation either, its black stone buildings like the moor's black stone walls and its shut cottage doors like the shut barn doors.

Plath makes skillful use of sound values, of multiple and quickly shifting images of hard substances, fire, the moon, and the color black, and of an effective stanza form to undergird her theme. No doubt inspired by an actual experience, she feels compelled to create distance through a third-person narrator speaking from the protagonist's point of view. Both the technical elements and the speaker serve to restrain the volatile emotions underlying the poem.

"Hardcastle Crags" begins with the explosive fireworks of the harsh consonants "k," "t," and "r" as the protagonist rushes through the "black / Stone-built town" with its "dark, dwarfed cottages," the sounds of her shoes reverberating against the streets and adjoining buildings; the consonance, quick tempo, and violent verbs convey the intensity of her mood, although it is neither explained nor described:

> Flintlike, her feet struck
> Such a racket of echoes from the steely street,
> Tacking in moon-blued crooks from the black
> Stone-built town, that she heard the quick air ignite
> Its tinder and shake
>
> A firework of echoes from wall
> To wall of the dark, dwarfed cottages.

These opening lines introduce the poem's major images: hard materials ("flint" and "steel"), fire ("quick," "ignite," "tinder," "firework"), the moon, and the color black.

As the protagonist leaves the village and approaches the moors, the tempo slows, the loud echoes die away, and the sinister sounds of the wind among the long grasses of the fields are heard:

>   the walls
> Gave way to fields and the incessant seethe of grasses
> Riding in the full
>
> Of the moon, manes to the wind....

The moon takes on a role that it plays often in Plath's poetry as a distant, unsympathetic observer of human vulnerability.

Following an extremely weak passage in which Plath describes the protagonist's total isolation, awkwardly alluding first to a West Yorkshire superstition[5] and then to the popular 50s song "Mr. Sandman, bring me a dream," stanzas 5–9 skillfully convey the oppressive nature of the moor through images of stone and iron as the woman is reduced to a pinch of flame on the verge of extinction. While she had hoped to find solace in nature, she is disappointed to discover indifference and potential hostility instead:

> All the night gave her, in return
> For the paltry gift of her bulk and the beat
> Of her heart, was the humped indifferent iron
> Of its hills, and its pastures bordered by black stone set
> On black stone.

Even the animals take part in this silent but devastating conspiracy against humanity. They are shut up in barns (in effect shutting her out) or they are asleep, as unresponsive as the stones of the pasture walls: the cows are "mute as boulders," the sheep drowse "stoneward," and the birds wear "granite ruffs." The entire landscape is totally self-sufficient, all-powerful, and enduring, neither needing nor acknowledging the existence of humanity, a brutal fact which is "Enough to snuff the quick / Of her small heat out." The image of frail human life as a "pinch of flame" is continued here in the protagonist's "small heat." Plath's use of "quick" suggests not only the protagonist's living matter, but also, and more significantly, its fragility and brevity.

The poem closes as "the weight / Of stones and hills of stones" threatens to crush the woman, described as quartz, a less impervious type of stone that can be broken down to "grit." Plath's shift from the metaphor of the human being as a tiny flame to that of quartz works well, juxtaposing one type of stone to another; as Annas notes, this final metaphor has been prepared for by the comparison of her feet to flint in the opening line (21). Terrified of annihilation, the protagonist departs:

> but before the weight
> Of stones and hills of stones could break
> Her down to mere quartz grit in that stony light
> She turned back.

The ambiguity of the ending leaves the poem's tensions unresolved.

The intricacy of the poetic structure is largely unobtrusive, revealing its complexity only upon close scrutiny; in this instance, Plath is able to blend it organically with the content. Its nine five-line stanzas have a rhyme scheme of ababa made of highly imperfect rhymes ("struck," "street," "black," "ignite," and "shake" in the first stanza, for example). While the meter is irregular, each stanza follows the same visual pattern with the first four lines becoming progressively longer, so that the brevity of the last line is jarring, particularly at the poem's end. As for the influence of Thomas, Lawrence, and Hughes detected by Rosenthal and Gall, they say, rightly I think, "No matter. She assimilates their apperceptive influence and makes it sufficiently her own.... We note the relationships, but they are simply tokens of a communion with other sensibilities, past and present, such as we find in even—perhaps especially—the greatest poetry" (37).

"Hardcastle Crags," a striking example of the Plathian theme of the menace of the universe toward the vulnerable individual, is among the finest of the early poems, largely avoiding excesses of diction and construction. While Plath chooses to employ a third-person narrator, she creates a highly original symbolic landscape to carry the emotional content. Rosenthal and Gall, who suggest that it "may be the best poem in *The Colossus*," praise it as a "relatively early instance of Plath's realized art" in that it is "on its way to the discovery of how to write at a pitch of pure intensity that is like being carried away by, yet somehow guiding, a runaway horse" (37). It is a powerful anti-Romantic vision of nature, not as consoling or uplifting, but as fiercely closed to human concerns and menacing in its might and longevity.

"The Thin People," originally entitled "The Moon Was a Fat Woman Once," was composed between September 1957 and June 13, 1958 when Plath read it at a recording session (Tabor 140); the "wallpaper / Frieze of cabbage-roses and cornflowers" no doubt reflects the "pink-rose-walled room" (J 183) of the Northampton apartment which the Hugheses occupied during the academic year. As noted above, there is some reason to suspect that it may have been produced in late May or early June of 1958 just prior to her recording it.

This brilliant poem, which has failed to receive the attention it deserves, presents yet another menacing force which preys on the sensitive and thus vulnerable human being: the haunting knowledge of the suffering and injustice of the world, represented by the starving peoples of the past. Plath ventures back to the realm of social and universal concerns as subject matter for poetry, her intention just prior to meeting Hughes. The starving people are, of course, quite literally thin, but are also thin in being ghostly apparitions that inhabit the minds of the sensitive and in removing the fullness of life from them. Plath reinforces their thinness by using the word "thin" eight times and by employing the "thinnest" stanza form, the couplet, so that the form here is organic to the content and not just a test of her technical capabilities.

The original starving people, remembered from the childhood of the narrator who speaks in the first-person plural for all sensitive human beings, seems to have come from Plath's own experiences at about the age of ten. In the short story "Superman and Paula Brown's New Snowsuit," written in 1955 when Plath (and the narrator/protagonist) was twenty-three, a young girl is disillusioned by her sudden recognition of the suffering and injustice of life both on a general and on a personal level. The former is revealed to her when she sees a World War II movie about starving prisoners of war which so shocks her that she vomits at the theatre and later has nightmares:

> [T]here was a war picture playing with [*Snow White*] ... about prisoners of the Japanese who were being tortured by having no food or water. Our war games and the radio programs were all made up, but this was real, this really happened.... After I went to bed that night, as soon as I closed my eyes, the prison camp sprang to life in my mind, and again the groaning men broke through the walls, and again they were shot down. (JP 272)

The same incident appears in "The Shadow," a short story written in 1959; as in the poem, the suffering figures do not stay in the dream but invade the protagonist's real world: "The hostile, brooding aura of the nightmare seeped out, somehow, to become a part of my waking landscape.... Prepared as I was for the phenomenon of evil in the world, I was not ready to have it expand in this treacherous fashion, like some uncontrollable fungus, beyond the confines of half-hour radio programs, comic book covers, and Saturday afternoon double features" (JP 148–9).

Plath was a socially and politically conscious person who reacted strongly to world events, as evidenced in letters to her mother; in November, 1956, for example, she wrote, "Well, between my private crisis [revealing her secret marriage to the Cambridge authorities] and the huge crisis aroused by Britain's incredible and insane bombing of Egypt, the universe is in a state of chaos" (322), and "the Hungarian and Suez affairs have depressed me terribly" (325). Often her personal crises paralleled global ones, and she frequently uses the latter as metaphors for the former. Here, however, she seems to intend the poem specifically as social protest; as Annas notes, it is one of the first with "an overtly historical/economic context and imagery.... The thin people are ... an externalization of social guilt" (43). While Bundtzen and Annas disagree over their identity, the former suggesting that they cannot be "clearly identified" (171) and the latter that Plath "specifically identifies [them] as victims of the Second World War" (43), it seems to me that Plath begins with the concrete, historical image from World War II but then expands it to symbolize the starving and poverty-stricken in general, a technique she used earlier in "All the Dead Dears."

The poem begins with the recreation of a childhood memory similar to those in the two short stories as the speaker describes the attempts made by sensitive people to deny the continuing existence of the starving and poor by relegating them to the movie screen and to the past, specifically to World War II:

> They
> Are unreal, we say:
>
> It was only in a movie, it was only
> In a war making evil headlines when we
>
> Were small that they famished....

After the war is over, they haunt "our bad dreams, their menace / Not guns, not abuses, / But a thin silence." Plath focuses on details traditionally associated with the suffering, details which demand pity from and evoke guilt in the sensitive; they cover their nakedness with "flea-ridden donkey skins," maintain an uncomplaining (but accusing) silence, and drink vinegar from tin cups, the latter a brilliant combination of the poverty of beggars and the suffering of Christ on the cross. The association of Christ is continued in the "insufferable nimbus of the lot-drawn / Scapegoat," the halo "insufferable" because it makes observers feel an unpleasant sense of guilt at their suffering.

The real horror of these haunting figures, however, is that they do not remain in newsreels, memories, or nightmares, but ultimately invade the everyday world:

> But so thin,
>
> So weedy a race could not remain in dreams,
> Could not remain outlandish victims
>
> In the contracted country of the head....

The words "outlandish" and "contracted" are particularly effective, the former meaning both "bizarre" and "remote from civilization" and the latter suggesting the limited area they occupy within memories and dreams; they clearly will expand their territory beyond so small a scope by invading the real world as well. The comparison of this inevitable move to the cutting away of the moon by the old woman in the fairy tale is an ironically appropriate choice since it involves food and eating.

As the speaker describes their movement out of the heads and into the lives of the sensitive, the tense significantly shifts from past to present:

Now the thin people do not obliterate

Themselves as the dawn
Grayness blues, reddens, and the outline

Of the world comes clear and fills with color.

They no longer disappear when dawn comes and dreams fade away, but remain in the daytime world where they take away its color and fullness, robbing it of what they themselves lack. It is a terrifying vision of how life loses its beauty, pleasure, and meaning when one is held in the powerful grip of some sinister fear or anxiety:

They persist in the sun-lit room: the wallpaper

Frieze of cabbage-roses and cornflowers pales
Under their thin-lipped smiles,

Their withering kingship.

Such is their power that it fades the rose and blue shades of the flowers in the wallpaper, an image haunting precisely because it is so domestic and ordinary.

From the bedroom they invade first the speaker's country and ultimately the whole world. As she realizes with horror, "We own no wildernesses rich and deep enough / For stronghold against their stiff / Battalions." Continuing the metaphor of the wilderness, she describes the thin people taking the fullness and color of an entire forest, rendering it as thin and gray as they are:

See, how the tree boles flatten
And lose their good browns

If the thin people simply stand in the forest,
Making the world go thin as a wasp's nest

And grayer; not even moving their bones.

This closing passage is effective in a number of ways. By using "See," the speaker forcibly involves the reader in the experience. Further, the wasp's nest simile is appropriate because it is both thin and gray. Finally, the sinister quality of the thin people's subtle and nonaggressive takeover is emphasized by their lack of movement or noise, anticipating the menacing mushrooms in the late 1959 poem. Their thinness, and that of the speaker's now bleak world, is emphasized in that the poem ends not with a couplet but with a single line.

Plath effectively welds technique and content in "The Thin People." In addition to the use of couplets to reinforce the concept of thinness, she employs repetition to create a sinister incantatory effect: "the thin people ... the gray people," "It was only ... it was only," "Not guns, not abuses," "so thin, / So weedy," "could not remain ... could not remain." Once the thin people come into the real world at line 24, however, the dreamlike repetition stops, emphasizing that move into reality. Further, Plath experiments skillfully with sound effects, keeping to a minimum the harsh consonants of which she is so fond and stressing instead the quiet, and in this context eerie, sounds of "l," "p," "n," and "s." The rhymes are varied, a combination of imperfect rhymes, exact repetition ("people," "people"), perfect rhyme ("They," "say"), and no rhyme at all ("flatten" has no rhyming equivalent).

Finally, the images and comparisons reinforce the content. The juxtaposition between thinness and grayness on the one hand and fullness and color on the other runs, sometimes subtly, throughout; gray, for example, is implied in the donkey skins and tin cups, and rose and blue in the wallpaper's roses and cornflowers. Starvation as opposed to eating well is reflected in the "stalky limbs" of the thin people versus the plump bellies of the mice and in the woman's "cutting fat meat" out of the moon until only "a rind of little light" is left. Finally, the actual war in which the thin people were victims is echoed ironically in the military images used at the poem's end to describe their insidious invasion of the world.

Although it has received little attention, "The Thin People" is significant in its blending of socially-conscious subject matter with Plath's highly personal perception of the human experience as menaced by sinister forces, in its simple yet organic technical devices, and in its appropriate and original imagery. It is indeed, as Hughes has noted, a "chilling" work ("Notes" 189).

There are only a few clues to the times of composition of the two remaining poems: "A Lesson in Vengeance" and "The Everlasting Monday." "A Lesson in Vengeance" was completed by February 28, 1958, as an unpublished portion of a journal entry notes that it was sent out to an unnamed magazine on that date (Smith College Library). A stilted allegory, it contrasts the direct ways in which sin or evil was dealt with in "the dour ages / Of drafty cells and draftier castles" with the more distanced and casual responses in recent times. Its two major examples from the past are the historical figures Suso, a German mystic of the 14th century who opposed contemporary evils, and Cyrus the Great, the 6th century B.C. ruler of Persia who, according to Biblical accounts, freed the Jews from their captivity in Babylon. Clearly Plath seems here to reflect the current dictum of Eliot and Pound that a poem must be intellectual and employ obscure allusions. While from a technical point of view "A Lesson in Vengeance" is particularly awkward in word choice and alliteration ("by such abuses / As smack of spite and the overscrupulous / Twisting of thumbscrews"), it demonstrates Plath's experimentation with yet another difficult rhyme scheme in that every line ends with "s."

"The Everlasting Monday" was written prior to April 26, 1958 since in an unpublished journal entry for that day Plath proposes *The Everlasting Monday* as the current title for her book of poetry, explaining that it captures "the Yeatsian idea of work, becoming fused with static being: a work and life of eternal Mondays, eternal launderings and fresh starts" (Smith College Library). Ironically, while this comment implies a hopeful tone and theme, the poem is rather the opposite, portraying Mondays as sterile and melancholic. The dominant image is the man in the moon as a poverty-stricken peasant reminiscent of Yeats's late poems on Jack: "The moon's man stands in his shell, / Bent under a bundle / Of sticks." The moon itself is described as cold and barren: "His teeth are chattering among the leprous / Peaks and craters of those extinct volcanoes." Clearly, however, the poem's most striking image is a domestic one, the light of this moon falling "chalk and cold" on the bedspread of the first-person plural speaker and thereby extending its bleakness into the human world. This poem, which has been virtually ignored by scholars, is tighter, barer, more chilling than most of the 1957 poems and deserves scrutiny as a mood piece or perhaps as an early expression of the hell of imaginative paralysis which constantly threatens the artist, a dominant theme in Plath's work as a whole.

NOTES

1. The giant may be associated with Hughes. Plath refers to him as "a huge Goliath" in a letter of April 29, 1956 (274), and the destructive male in "The Queen's Complaint" is also a giant.

2. In the original version, the following lines describe the male visitor's aversion to the head:

> In distaste he pointed at it:
> Brickdust-complected, eyes under dense lid
> Half-blind, that derisive pout—

Rude image indeed, to ape with such sly treason
Her dear face: best rid
Hearthstone at once of the outrageous head.

3. A source which may have influenced Plath's description of the father is Alfred Noyes's children's poem, "When Daddy Fell into the Pond."

4. In "Dialogue Over a Ouija Board," when Sybil states that she prefers "To picture some other party speaking through / Our separate veins and this glass mouth," Leroy replies, "Oh, you're / Going to get Gabriel's thumb into the pie / If you must butcher Mother Goose to do it. / Gabriel or Beelzebub" (CP 280).

5. The West Yorkshire superstition that a mist can dissolve into the figure of a recognizable ghost also appears in her short story "All the Dead Dears" (JP 196–203).

S A N D R A M . G I L B E R T

A Long Hiss of Distress:
Plath's Elegy on the Beach at Berck

Berck est une station à la fois balneaire, familiale et medicale climatique.
Guide Michelin, Nord de la France,
Champagne, Ardennes (1980)

I still remember the curious, and indeed curiously chilling, combination of bafflement and envy with which I read "Berck-Plage" when it first came out in a magazine—a British journal like *Granta* or *Encounter*, as I recall, though I'm not sure which. My bafflement was generated by my envy or maybe the other way around. I was both puzzled and piqued by what I understood was far beyond my writerly (and even readerly) grasp: a presiding tension that gave shape, depth, and mystery to the poem, a tension between coolly controlled formal precision, on the one hand, and on the other, enigmatically, almost mystically daring metaphorical leaps. The strangely sinister mackerel-gatherers "handling the black and green lozenges like the parts of a body" scared me, even though (or perhaps because?) I didn't understand why and how they mattered in this gravely elegiac work. I was inexplicably sickened by the riddle of the passing priest, with his "high, dead, toeless foot," by the "obscene bikinis" and the furtive lovers who weirdly "unstick themselves" behind "concrete bunkers," by the plight of the "onlooker, trembling," who is drawn "like a long material // Through a still virulence," and by the "weed, hairy as privates" that this cryptic observer confronts. As for the at first dying,

From *Field* 59 (Fall 1998): pp. 30–38. © 1998 by Oberlin College.

then dead old man at the center of the piece, with his "wedding-cake face in a paper frill" and his lost "eye-stones, yellow and valuable," his useless "tongue, sapphire of ash," those prophetic anxieties that, like most aspiring poets, I carefully cultivated, made his meaning all too clear to me, though I had as yet faced few mortal losses in my own life.

I came across "Berck-Plage" in the early sixties—maybe after Plath's death, maybe not—but I'd been following her career with fascination for nearly a decade, ever since I was transfixed by an unnerving story she published in the girls' magazine *Seventeen*, when she must have been little more than that age herself and I was still in my "pre-teens." Now, as I journeyed into my twenties, I was a barely published poet, a part-time graduate student, and a full-time mother of two—soon to be three—babies, living in Kew Gardens, Queens, and Byronically stalking apart in "joyless reverie" from the other mothers at the playground, whom I scorned for what I considered their bovine cheerfulness. Plath was just enough ahead of me—four or five years older, I gathered—so that I could be secretly competitive without being as overwhelmingly daunted by her achievements as I would be by those of an exact contemporary. That I too had been Guest Managing Editor of *Mademoiselle* (albeit five years after she was) during the triumphant "prize" month she later so devastatingly portrayed in *The Bell Jar*—that I'd indeed worked closely with Cyrilly Abels, the very "Jay Cee" of that novel—cemented what I considered an obscure bond between my own quotidian domesticity and the more glamorous life of this author strolling a European beach of which I'd never heard.

Until around the time I first read "Berck-Plage," however, I'd been disappointed by Plath's poems (which is to say, in all honesty, I'd been rather relieved by their apparent docility, their "good girl" decorum). Though I knew I myself might seem just the kind of dutiful young "wife/mother" produced like vanilla wafers by the cookie-cutter culture of mid-century America, I didn't want to be a "good girl" in poetry, even though I had no very clear idea how to stop being one. Of course, most of the Plath verses I'd been reading had been the relatively careful texts of *The Colossus*, rather than the great *Ariel* poems, which I was just beginning to read when I stumbled on "Berck-Plage." Looking back now on those baffled, envious, really quite astonishing reading experiences, I realize how lucky it was for me that I *could* "stumble" on the *Ariel* poems. In the early sixties, Plath's vehement last words swam randomly, haphazardly into my ken, and even when, later, I began seeking them out, knowing she had lost her life (although not quite how or why) and eager to see what she had left behind, I remained for quite a while an innocent, if no longer a random, reader. None of her poems had yet been privileged over any other: she was not yet the figure of melodrama who became notorious as the "poetess" of "Daddy." Rather, she was someone from a college cohort just a little ahead of my own who had suddenly written a number of unfathomably compelling poems (including "Daddy") that kept emerging along with odd, unverifiable rumors about the circumstances of her death.

Compelling, compulsive, almost compulsory reading. That was the point about the poems themselves. Whatever their author's story—and no one I knew could explain it to me, at least for a while—there were the poems. Scorching the page with a kind of fatality. Hissing through the page. Burning the paper. Weird. I had never seen anything like them, nor have I since. I even wrote, and eventually published, a poem of my own "Her Last Sickness"— whose title reflects my sense of a feverishly brilliant malady at play in these breakthrough finalities.

"Berck-Plage" wasn't, to be sure, the most scorching of Plath's late works. I'd reserve that adjective for (besides "Daddy" and "Lady Lazarus") "Fever 103," "Getting There," "Stings," and a few others. But what I've called its "metaphoric leaps" had a disciplined dazzle that I sensed was rooted in something hectic, something that in lesser hands would be out of control. At the same time, control—as I noted earlier—was also crucial in the poem, which has a surprisingly dispassionate as well as somber tone, despite its speaker's sometimes almost paranoid edginess ("Why is it so quiet, what are they hiding? ... Obscene bikinis hide in the dunes.... These children are after something, with hooks and cries"). Indeed, studying the piece today, I begin to suspect that what I'm calling "control" or "discipline" is the flip side of a kind of madness, a narrative estrangement from disturbing subject matter that makes it possible for Plath the artist to fashion such material into a superb elegy that is both deeply moving and deeply skeptical. For "Berck-Plage" is, of course, an elegy, perhaps the finest one this often indefatigable mourner giver produced, though the gravity of its lamentation has been overlooked in favor of the more conventionally confessional "family elegies" the writer addressed to her father.[1]

Like so many strong elegies, "Berck-Plage" juxtaposes the world of the desirous flesh—"those dying generations at their song"—with the *timor mortis* that the very processes of generation inevitably beget. Carnal appetites flourish on Plath's beach, bordered by the sea, that "great abeyance" of the solid and known, but so does fear, in the person of the deathly Father, a priest who no doubt "plumbs the well of his book" to uncover the awful truth of ashes to ashes, dust to dust. For on this "sandy damper" that stretches for miles, the earth is quite literally the ground of a hospital where the "onlooker, trembling" observes the hosts of "Things, things— / Tubular steel wheelchairs, aluminum crutches" that have been amassed to stave off death, but where, nonetheless, a representative old man is inexorably "vanishing" on "a striped mattress in one room." His death in section 3, a little more than halfway through the seven-part poem, sets off the work's remaining (and its major) action: the laying out of his body ("They propped his jaw with a book until it stiffened / And folded his hands, that were shaking: goodbye, good-bye"), the problematic condolences of mourners ("It is a blessing, it is a blessing") as they confront the "long coffin of soap-colored oak ... and the raw date / Engraving itself in silver with marvelous calm"); the rituals of wake and funeral ("the pallors gather— // The pallors of hands and neighborly faces, ... while the hills roll the notes of the dead bell") and the final resolution of burial, attended by the poem's speaker, "dark-suited and still, a member of the party."

"A member of the party": that Plath, as it turned out, was literally one of the mourners who followed the coffin of her neighbor Percy Key to its "stopping place" in Devonshire powerfully testifies to the conscious craft with which she fashioned this apparently seamless work. For the old man who is said to "vanish" at the center of "Berck-Plage" (and presumably therefore at or near the "real" Berck-Plage) did not actually expire anywhere near the beach in northern France where the poem's protagonist moves "smilingly" though she knows she is "not a smile" and fears her heart is "too small to bandage" the "terrible faults" of the children who are "after something, with hooks and cries." When I first read "Berck-Plage," of course, I knew as little about someone in Devon named Percy Key as I did about the town of Berck, on the shore of Picardy—which is to say I knew nothing of either. Instead, I assumed that the episode the poem purports to represent was a single coherent event that took place at a sea-side hospital—in France or Belgium. Nor did I learn the "truth" about the work's sources until decades later when Ted Hughes explained that "Berck-Plage" is a beach in Normandy "which SP visited in June 1961" and where "there was a large hospital for mutilated war veterans and accident victims—who took their exercise along the sands." Added Hughes, the "funeral in the poem is that of Percy Key [an elderly neighbor] who died in June 1962, exactly a year after her visit to Berck-Plage."[2] Later still, I discovered in the old Green Michelin that has provided me with an epigraph here what Hughes himself evidently didn't realize (and what explains the importunate children with "hooks and cries"): that Berck, with its "immense plage de sable fin, tres sure," is "mondialement connu pour le traitement des malades osseuse, specialement chez les enfants," but that "ces affections, y compris la tuberculose osseuse, ne sont pas contagieuses, aussi les malades peuvent-ils mener une vie sociale normale."[3]

Although over the years I've examined a number of the Plath materials held at the Smith College Rare Book Room and Indiana University's Lilly Library, I don't remember ever looking at drafts of "Berck-Plage." It seems likely, however, that surviving pages might show the poem starting with jottings on the beach at Berck—jottings that mingled observations "balneare" ("Electrifyingly colored sherbets" floating above the long "sandy damper"), "familiale" (bikinis, children, "white sea crockery") and "medicale" (wheelchairs, crutches, "a green pool ... Sick with what it has swallowed," and even a priest whose black boot "is the hearse of a dead foot" not unlike the gangrenous foot of that bastard "Daddy").[4] Whether or not my conjecture is right, however, the work's genius is evident in the skill with which Plath brought such real or hypothetical "balneare, familiale et medicale" notations to bear on the elegiac tradition in which she undertook to compose a work memorializing the death of her octogenarian neighbor, Percy Key. For as in T. S. Eliot's "East Coker," in which the "whole earth is our hospital/ Endowed by the ruined millionaire," the sanitoria at Berck-Plage become monitory establishments, with each crutch and wheelchair a *memento mori* meant to warn all alike—sick or well, consumers of sherbets or wearers of obscene bikinis, mackerel gatherers or trembling onlookers—that priestly death comes always and inexorably closer with his "black boot [that] has no mercy for anybody."

To be sure, from the early "Morning in the Hospital Solarium" to the late "Tulips," "In Plaster," "The Surgeon at 2 a.m.," and "Paralytic," hospitals had long had special significance for Plath, who also fictionalized medical scenes in such prose writings as "Johnny Panic and the Bible of Dreams" and *The Bell Jar*. Perhaps, however, the sheer strangeness of the beach at Berck—both its foreignness and its uncanny juxtapositions of jovial holiday-making and sorrowful cure-taking, of, that is, the "balneare, familiale et medicale"—fosters the tone of solemn estrangement that governs the piece from the start. Certainly such distancing is apropos, like muffled drums, in the presence of death, but this beautifully crafted elegy has, throughout, a firmness of defamiliarization that seems singularly suited to the "immense plage de sable fin, tres sure" on which it is so resonantly set.

The aesthetic processes that shape such defamiliarization are, moreover, strikingly ironic. On the one hand, as priestly death stalks the living, human beings are disassembled into fragments of themselves, with the "toeless foot" of doom drawing ever nearer to the "shrunk voices // Waving and crutchless" of the bathers and to the "confectioner's sugar" of breasts and hips hidden in the dunes, while the "green pool" sick from swallowing "limbs, images, shrieks" and the "weed, hairy as privates" prefigure the "red ribs" and "mirrory" surgical eye that will soon appear, along with the "eye-stones" and tongue of the dead man, the pallid "hands and neighborly faces" of mourners, and the crusted "blood of limb stumps" evoked by the red earth of the graveyard. On the other hand, as the living disintegrate into body parts, inhuman objects ("Things, things") take on an almost surrealistically autonomous existence: "Electrifyingly-colored sherbets ... travel the air in scorched hands" as if of their own volition; "washed sheets fly in the sun"; the "raw date" of the old man's death engraves "itself with marvelous calm." Finally, indeed, the thoughts of his widow are "Blunt practical boats // Full of dresses and hats and china and married daughters," as if there were no distinction between people and possessions, and the "actions" of the dead man have solidified "like living-room furniture, like a decor," while the trees with serene composure "march to church."

Such processes of distancing and estrangement set the scene with extraordinary effectiveness for the climactic moment of "Berck-Plage"—the moment when the "naked mouth" of earth opens, "red and awkward," to swallow the coffin of the dead man, who turns out to have been one Percy Key but obviously signifies Everyman. I don't think I noticed, when I was first seized by the austere ferocity of this elegy, how carefully—how theologically!—Plath prepares for such a denouement, from the very beginning of the work dressing death in the black cassock of a priest and juxtaposing his affectation of piety with the cryptic (and perhaps desperate) ritual of the mackerel-gatherers, who "wall up their backs against him" to handle "the black and green lozenges [of fish] like the parts of a body." But if only unconsciously I must have been gripped by the fatality with which the sacramental "lozenges" of dead mackerel dissolve into the distanced and defamiliarized "lozenge of wood" in which the body parts of the dead man have been secreted. And I must have at least intuited, too, the bitter skepticism that shaped the transformation of priestly death (from the poem's beginning) into, at the end, a hopeless human priest who is merely a "tarred fabric, sorry"—in several senses—and "dull," though he presides dutifully over the ceremonial futility with which the "coffin on its flowery cart like a beautiful woman, / A crest of breasts, eyelids and lips" (echoing the obscenely titillating breasts and hips of section 2) storms the hilltop graveyard.

Nor did I quite appreciate, I'm sure, the brilliance with which Plath assigns the poem's final vision to a group of children in a "barred yard"—children who in their representation of mortal innocence and fleshly entrapment surely share with the children in section 3 the "terrible faults" the speaker cannot "bandage." From their (ironically) naive perspective, the last communion in which the earth must swallow a eucharistic "lozenge of wood" is a "wonderful thing." But the speaker—and I believe I trusted her, even though I was a "twenty-something" baffled and envious would-be competitor—knows better. Though "the sky pours into the hole" in the graveyard "like plasma," she concludes, "there is no hope, it is given up." And "it" here has of course multivalent references. Most obviously "it" is the lozenge/coffin that must be "given up" to the voracious earth mouth. But, too, "it" is hope for some ritual of redemption from the "sorry and dull" human priest. And "it" is even the sky, which only pours *like* plasma but can neither resuscitate the dead one nor offer him and his mourners the promise of a heavenly home.

Whether sacrifice or surrender, says this classic mid-century elegy, giving up is what one does in the face of death. Yet at the same time the circumstances of defeat must be scrupulously recorded and set against the oncoming priest of the grave—the living must "wall up their backs against" his "black cassock" and his "high, dead, toeless foot" as the mackerel gatherers do—even if the details out of which they build their defenses are as nauseating as the "Limbs, images, shrieks" that have sickened the eye of the innocent green pool among the dunes. In this respect, I think even my earliest readings of "Berck-Plage" prepared me for at least a few arguments I might now want to make about late twentieth-century public as well as private procedures for mourning and perhaps, more generally, about the theological "damper" on which our aesthetic now locates itself. To be sure, the skeptical resignation with which Plath gives "it" (the coffin, hope, the sky) up at the end of her bleak elegy is hardly unprecedented. The "melancholy, long, withdrawing roar" of the "Sea of Faith" had been heard by Matthew Arnold, among others, more than a century earlier. But the Channel dividing Berck-Plage from Dover Beach is obviously even more historical than geographical. On "the French coast the light / Gleams and is gone," mourned Arnold, but he insisted that "the cliffs of England stand, / Glimmering and vast, out in the tranquil bay" and imagined that there might still after all be something substantive to fight about, even if the battle was joined by "ignorant armies" who clash by night. For Plath, though, the sea that primordially "crystallized" body parts, limbs, images, shrieks, simply "Creeps away, many-snaked, with a long hiss of distress." I suspect it was that long, that devastating and devastated hiss of distress I found so eerily compelling in "Berck-Plage" almost, now, four decades ago.

NOTES

1. For a fine and influential discussion of the "American family elegy" see Jahan Ramazani, *Poetry of Mourning: The Modern Elegy from Hardy to Heaney* (Chicago: University of Chicago Press, 1994).

2. I am quoting Hughes' footnote to "Berck-Plage" in Plath's *Collected Poems* (New York: Harper & Row, 1981), but he also offered much the same explanation of the poem's origins in "Notes on the Chronological Order of Sylvia Plath's Poems," in *The Art of Sylvia Plath*, ed. Charles Newman (Bloomington: Indiana University Press, 1970), pp. 187–95.

3. *Guide de Tourisme: Michelin, Nord de la France, Champagne, Ardennes* (Paris: Pneu Michelin, 1980), p. 57. Interestingly, the Michelin *Guide* goes on to note that this "centre

de cure" which in 1980 consisted of six establishments with three thousand beds among them "est ne du devouement d'une humble femme, Marianne Brillard, dite Marianne 'toute seule' parce qu'elle avait perdu son mari et ses quatre enfants, qui recevait, vers 1850, les petits soffreteux, malingres ou scrofuleux" (57). The benevolence and devotion of the long-suffering Marianne contrasts dramatically with the insistence of Plath's speaker that "I am not a nurse, white and attendant" as well as with her assertion that her own "heart [is] too small to bandage [the] terrible faults" of the children who seem to be following her "with hooks and cries."

4. Jack Folsom, of Montana State University, has published on the Internet an essay discussing death and rebirth in "Berck-Plage," which also offers some information on the variant drafts that are evidently held at Smith but though he studies evolving versions of the poem he doesn't indicate whether the Berck-Plage passages seem to have begun earlier (or separately) than the Percy Key material.

CAROLINE KING BARNARD HALL

Transitional Poetry

If "The Stones" is the "first eruption" of that final, excellent voice, however, it does not herald immediate success. There are a number of poems Plath wrote between 1959, the year before publication of *The Colossus*, and early 1962 that may be accurately termed transitional. These poems, collected in *Crossing the Water* and designated "transitional poems" on the volume's title page, belong to the three-year period that followed Plath's second visit to England. This was the time of the Hugheses' two years in London and their first year in Devon, an interval ending sometime near the breakup of their marriage and Ted's departure from home. It was not, on the whole, either a happy or a productive time for Plath. To be sure, her two children were born in these years—Frieda Rebecca in 1960, and Nicholas Farrar in 1962. But it was a time when Plath often felt choked by domesticity, as she said, and when she suffered continuing poor health.

The poems that we may call transitional generally reveal neither the honesty of the early poems nor the power of the late ones. To be sure, a number of poems that properly belong to Plath's late period were written also during 1960–1962; the distinction between "transitional" and "late" must be made on the basis not only of composition date but also of style and approach. Indeed, the transitional volume *Crossing the Water* is aptly named, for the poems of this period do evince, variously, a kind of stepping-stone

From *Sylvia Plath, Revised*: pp.67–82. © 1998 by Twayne Publishers.

quality, or a sense of floundering, of being neither on one shore nor the other. At the same time, they also represent an important stage in Plath's poetic development.

In the interest of accuracy, it should be noted both that the *Crossing the Water* poems were collected and published by Plath's estate eight years after her death and that, like the early volume *Colossus*, the contents of the American and British editions differ slightly. The 10 early poems not included in the American *Colossus* are printed in the American version of *Crossing the Water*. And there are six transitional poems in the English volume that do not appear in the American. These poems—"Pheasant," "An Appearance," "Event," "Apprehensions," "The Tour," and "Among the Narcissi"—are included instead in the American edition of *Winter Trees*. By their nature, however, these six poems seem to belong to Plath's transitional period, and they shall be treated here as such.

We can date the composition of these 33 transitional poems with the aid of *Crystal Gazer* and *Lyonnesse* (both published in 1971), the "Six Poems" published in *The New Yorker* in 1971, the poems that appear in the appendix to *The Art of Sylvia Plath*, and the table of contents of *The Collected Poems*. According to these sources (whose information again conflicts in a few instances), "Private Ground" and "Poem for a Birthday" were composed in 1959; "Stillborn," "On Deck," Sleep in the Mojave Desert," "Leaving Early," "Love Letter," "Magi," "Candles," "A Life," and "Two Campers in Cloud Country" were written in 1960; "Parliament Hill Fields," "Whitsun," "I Am Vertical," "Insomniac," "Wuthering Heights," "Blackberrying," "Finisterre," "The Surgeon at 2 A.M," "Face Lift," "Heavy Women," "The Babysitters," "In Plaster," "Widow," "Mirror," "Zoo Keeper's Wife," and "Last Words" were composed in 1961; and "Among the Narcissi," "The Tour," "Pheasant," "An Appearance," and "Apprehensions" were written in 1962.

STRUCTURAL TRANSITIONS

Plath's transitional work reveals, in several ways, the poet's continuing quest to achieve her own style. For one thing, the stepping-stone quality of these transitional poems is revealed in their structure; the mutation in Plath's use of rhymes, rhythms, sounds, and stanza forms from the early to the late poems is a process instructive to follow in tracing her gradual achievement of economical expression. John Frederick Nims accurately, and closely, describes the differences in these specific components in the *Colossus* and *Ariel* poems; he observes a "less obtrusive" attention to sound effects and at the same time a stronger emphasis on "ghostly," irregular end rhymes in *Ariel*, a more obvious attention to short stanzas combined with a near abandonment of formal end-rhyme and stanza constructions, and a change from metrical experimentation in *Colossus* to an almost exclusive use of iambs in *Ariel*.[1]

We can see these changes occurring in the transitional poems. In stanza form, the early poems are far more conventionally structured than the late, and a partial survey simply of the kinds of stanza structures Plath progressively employs reveals the tendency of her poetry toward greater structural freedom and verbal elasticity. For example, in the early poems there are five villanelles and one sestina, but there are none among the transitional or late works. Further, in *The Colossus*, 12 poems are written in three-line stanzas of which six are terza rima. In *Crossing the Water*, of seven poems written in three-line stanzas, only three are terza rima. In *Ariel*, there are no terza rima constructions in the 11 poems written in three-line stanzas. Throughout her work, then, Plath seems comfortable writing in three-line stanzas; she retains this structure but moves away from her early employment of the highly schematized terza rima and villanelle toward use of a freer three-line form.

This movement toward flexibility and brevity can be dramatized also by simply cataloging different stanza lengths in Plath's early, transitional, and late work. *The Colossus* contains one poem written in two-line units with irregular end-rhyme; *Crossing the Water* has none; *Ariel* has nine. In *The Colossus* there are 11 poems in four-line stanzas, 8 poems in five-line stanzas, and 17 poems in stanzas of six or more lines; *Crossing the Water* contains no four-line and six five-line stanza poems, and *20* poems in stanzas of six or more lines; in *Ariel*, 3 of the poems are written in four-line stanzas, 15 in five-line, and only 5 in stanzas of six or more lines. After experimentation in long stanzas, then, Plath generally returns in her late work to shorter, more economical, and more flexible stanza forms.

The trend is toward a simpler, more direct, and more emphatic verse. This same trend may be observed in Plath's use of rhythms and diction. Nims observes that whereas the predominant metrical pattern of *The Colossus* is the syllabic line, the nearly exclusive pattern in *Ariel* is the iambic. The poems in *Crossing the Water* are written in the earlier mode. The diction of *Colossus*, says Nims, "is always distinguished and elegant" but is "a written language rather than a spoken one." In *Ariel*, on the other hand, we hear "a real voice in a real body in a real world."[2] Again, *Crossing the Water* belongs more to the *Colossus* than to the *Ariel* category.

This change in Plath's poems from a written to a spoken language is one observed not only by a number of critics but also by the poet herself. Douglas Cleverdon suggests that Plath's composition of the voice play *Three Women*, and her experience in broadcasting this and other poetry over the BBC from 1960 on, may well have marked the turning point between poems not meant to be read aloud and poems intended to be.[3] A. Alvarez, too, observes a difference "between finger-count" in Plath's early poems and "ear-count" in the late; "one measures the rhythm by rules," he contends, whereas "the other catches the movement by the inner disturbance it creates."[4] On this subject, we may indeed invoke the poet herself, who, in a 1962 interview and reading of her own work, claimed that designing her poems to be effective when read aloud "is something I didn't do in my earlier poems. For example, my first book, *The Colossus*, I can't read any of the poems aloud now. I didn't write them to be read aloud.... These ones ... that are very recent, I've got to say them, I speak them to myself and I think that this in my own writing development is quite a new thing with me, and whatever lucidity they may have comes from the fact that I say them to myself, I say them aloud."[5]

This observation is certainly accurate. Because of their syntax, for one thing, a number of Plath's early poems yield very reluctantly to being read aloud. The Petrarchan sonnet "Mayflower" (1955) offers one example of this unwieldy syntactical aspect in the early work. In it, the occasional dropping of the definite and indefinite articles lends a jerky, abrupt quality to the line flow—not the calculated, effective abruptness of such late poems as "Lady Lazarus," but a disrupting jerkiness that requires distracting pauses in the reading:

> Throughout black winter the red haws withstood
> Assault of snow-flawed winds from the dour skies
> And, bright as blood-drops, proved no brave branch dies
> If root's firm-fixed and resolution good.[6]

Other early poems, such as "Wreath for a Bridal" (1956), offer either a similar sort of disruptive ellipsis, or unexpected syntactical inversions, so that the reader becomes at times unsure of the function of certain words: "Now speak some sacrament to parry scruple / For wedlock wrought within love's proper chapel."[7] "The Goring" (1956) offers similar difficulty: "Arena dust rusted by four bulls' blood to a dull redness, /.../ Instinct for art began with the bull's / horn lofting in the mob's / Hush a lumped man-shape."[8] This crowding of words and figures that requires such deliberate, careful reading is, of course, not in itself a flawed technique. Such a poetic style can be highly effective— as used, for example, by Dylan Thomas. But, although Plath experiments with this technique in her early work, she later discards it for a more natural, spoken cadence. By the time of the transitional poems, Plath employs a much smoother syntax.

This change in oral quality from Plath's early to her late work is observable not only in the poems' syntax but in their employment of diction and sound as well. As Nims points out, "the sound of words—any page of

Sylvia Plath shows her preoccupation with it. *The Colossus* shows a concern almost excessive, unless we see it as a preparation for *Ariel*."[9] In this aspect as in most of the others, the *Crossing the Water* poems indicate transition. A reader is almost constantly aware in the early poems of technical experimentation, especially in sound (and in related diction); there, sound effects are often effective and impressive, but often obtrusive as well:

> And he within this snakedom
>
> Rules the writhings which make manifest
> His snakehood and his might with plaint tunes
> From his thin pipe.
>
> Hard gods were there, nothing else.
> Still he thumbed out something else.
> Thumbed no stony, horny pot,
> But a certain meaning green.[10]

By the time of the late poems, this tongue-twisting quality is abandoned; diction is more natural, words are more easily spoken, sound effects are more appropriate, and the line-flow is more economical. This change is already occurring in the transitional poems. There, Plath continues her experimentation with internal rhymes, and with alliteration, assonance, and consonance. But the effects throughout are less obtrusive than in the earlier poems—sometimes only slightly less so, as in the transitional "Insomniac":

> The night sky is only a sort of carbon paper,
> Blueblack, with the much-poked periods of stars
> Letting in the light, peephole after peephole—
> A bonewhite light, like death, behind all things.[11]

and more often decidedly less so, as in "Event":

> The moonlight, that chalk cliff
> In whose rift we lie
> Back to back. I hear an owl cry
> From its cold indigo.[12]

This transitional experimentation points toward two very different aural aspects of the late poems; Plath's increasing control over her sound effects in *Crossing the Water* allows not only the powerful subtlety of such late poems as

"The Moon and the Yew Tree" or "Little Fugue" but also the effective and obvious rhymes of such poems as "Lady Lazarus" and "Daddy."

CUT-PAPER PEOPLE

In all aspects of form, then, the transitional poems reveal the changes from the early to the late ones. At the same time, many seem peculiarly lifeless. Indeed, what is significant about them is their very quality of literariness and of falseness to real experience. Though it is true that the early poems seem often artificially contrived, they nonetheless manage to evince sometimes a kind of raw force. It is not the disciplined, controlled power of the late poems, in which, to quote Richard Wilbur's comment on poetry in general, "the strength of the genie comes of his being confined in a bottle."[13] But a real voice does break through in such early poems as "The Stones," "Full Fathom Five," "The Eye-Mote," and "Two Views of a Cadaver Room." We hear this real voice seldom in *Crossing the Water*.

The title poem of this transitional collection seems to express the nature of the whole group. It begins:

Black lake, black boat, two black, cut-paper people.
Where do the black trees go that drink here?
Their shadows must cover Canada.

Like the figures described in this scene, "Crossing the Water" seems colorless, two-dimensional, cut-from-paper. Clearly, Plath's ability, newfound in her composition of "The Stones," to "let herself drop, rather than inch over bridges of concepts," has not yet emerged as a consistent impulse. About the *Colossus* poems one might say that the forced, stylized quality results from the poet's vigorous experimentation with the materials of her craft. In the transitional poems, however, the lack of spontaneity appears to result rather from a certain self-consciousness on the poet's part.

Helen Vendler makes a similar observation. "The withdrawal of affect," she writes, "annihilates not only nature but people." She uses the examples of "Two Campers in Cloud Country" and "Whitsun" to show that people are no more than "stick-figures," and she comments further that "Face-Lift" reveals a "falseness to the wellsprings of life from which metaphors are drawn." The main problem with the poems in this volume, says Vendler, is that "an undeniable intellect allegorizes the issues before they are allowed expression."[14]

Two manifestations of this self-conscious intellectualizing in *Crossing the Water* are the poetry's surprisingly undramatic quality and the comparatively large number of landscape poems. In both the earlier and the later poetry, the speaker assumes an identifiable voice, an individual identity, so that the poems themselves present a clear dramatic situation. In *The Colossus*, for example, we hear the voice of a woman agonizingly confronting the sirens' temptation, or the voice of a daughter trying to come to terms with a very specific father relationship, or the voice of a proliferating mushroom family, or the voice of a spinster shakily committed to self-denial. Even in the landscape poems, such as "Hardcastle Crags" or "Point Shirley," the speaker is given a special identity and is surrounded by a particular, believable landscape for a specific and evident reason.

In *Ariel*, the same dramatic concreteness prevails. Here, there are virtually no landscape poems in the earlier sense of an identifiable natural setting for the speaker's activities. For by this time, external settings have become internalized, so that they serve only as functions of the speaker's unique vision. (For example, moonlight in "The Moon and the Yew Tree" becomes "the light of the mind," and golden apples and leaves and flowers in "Letter in November" are "the mouths of Thermopylae.") And throughout the volume, the identifiable speaker acts and talks in a clear dramatic context— a Jew victimized by a Nazi, for example, or a mother poignantly warning her child of his probable fate, or an onion-chopping housewife cutting her thumb.

But in *Crossing the Water*, we find very little dramatic concreteness and hear mainly an amorphous voice, as evinced, for example, in the first stanza of "Magi":

> The abstracts hover like dull angels:
> Nothing so vulgar as a nose or eye
> Bossing the ethereal blanks of their face-ovals.

Here as elsewhere in the volume, the poet seems sharply conscious of herself so that her poems' characters and situations remain more or less abstract. Further, there are among these transitional works more landscape poems than appear proportionately in the work of the other periods. In them, the speaker is "I," and "I" is occasionally accompanied by "you." Generally one has the impression that "I" and "you" and the surrounding landscape exist to express an idea the poet has—an idea that, struggling for expression, renders the specifics of the poem subordinate and lifeless. In "Wuthering Heights," for instance, both speaker and landscape display a substanceless quality:

> The horizons ring me like faggots,
> Tilted and disparate, and always unstable.

> Touched by a match, they might warm me,
> And their fine lines singe
> The air to orange
> Before the distances they pin evaporate,
> Weighting the pale sky with a solider colour.
> But they only dissolve and dissolve
> Like a series of promises, as I step forward.

In "Two Campers in Cloud Country," in which the idea is the person's desire for self-effacement in an indifferent landscape, effacement occurs even before identity can be established:

> Well, one wearies of the Public Gardens: one wants a vacation
> Where trees and clouds and animals pay no notice;
> . . . .
> The Pilgrims and Indians might never have happened.
> Planets pulse in the lake like bright amoebas;
> The pines blot our voices up in their lightest sighs.

Similarly, characters fail to become real beings in a number of the other poems of *Crossing the Water*. "A Life," for example, seems to have both speaker and listener—someone is giving various orders to someone else—but we remain unsure of who they are or what they are doing or why they are doing it:

> Touch it: it won't shrink like an eyeball,
> This egg-shaped bailiwick, clear as a tear.
> . . . .
> Flick the glass with your fingernail:
> It will ping like a Chinese chime in the slightest air stir
> Though nobody in there looks up or bothers to answer.

An interesting companion to these observations is the fact that these transitional poems are quite humorless. We cannot be certain whether this characteristic is a cause or an effect of overintellectualization and lack of spontaneity; it is observable, however, that with a very few exceptions, these poems lack the wit, the drollery, and even the bitter, mocking humor of both the early and the late work. To be sure, there is a witty line or two, for example in "Leaving Early": "Lady, your room is lousy with flowers." And we can hear the humorous satire of the early poem "A Winter's Tale" in the transitional "On Deck":

The untidy lady revivalist
For whom the good Lord provides (He gave
Her a pocketbook, a pearl hatpin
And seven winter coats last August)
Prays under her breath that she may save
The art students in West Berlin.

or the mocking tones of early and late poems in "The Tour":

O maiden aunt, you have come to call.
Do step into the hall!
. . . .
And *this*
Is where I kept the furnace,
. . . .
It simply exploded one night,
It went up in smoke.
And that's why I have no hair, auntie, that's why I choke.[15]

As a group, however, the transitional poems are quite sober.

Another poem in *Crossing the Water* that seems expressive of the whole group of transitional poems is "Stillborn," in which the poet herself announces her dissatisfaction with her work:

These poems do not live: it's a sad diagnosis.
They grew their toes and fingers well enough,
Their little foreheads bulged with concentration.
If they missed out on walking about like people
It wasn't for any lack of mother-love.

O I cannot understand what happened to them!
They are proper in shape and number and every part.
They sit so nicely in the pickling fluid!
They smile and smile and smile and smile at me.
And still the lungs won't fill and the heart won't start.

REFINEMENT OF IMAGERY

But even though the poems of this volume may show less life and humor than the early or late poems, they are valuable not only as formal transitions but

as transitions in their use of imagery as well. In this group of poems, Plath
seems to have culled from the early work the relatively small group of images
she will use later, and here she uses them over and over again in various
combinations. One might speculate that without this time to become totally
familiar with her system of imagery, she might not have succeeded in using it
as brilliantly as she does in the poems that follow.

In the poem "Private Ground," for example, we find an explanation,
clearer probably than any in *Ariel*, of the meaning of the familiar death images
of frost, glitter, and reflection:

> All morning, with smoking breath, the handyman
> Has been draining the goldfish ponds.
> They collapse like lungs,
> . . . .
> I bend over this drained basin where the small fish
> Flex as the mud freezes.
> They glitter like eyes, and I collect them all.
> Morgue of old logs and old images, the lake
> Opens and shuts, accepting them among its reflections.

The mirror, too, is an image that belongs to this particular group of death
figures. Plath uses it in conjunction with the color white (another, related figure
for death's blankness) in "Last Words": "My mirror is clouding over— / A few
more breaths, and it will reflect nothing at all. / The flowers and faces whiten
to a sheet." And in the poem "Mirror," Plath offers a detailed exploration of
the special connotations this image has for her. We can recognize here the
particular relation with death (and drowning) of such figures and allusions as
candlelight and moonlight, silver, water, and narcissi:

> I am silver and exact. I have no preconceptions.
> . . . .
> Now I am a lake. A woman bends over me,
> Searching my reaches for what she really is.
> Then she turns to those liars, the candles or the moon.
> I see her back, and reflect it faithfully.
> . . . .
> Each morning it is her face that replaces the darkness.
> In me she has drowned a young girl, and in me an old woman
> Rises toward her day after day, like a terrible fish.

Related to the effacement imagery of water, and of whiteness and blankness, is the mythological allusion to Lethe, used so effectively in the late poems "Amnesiac" and "Getting There":

Planets pulse in the lake like bright amoebas;
The pines blot our voices up in their lightest sighs.

Around our tent the old simplicities sough
Sleepily as Lethe, trying to get in.
We'll wake blank-brained as water in the dawn.
                    ("Two Campers in Cloud Country")

Further, "Face-Lift," a poem where the woman's face-lift operation sounds very much like suicide, shows clearly, and for the first time, the reincarnation image so common in Ariel: "Mother to myself, I wake swaddled in gauze, / Pink and smooth as a baby."

And the saint–sinner conflict, so thematically central to the early poetry, is evident in this transitional work as well but with a significant difference. Whereas in the *Colossus* poems Plath chose to express this split in separate, opposing poems ("Spinster" versus "Strumpet Song," for instance), here she expresses it within a single poem, "In Plaster":

I shall never get out of this! There are two of me now:
This new absolutely white person and the old yellow one,
And the white person is certainly the superior one.
She doesn't need food, she is one of the real saints.
. . . .
I used to think we might make a go of it together
After all, it was a kind of marriage, being so close.
Now I see it must be one or the other of us.
She may be a saint, and I may be ugly and hairy,
But she'll soon find out that that doesn't matter a bit.
I'm collecting my strength; one day I shall manage without her,
And she'll perish with emptiness then, and begin to miss me.

This technique of manifesting conflicting aspects of the self within a single speaker emphasizes the desperate, intense aspect of the split. And after experimenting with this technique in "In Plaster," Plath skillfully reemploys it in such late poems as "Lesbos" and "Fever 103°."

Toward *ARIEL*

Plath's transitional poems, then, are developmentally significant in several ways. And in this light, even their failures are important, for they reveal the poet's continuing efforts to shape the materials of her craft to her special use, to find her own voice. Furthermore, it would be inaccurate to imply that there are not some very fine poems among them. In a few instances, Plath seems not to have been able to maintain the intellectual defenses that denied life and power to so many of these transitional poems, and she created instead the direct, affecting kind of poem that was to become the predominant mode of the final work.

One of these poems is "Private Ground." Outstanding for its skillful use of sound and rhythm, this poem reflects the change in oral quality from Plath's early to her late work; it catches the reader's attention in the cadences of the very first line: "First frost, and I walk among the rosefruit," and continues throughout to evince a very readable and spoken texture.

Another fine poem in *Crossing the Water* is "Blackberrying." Belonging to the landscape tradition of such earlier poems as "Point Shirley" and "Watercolor of Grantchester Meadows" and of so many transitional poems, this work shows one direction Plath's verse was going:

> Nobody in the lane, and nothing, nothing but blackberries,
> Blackberries on either side, though on the right mainly,
> A blackberry alley, going down in hooks, and a sea
> Somewhere at the end of it, heaving.

The plain description of the external landscape in this poem is powerful and lively. But beyond that, rhythms and word sounds afford to the experience a distorted quality suggesting that this landscape is internal as well:

> Blackberries
> Big as the ball of my thumb, and dumb as eyes
> Ebon in the hedges, fat
> With blue-red juices. These they squander on my fingers.
> I had not asked for such a blood sisterhood; they must love me.
> They accommodate themselves to my milkbottle,
> flattening their sides.

"The Surgeon at 2 a.m." shows a similar and more pronounced external–internal distortion. Performing his operation in a white, sterile environment, the surgeon describes a procedure belonging more to the nightmare (appropriately, the time is 2:00 a.m.) than to the operating room:

The white light is artificial, and hygienic as heaven.
The microbes cannot survive it.
They are departing in their transparent garments, turned aside
From the scalpels and the rubber hands.
The scalded sheet is now a snowfield, frozen and peaceful.
The body under it is in my hands.
As usual there is no face. A lump of Chinese white
With seven holes thumbed in.

Notice, too, the imagery of white, cold, and freezing, of flowers, color, and blooming, of hooks (specifically used in "Blackberrying" as well), and of perfection, so familiar in the later poems:

It is a garden I have to do with—tubers and fruits
Oozing their jammy substances,
A mat of roots. My assistants hook them back.
Stenches and colours assail me.
This is the lung-tree.
These orchids are splendid. They spot and coil like snakes.
The heart is a red-bell-bloom, in distress.
. . . .
The blood is a sunset. I admire it.
I am up to my elbows in it, red and squeaking,
Still it seeps up, it is not exhausted.
So magical! A hot spring
I must seal off and let fill
The intricate, blue piping under this pale marble.
. . . .
It is a statue the orderlies are wheeling off.
I have perfected it.

In the speaker's cool fascination with fantastic, horrible events, this poem is as excellent as any in the *Ariel* collection.

Finally, in "Widow" (1961) a number of major motifs from the early poems are drawn together and treated with brutal honesty; problems with father, sex, love, despair, and frustration meld with the poet's intense energy and skill to produce, truly, "the first eruption of the voice that produced *Ariel*." The poem poignantly records the sensations of rejection, loneliness, and loss that may have reflected Plath's own feelings at the time about her failing marriage. And it also succeeds in presenting the drained voice and the bare confrontation with the void that are such compelling qualities in the late poetry. The poem's first two stanzas, in a calm, almost exhausted mood, begin with these lines: "Widow. The word consumes itself— /... / Widow. The dead syllable, with its shadow / Of an echo...." Intensity builds in stanzas three and four as the mood shifts gradually from numbness to animosity and the poet confuses husband with father:

> Widow. The bitter spider sits
> And sits in the center of her loveless spokes.
> Death is the dress she wears, her hat and collar.
> The moth-face of her husband, moonwhite and ill,
> Circles her like a prey she'd love to kill
>
> A second time, to have him near again—

And the intensity reaches its climax in stanza five:

> Widow: that great, vacant estate!
> The voice of God is full of draughtiness,
> Promising simply the hard stars, the space
> Of immortal blankness between stars.

The intensity begins to subside as animosity recedes: "Widow, the compassionate trees bend in, / The trees of loneliness, the trees of mourning." The poem closes in relative calm as the poet expresses her sense of helpless isolation:

> A bodiless soul could pass another soul
> In this clear air and never notice it—
> One soul pass through the other, frail as smoke
> And utterly ignorant of the way it took.
>
> This is the fear she has—the fear
> His soul may beat and be beating at her dull sense
> Like blue Mary's angel, dovelike against a pane
> Blinded to all but the grey, spiritless room
> It looks in on, and must go on looking in on.

The special combination of desperation and restraint, of power and control so striking in the final poems is evident here. Still, the poems of this transitional period are relatively subdued compared with those in *Ariel* and *Winter Trees*, subdued indeed because of their special, and necessary, transitional aspect.

In the poetry of *Crossing the Water*, Plath's technique is in the process of becoming, of developing from an experimental to a finely honed and natural mode. It is in the transitional work that the change in oral quality occurs, so that we see, in the individual poems of this period, the shift in her verse from a written to a spoken language. Moreover, the poet's self-consciousness, responsible for the mediocrity of so many of these transitional poems, is perhaps a necessary qualification for the precision of the late work; here, the poet comes to know herself so that her attitudes can be expressed rather than explained in her final poetry.

For there, in the poems of *Winter Trees* and *Ariel*, there is little search for new meaning and no self-pity whatever. The writing in the late poems exudes a sense of feverish necessity whose motivation is, as Stephen Spender observes, "pure need of expression."[16] Indeed, Plath herself announces there that "The blood jet is poetry, / There is no stopping it."[17]

NOTES

1. John Frederick Nims, "The Poetry of Sylvia Plath—A Technical Analysis," in *The Art of Sylvia Plath*, 140–52.

2. Nims, 147–48, 151–52.

3. Douglas Cleverdon, "On *Three Women*," in *The Art of Sylvia Plath*, 227–29.

4. A. Alvarez, "Sylvia Plath," in *The Art of Sylvia Plath*, 60.

5. Sylvia Plath, "Sylvia Plath," interview by Peter Orr, in *The Poet Speaks*, ed. Peter Orr (London: Routledge & Kegan Paul, 1966), 170; hereafter cited in text as *TPS*.

6. Sylvia Plath, "Mayflower," in *Lyonnesse*, 3.

7. Sylvia Plath, *Wreath for a Bridal* (Frensham: The Sceptre Press, 1970), unpaged.

8. Sylvia Plath, "The Goring," in *Crystal Gazer*, 14.

9. Nims, 140.

10. Sylvia Plath, "Snakecharmer," "The Hermit at Outermost House," in *The Colossus*, 9, 54.

11. Sylvia Plath, "Insomniac," *Crossing the Water*, 10–11.

12. Sylvia Plath, "Event" *in Winter Trees* (New York: Harper & Row, 1972), 16.

13. Richard Wilbur, "The Genie in the Bottle," in *Mid Century American Poets*, ed. John Ciardi (New York: Twayne Publishers, 1950), 7.

14. Helen Vendler, "Crossing the Water," *New York Times Book Review*, October 10, 1971, 4, 48.

15. Sylvia Plath, "The Tour," in *Winter Trees*, 37–39.

16. Stephen Spender, "Warnings from the Grave," *New Republic* 154 (June 18, 1966): 23; hereafter cited in text.

17. Sylvia Plath, "Kindness," in *Ariel* (New York: Harper & Row, 1966), 82.

CHRISTINA BRITZOLAKIS

Gothic Subjectivity

Plath's exploration of the enigmatic or 'oracular' origins of poetic voice precipitates a crisis of the generic codes of authority which govern the relation between self and objects. In Romantic tradition, the lyric subject is traditionally constituted by the activity of metaphoric identification with the natural object, also known as anthropomorphism. For Plath, the Romantic dialectic between subject and object is always in danger of being frozen or collapsed. Her work presents her readers with the paradox of an intensely subjective poetry, filled with assertions of the first person singular, in which the poetic 'I' is almost always articulated as incomplete, lacking, or victimized, and the natural world as either reified, deprived of vitality, or actively hostile. The anthropomorphic quest for identities between the mind and natural objects, instead of sustaining the lyric subject, turns out to endanger its very existence.

I have already suggested that the construction of space, time, and subjectivity in Plath's poetry tends to be governed by tropes of spatial imprisonment and suffocation which announce an 'awful birthday of otherness' (JP 221). In this chapter, I shall show how the placing of lyric voice under the sign of a 'Gothic' or doubled subjectivity undermines the empirical (spatial and temporal) correlatives of the poem's narrative. By staging a return of the repressed within the conventions of lyric voice, Plath reinvents the

From *Sylvia Plath and the Theatre of Mourning*: pp. 101–134. © 1999 by Christina Britzolakis.

psychic landscape as a theatre of mourning. This process of haunting or phantasmatic invasion is pushed to its limit in the later poems, in which the subject appears as an effect of various forms of rhetorical doubling, irony, theatricalism, impersonation, and mimicry at the expense of the 'objective' or 'external' world. The element of doubling involved in poetic performance becomes an agent of uncanny defamiliarization in the text.

Gothic literature, it has been argued, typically combines a 'fearful sense of inheritance in time with a claustrophobic sense of enclosure in space'.[1] For Plath, the literary-historical sign 'Gothic' forms a secret link between the polarized male and female legacies of writing which the daughter-in-mourning inherits. Freud's famous essay on 'The "Uncanny"' points out that the German term *unheimlich* (uncanny) literally means unhomely, and argues that what is now regarded as 'uncanny' must once have been familiar or 'homely'.[2] Ghosts threaten the feminine realm of the home, the proper or the domestic. Plath's tendency to conflate metaphors of psychic and spatial enclosure taps into the conventions of Gothic romance, historically coded as feminine; at the same time, it exploits the ironic possibilities of that archive of masculine literary fantasy which Mario Praz called 'the Romantic agony'.[3] Her alternation between the roles of persecuted heroine and avenging female demon connects the drama of literary inheritance with the themes of ambition, domesticity, and revenge.

THE UNCANNY MARRIAGE OF MIND AND NATURE

> I am inhabited by a cry
>   'Elm'

The Romantic and post-Romantic poem has frequently been seen as uniting the poet's consciousness with objects by means of an expressive act directed from inside to outside. In *The Mirror and the Lamp* (1953), M. H. Abrams describes a shift within Romantic critical theory from metaphors of imitation to metaphors of expression, from the mind as passive receptor or register to the mind as active projector; a shift seen as 'an attempt to overcome the sense of man's alienation from the world by healing the cleavage between subject and object, between the vital, purposeful, value-full world of private experience and the dead, postulated world of extension, quantity and motion'.[4] Like Harold Bloom, he sees the Romantic lyric in terms of figures of a 'capable' imagination, a spirit informing and shaping inhuman nature to human purposes. Abrams's highly influential conception of 'Natural Supernaturalism' implies, as Mary Jacobus has pointed out, a 'spousal union' of mind and nature in which the mind is implicitly seen as the active, masculine partner and nature as the feminized object of perception.[5]

If what is primarily at stake in the Romantic ideology of lyric is the freedom and power of the mind in relation to the natural object, there is, for Plath, nothing 'disinterested' about that relation. She often envisages the relation between self and natural objects in hierarchical and gendered terms. In 'Ode for Ted', the primal act of naming is underwritten by a biblical marriage metaphor: 'how but most glad / could be this adam's woman / when all earth his words do summon / leap to laud such man's blood!'. In 'Watching the Water-Voles' (c. 1958), an unpublished piece of humorous journalism on the wildlife of Grantchester Meadows, she writes: 'My husband enjoys calling animals, and often, to my delight, they come to the call.' In a scene which recalls the 'owl-hooting' passage of the *Prelude*, his 'hooing' elicits a response: 'The owls did seem to be answering Ted as well as each other'.[6] By contrast, her own unsuccessful attempts to emulate this Wordsworthian conversation are travestied. In the journals, creative blockage, failure of figurative capacity, and an impotent or disempowered relation to nature are recurrent themes: 'It is as if my mind stopped and let the phenomena of nature—shiny green rose bugs and orange toadstools and screaking woodpeckers—roll over me like a juggernaut—as if I had to plunge to the bottom of nonexistence, of absolute fear, before I can rise again' (*J* 251). Such passages lament a failure of anthropomorphism, of the metaphoric activity which identifies the human with the inhuman, and a fear of the fading or defeat of subjectivity in the face of a densely particularized, machine-like universe.

Plath tends to foreground the process of metaphoric identification itself as the drama of the poem. The two varieties of anthropomorphism most common in her poetry are prosopopoeia, the fiction by which an absent or voiceless entity is endowed with a face or voice, and apostrophe, the figure of address, often seen as a subcategory of prosopopoeia, which purports to vivify inanimate objects. Both, according to Paul de Man, manifest 'the inside/ outside pattern of exchange that founds the metaphor of the lyrical voice as subject'.[7] For de Man, the Orphic myth of lyric utterance as the metaphoric transfer of consciousness from subject to object contains within itself its own reversal. To invoke, through anthropomorphism, a 'correspondence' between the inwardness of the subject and the outside world, is to risk the loss of that very autonomy and centrality of poetic voice which invocation claims. Objects external to the self can then appropriate the subjectivity that ought to pertain to poetic voice, leading to an emptying out of lyric voice, a loss of inwardness, and a subjection of the 'I' to the non-human. The taking on of the voice of the other which constitutes lyric subjectivity paradoxically foregrounds a negativity inherent in the notion of the subject.[8] The term

prosopopoeia derives from the Greek *prosoposon poiein*, to confer a mask;
Pierre Fontanier in 1830 defined this figure as 'somehow staging [mettere en
quelque sort de scene] those who are absent, the dead, supernatural beings
or even inanimate beings'.[9] If prosopopoeia names identification with the
natural object as constitutive of lyric voice, it also, as Fontanier's definition
suggests, stages a metaphoric return of the dead.

Plath is acutely aware of the instability of the founding metaphors of lyric
voice. Her psychic landscapes tend to turn prosopopoeia—the endowment of
the natural object with voice and its staging as a mask or mouthpiece for the
poet's subjectivity—into a Gothic drama of the haunting of the subject. The
subjective relation to the natural object alternates between the psychic tropes
of projection and incorporation. On the one hand, the natural world takes
on an appearance of active malignity which imperils the inwardness of the
subject (as in 'Wuthering Heights' and 'Blackberrying'). Anthropomorphism
becomes the plot of the poem, a plot involving a sinister conspiracy of natural
objects against the self. On the other hand, the natural world is organized
around metaphors of spatial enclosure, and coded as the scene of repetitive
and obsessive psychic rituals (as in 'The Moon and the Yew Tree' and 'Little
Fugue').

Plath's psychic landscapes thus explore what de Man calls 'the uneasy
combination of funereal monumentality with paranoid fear that characterizes
the hermeneutics and pedagogy of lyric poetry'.[10] 'Wuthering Heights' is, as
its title suggests, a poem haunted by Emily Brontë's myth of the elemental
marriage between mind and nature. The house, whose ruins have merged
into the landscape, has left behind a ghostly linguistic residue: 'Of people the
air only remembers a few odd syllables / It rehearses them moaningly: Black
stone, black stone'. The speaker alternates between the fairy-tale figure of
the bereft child, exposed to the hostile elements, and the witch/martyr figure
whom 'the horizons ring ... like faggots'. The natural world appears to the
speaker as an actively hostile force threatening her with extinction; all of its
elements seek to reduce her to their common denominator: 'The sky leans
on me, me, the one upright / Among all horizontals'. Her gaze is usurped by
its objects; in the third stanza, for example, the 'pupils' of the grotesquely
maternal sheep (whose 'grandmotherly disguise' echoes the story of Little
Red Riding Hood and the wolf) become 'black slots', which turn her into a
meaningless cypher, 'a thin, silly message'. As in the later poem 'The Rabbit
Catcher', a rewriting of D. H. Lawrence's 'Rabbit Snared in the Night' the
landscape becomes a metaphorical trap set for the speaker. Whereas, in 'The
Rabbit Catcher', the persecutory threat is ultimately located in a Heathcliff-
like lover/hunter figure, deeply related to the landscape and natural creatures,
and linked to the barbarous cruelty of the heath through his will to destroy, in

'Wuthering Heights' the menace is far less localized. Moreover, the speaker's apparently complete victimization and lack of authority are belied by the poem's assertive rhetorical syntax. Its discourse oscillates, in paranoid fashion, between egocentricity and terrified passivity.

This drama of identification with inanimate nature is accompanied by a proliferation and foregrounding of rhetorical figures of voicing. In two of the poem's manuscript drafts, 'Grass at Wuthering Heights' and 'The Grass', the prosopopoeic gesture, which invests voice and consciousness in the natural object, is compulsively repeated.[11] In the course of a series of increasingly elaborate personifications, the grass becomes a collective 'medium' for the 'voice of the wind'. It is also personified, through a rhetoric of remembering, forgetting, and repetition, as 'a true mourner'; the 'grasses' alternately 'remember' and 'suffer from amnesia'; 'nothing is too trivial for them to reiterate'. This rhetoric of mourning turns the natural object into an arena for a ghostly play of influence. By relocating the Romantic iconography of natural inspiration, oracular possession, and prophecy entirely within the natural object, Plath foregrounds an uncanny dimension within the lyric paradigm itself, as the scene of a potentially overwhelming invasion of otherness.

The intensity of Plath's investment in metaphors of lyric voice is marked by the recurrence in her poems of apostrophe, the figure of address. Richard Marovich's concordance to *The Collected Poems* lists no fewer than sixty-nine instances, their frequency increasing greatly in the later poems.[12] To apostrophize is to purport to vivify inanimate objects, in a reactivation of the Orphic myth of poetry. The linguistic structure of the apostrophic utterance engenders a prosopopoeia because it assumes or predicates a responsive human consciousness in inanimate objects.[13] Yet apostrophe, as Jonathan Culler has pointed out, does not trope on the meaning of a word but on the poetic activity itself. It is at once embarrassingly naïve and self-conscious, primitive and posturing. The invocation is, he argues, an archaic figure of 'vocation' which calls up the spirit of poetry. 'The poet makes himself a poetic presence through an image of voice, and nothing figures voice better than the pure "O" of undifferentiated voicing: in Fontanier's phrase, "the spontaneous impulse of a powerfully moved soul"'.[14] It is 'the sign of a fiction that knows its own fictive nature', i.e. of lyric self-reflexivity.[15] Within a psychoanalytical rather than a purely figural perspective, of course, apostrophe appears as an obsessive gesture, a magical charm which wards off the narcissistic fear that one will *not* see oneself reflected in objects, and therefore an instance of what Freud calls 'the belief in the omnipotence of thoughts'.[16] As a sign of lamentation, an attempt to bring something back that is no longer present, it roots metaphoric identification in lack. The anxiety of poetic voice the need to constitute the 'I' through figures of voicing—shadows the claim to establish a relationship between self and other.

The apostrophic nature of Plath's writing is announced by the Plathian moon-muse, who is endowed with 'the O-gape of complete despair' ('The Moon and the Yew Tree'), a grimace of frozen utterance. The lack or disturbance that sounds within this figure of abortive voicing finds a highly aural vocalization in 'Elm'. The origin of the 'voice' that is described as 'echoing, echoing' through the tree is inscribed as a series of questions which circle back on themselves:

> Is it the sea you hear in me,
> Its dissatisfactions?
> Or the voice of nothing, that was your madness?
>
> Love is a shadow.
> How you lie and cry after it
> Listen: these are its hooves: it has gone off, like a horse.

The elm bears a complex relation to the locality of Court Green in rural Devon, where Plath was settled with Ted Hughes and her two children. Ted Hughes states that 'The house in Devon was overshadowed by a giant wych-elm, flanked by two others in a single mass, growing on the shoulder of a moated prehistoric mound'.[17] The elm is a witchy, primeval mother figure, governed by the deathly moon-mother, who, like the elm tree at the gates of hell in Book VI of *The Aeneid*, harbours nightmarish monsters in her branches, and who 'know[s] the bottom with [her] great tap root'. She constitutes an ironic inversion of the idyll of the 'earth mother' (*J* 3120, celebrated in many of Plath's letters and journals. Through an act of aural projection/impersonation, the speaker gains access to an 'other space' profoundly troubling to the 'homely' space of married domesticity. This space is inhabited by an unlocalizable 'cry', which metamorphoses into the bat-like 'dark thing' gestated by the tree, and is finally given a Medusan face:[18]

> What is this, this face
> So murderous in its strangle of branches?—
> Its snaky acids kiss.
> It petrifies the will. These are the isolate, slow faults
> That kill, that kill, that kill.

The closing lines of the poem constitute a revelation, within the natural object, of the *unheimlich*; they announce a disintegration and hallucinatory defacement of the speaking subject. At the same time, apostrophe turns into incantation, in a reversion to primitive rituals of verbal power over reality. The haunting of the elm becomes a metaphor for the recovery of a terrifying maternal double which 'petrifies the will'.

In the manuscript drafts of 'Elm', the crisis of subjectivity staged in the poem is far more explicitly connected with the terrifying, creative-destructive power of the maternal body.[19] The elm is described as 'huge, like a laboring woman' (2a); 'she would undo everything; she would see the end of it' (2a). The aural reverberation of this maternal negativity is described as a 'voicebox of desolations' (2b). The drafts show the emergence, as Ted Hughes suggests in an appended note, of key features of Plath's later style, which she herself conceived of as more 'spoken' than 'written'.[20] In the course of the drafts, the focus shifts from the sound of the wind in a tree to the elm itself, and from the elm as third-person protagonist to a first-person discourse which 'voices' the elm. At one point, the poem is entitled 'The Elm Speaks', suggesting an animistic dramatic monologue. From the outset, however, the anthropomorphic relationship between the 'I' and the elm is seen as perverse, as not conforming to the 'proper' relations between human subject and natural object:

> Do I need such a false relation?
> She upsets me some way.
> It is stupid, this relationship.
> I am a person. She is my subordinate.
> She is a tree on my property.
>
> (3a)

Plath's revisions show a tendency to translate declarative statement into rhetorical question, exclamation, and apostrophe. The apostrophic and hallucinatory mode of 'Elm' marks a shift towards a more performative rhetoric of vocal utterance; the published poem contains seven rhetorical questions, two exclamations, and one imperative in the space of fourteen three-line stanzas. The trope of uncanny metamorphosis is paralleled by a rhetorical movement towards the mode of direct address.

Plath's psychic landscapes tend to foreground the drama of metaphoric identification itself, as one involving the return of archaic or repressed aspects of subjectivity. In this drama, figures of orality and of wounding become interchangeable. The phrase 'stigma of selfhood', written in the margin of one of the drafts of 'Elm' (2c), recalls Freud's image of melancholia as a narcissistic 'open wound ... drawing to itself cathectic energies ... from all directions, and emptying the ego until it is totally impoverished'.[21] In 'Tulips', the flowers, which are initially seen as hostile to the speaker's existence ('the vivid tulips eat my oxygen'), eventually 'hurt' the speaker back into life and writing 'with their sudden tongues and their colour'. In 'Poppies in July', an extended apostrophe, the speaker's attraction towards the blood-red colour of the poppies, with its violent associations of bodily wounding, becomes a perverse celebration, a parody of heterosexual marriage: 'if my mouth could marry a hurt like that!'. 'Poppies in October' juxtaposes the epiphanic 'love-gift' of the flowers with a denatured urban mass-humanity in Poundian imagist mode:

> O my God, what am I
> That these late mouths should cry open
> In a forest of frost, a dawn of cornflowers.

In this prosopopoeia, the flowers become 'late mouths' which 'cry open', miming the apostrophic gesture. The rhetorical question ('what am I') poses the question of the engendering of subjectivity itself, through the lyric 'cry'. The effect, as so often in the later poems, is one of stunning dramatic immediacy. Although intensely subjective moments of this kind in Plath's work have almost invariably been read as expressive of biographically specific personal and local states of feeling, they tend rather to foreground their own figural structures. Through the self-reflexive dimension of her figurative language, Plath reinvents the lyric as the vehicle for a crisis of subjectivity which cannot be confined to a biographical narrative.

CRYPTOGRAPHIES

The Plathian emblem of the wound/cry suspends lyric subjectivity between rhetorics of speech and of silence; gestures of voicing and invocation tend to become interchangeable with figures of a repression and muting of voice. Indeed, Plath's psychic landscapes are often organized, either implicitly or explicitly, around the central image of a crypt, in which an enigmatic and unspeakable loss is immured. At the same time, they are self-consciously placed under the sign of a 'Gothic' cultural inheritance, according to which, as Eve Kosofsky Sedgwick writes:

> It is the position of the self to be massively blocked off from something to which it ought normally to have access. This something can be its own past, the details of its family history; it can be the free air, when the self has been literally buried alive; it can be a lover; it can just be all the circumambient life, when

the self is pinned in a death-like sleep ... The inside life and the
outside life have to continue separately, becoming counterparts
rather than partners, the relationship between them one of
parallels and correspondences rather than communication.[22]

The Gothic crypt is linked with psychic obstruction, a repression and muting
of voice, a thematic of 'the unspeakable' and a tendency towards narrative
involution. For Plath, as for Poe and the early Eliot, poetic discourse is
haunted by the threat of imprisonment within the words of others. Literary
tradition itself becomes a tortuous and labyrinthine structure, a crypt or
haunted house.

     The manuscripts of 'Private Ground', a poem begun at Yaddo in 1959
under the title 'In Frost Time', but completed only in 1961, highlight this
Gothicizing of the poet's relation to writing and to cultural history. 'Private
Ground' locates the speaker in a garden coded as an elegiac, meditative enclave of
high culture, in which the speaker walks among 'the marble toes / Of the Greek
beauties you bought off Europe's relic heap / To sweeten your neck of the New
York woods.' The implied, though unnamed addressee, is the financier Spencer
Trask, original owner of the estate at Yaddo, the artists' colony where Plath and
Hughes spent some months in 1959. In the longer manuscript version, 'In Frost
Time', this brooding paternal presence plays a much larger part in the poem.
Two stanzas excluded from the published (1961) version project the speaker out
of the ostensible setting into another scene, a non-place in which the psychic and
the cultural cross over and infect each other:

     White shadows melt and shrink in the late sun.
     I try to forget my room,
     Charitable and tidy as a room in an asylum.
     Off and on, now, my heart
     Starts to knock in its hysterical chimney: Let me out.
     I want to kill it like a bird.

     Your black firs usurp my light. My bed extends.
     One foot in the Tyrol and the other stubbed somewhere
     In manic-depressive Prussia,
     I'm almost at home here. Gargoyles
     Contort your cabinets; on your mantel
     The ghost of Wagner glooms among the Bayreuth beersteins.[23]

The manuscript stanzas insert a subjective process *within* the elegiac
contemplation of the rose garden at Yaddo. They invoke an unnamed, spectral

other, announced by the shift to direct address in the second stanza, who casts a shadow upon the speaker ('your black firs usurp my light'). The 'you' is a pastiche of stock 'Gothic' images (gargoyles, Wagner) and the phantasmagoria of familial memories. While ostensibly addressing the original owner of the Yaddo estate, Spencer Trask (on whose 'private ground' the speaker is intruding), it recalls a number of other representations in Plath's writing of the perverse Oedipal father figure or 'black man'. This Gothic apparition all too clearly violates the naturalistic-empirical framework of the published version of the poem, from which he is excluded.

The structure of this fantasy is that of Gothic romance: a victim-heroine is persecuted by a male seducer/antagonist whose house contains guilty secrets. Such narratives have often been linked with Freud's theory of the incestuous fantasy or primal scene, which governs the Oedipal father–daughter relation, and which he saw as the origin of hysterical symptoms. Eve Kosofsky Sedgwick, for example, argues that the heroine of the genre is 'a classic hysteric', its hero 'a classic paranoid'.[24] In the lines quoted above, the metaphor of the heart which 'knocks in its hysterical chimney' explicitly aligns the speaker with the anachronistic figure of the Freudian hysteric, whose psychic disorder is converted into pathological bodily symptoms. In hysteria, according to Freud and Breuer, reveries that are charged with emotion ('brooding') give rise to a 'splitting of mind' or 'hypnoid' state. A zone of repressed psychic contents—memories, ideas, and wishes—is split off from consciousness in a kind of internal quarantine.[25]

It is worth noticing, however, that the composite parental ghost of 'In Frost Time' is androgynous, reaching back into the ancestral histories of both Otto and Aurelia Plath (the speaker's bed has 'one foot in the Tyrol and the other stubbed somewhere / In manic-depressive Prussia'). There is clearly a maternal as well as a paternal Gothic plot encrypted within this palimpsest of family history, cultural tradition, psychoanalysis, and fantasy.[26] In a later discarded stanza the speaker alludes to a famous Gothic image, Henry Fuseli's painting 'The Nightmare' (1781):

> And you seem like the dreaming woman the incubus squats on
> In Fuseli's painting. Helpless as a dummy, she droops
> Back over the fat pillows,
> Hair and arms trailing like drapery.
> In midair, the horse's head
> Hangs with its steamed white eyeballs.[27]

In this Freudian reinscription of Fuseli's image, the 'dreaming woman' appears as a passive vehicle of fantasy, devoid of autonomous volition and awareness.

However, it is unclear whose fantasy is being staged. If, in the two stanzas quoted earlier, the speaker presented herself as suffering from a 'hysterical' male identification, here the male apparition or phantasm itself appears to be haunted by the feminine. The personal pronoun moves across gender boundaries within the structure of address, producing a highly unstable identification. In another draft of the manuscript, the speaker announces 'I am the daughter of your melancholy'.[28] The figure of the hysteric crosses the boundaries of gender, splitting and dislocating the subject.

Plath's Journals for September–November 1959 repeatedly invoke metaphors of hysteria and demoniacal possession to describe a state of creative paralysis and blockage, of being 'verbally repressed' (J 316). 'I feel a terrific blocking and chilling go through me like anesthesia' she writes (J 316), and 'When Johnny Panic sits on my heart I can't be witty, original or creative'. The images of the trapped 'panic' bird and the sterile, hospital-like bedroom run through passages voicing fears of becoming overly dependent upon her husband, of lapsing into torpid domesticity, and of the failure of her professional ambitions. She writes a short story which she describes as 'a ten-page diatribe against the Dark Mother. The Mummy. Mother of Shadows ... the monologue of a madwoman', and laments that unlike Jung, one of whose case histories the story turns out to resemble, she is 'the victim rather than the analyst' (J 318). She also tries hypnotizing herself by a method learnt from Ted Hughes (J 313).

'In Frost Time' enfolds within the speaker's discourse a secret topology which is then excluded by the process of manuscript revision. In their reading of Freud, the psychoanalysts Nicholas Abraham and Maria Torok identify incorporation as a type of failed or refused mourning whereby the other is secreted within oneself. The emblem of incorporation is, they argue, the crypt, 'an enclave ... a kind of artificial unconscious lodged in the midst of the ego' which turns the self into a 'cemetery guard'.[29] The architecture of the crypt is that of an archive of texts and images, within which a lost object is figuratively kept alive as a stranger or 'living dead'. Plath's psychic landscapes are structured around such rituals of incorporation or encrypting. A highly formal and coded scheme of imagery is linked with an inexplicable state of mourning, a deadlock of creativity, and a crisis of vocation. In 'The Moon and the Yew Tree', the landscape is constructed as an 'objective correlative' which signals psychic as well as spatial enclosure:

> This is the light of the mind, cold and planetary.
> The trees of the mind are black. The light is blue.

The opening lines reflect upon the poem's own process of composition, invoking a set of willed equivalences between inside and outside. Ted Hughes notes that 'The Moon and the Yew Tree' was written as an exercise assigned by him, and the childlike syntax mimes the dreamlike passivity of a hypnotic subject or of a pupil learning to write:[30]

> The yew tree points up. It has a Gothic shape.
> The eyes lift after it and find the moon.
> The moon is my mother.

If the 'I' is positioned as an empty vessel filled by the lore of the teacher-mesmerist, the landscape is structured in a quasi-pictorial, highly deterministic way around two images: the white, spherical outline of the moon, starkly juxtaposed with the black, vault-like, 'Gothic' shape of the yew. Both are, in different ways, emblems of mourning. Romantic tradition links the yew tree with death, oracle, prophecy, and the 'spirit of place' or *genius loci*.[31] In Wordsworth's 'Yew Trees' (1815) it is a 'natural temple', 'nor uninformed with Phantasy'.[32] Tennyson addresses it in 'In Memoriam' (1850) as 'Old Yew, which graspest at the stones / Which name the underlying dead'.[33] The 'voices shaken from the yew tree' in T. S. Eliot's 'Ash-Wednesday' (1930) are linked with Christian prophecy.[34] If the yew is a medium of transmission for the ghostly paternal voices of literary tradition, the moon is a token of 'blank' mourning, a negative inscription of maternity which inverts Romantic lunar symbolism and refuses empathetic identification ('The moon is no door'). The speaker aligns herself with the hag-like, unregenerate moon as an outlaw, beyond the intercession even of that icon of maternal 'tenderness', the Virgin Mary. With its 'O-gape of complete despair', the moon is the 'muse' of female patienthood or 'castration' (compare 'The Rival': 'her O-gape grieves at the world'), although it is also, at least potentially, an ironic masks whose stock Gothic properties are parodied ('Her blue garments unloose small bats and owls'). 'The Moon and the Yew Tree' is an allegory of creative impossibility. Trapped between a forbidding paternal inheritance and a despairing maternal dispossession, the 'I'/eye announces its defeat at the end of the first stanza: 'I simply cannot see where there is to get to'. The set subject leads nowhere; the conclusion of the poem can only repeat, in a kind of tautology, the dualistic regime of the 'bald and wild' moon and of the yew tree whose 'message' is 'blackness—blackness and silence'.

In Plath's poetry; the encrypting of landscape appears as the effect of a traumatic temporality, which replaces recollection (the narrative sequence of memory) with repetition. This traumatic temporality also generates an occult traffic between personal and public memory. Like 'The Moon and the Yew Tree', 'Little Fugue' inscribes itself, at one level, as a parodic 'exercise' performed under male tutelage. It has been linked with Robert Graves's description in *The White Goddess* of an ancient poetic technique of meditation and invocation—a spontaneous or automatic 'finger writing' produced by concentrating on a visual object and repeating its elements—through which the 'oracular' poet is supposed to call up the spirits of the dead.[35] 'Little Fugue' also declares, through its title, a minor repetition (or mimicry) of Beethoven's *Grosse Fuge*. The 'fugue' brings together musical and psychoanalytical metaphors of memory and forgetting. A musical fugue is a contrapuntal form, with two or more short melodies, successively taken up by different parts or 'voices' and interwoven with each other; a psychoanalytic 'fugue' is a hysteria marked by wandering or departure from home, accompanied by a forgetting of the past, which may itself be later forgotten.

In 'Little Fugue', linear temporality is systematically occluded, scrambled, and dismembered by obsessive verbal ceremonials. Narrative sequence is replaced by a series of paired *motifs*: yew/clouds, black/white, fingers/eyes, touch/vision, father/daughter, presence/absence, voice/echo, Grosse Fuge/little fugue, phallus/hymen, past/present. Within this bipolar pattern of substitutions, the speaker's voice occupies the position of the negative term. On the level of sound, too, the method is contrapuntal, using homophonic puns—yew/you, eye/I, mourning/morning. The highly coded and self-referring use of sound patterns anticipates the tactic of later poems such as 'Daddy', 'Lady Lazarus', 'Ariel', and 'Sheep in Fog'. The poem's elaborate quasi-musical repetitions of sound and image inscribe a compulsive marshalling and arranging activity, the elaboration of a talismanic code:

> The yew's black fingers wag;
> Cold clouds go over.
> So the deaf and dumb
> Signal the blind, and are ignored.

A pattern of non- or mis-translation spreads through the sensory, somatic, psychic, and textual orders, turning the natural world into a collection of fragmentary, cryptic signs manipulated by a numbly desensitized speaker. Narrative is obstructed by catachresis, a disturbance of figurative language in which a word which belongs in one sensory dimension of meaning is used in another ('I see your voice'): a 'derangement of the senses' not in Rimbaud's ecstatic mode but in the mode of mourning. The phallic, admonitory finger imagery which runs through the poem portends a maiming and muting of voice, the threat of non-speech as well as of non-hearing and non-seeing.

Like 'The Moon and the Yew Tree', 'Little Fugue' is dominated by the image of the yew tree as a medium of transmission for ancestral (and predominantly paternal) voices. An early draft of the poem describes the yew as a 'go-between' that 'talks for the dead' and as 'a tree of poems, of dead men':

> The yew is many-footed
> Each foot stops a mouth
> So the yew is a go-between:
> It talks for the dead.
>
> A deaf man perceives this.
> He hears a black cry.
> The dead talk through it.
> O the voice of my masters.[36]

The yew tree is linked with the paternal metaphor or Name-of-the-Father, with cultural inheritance, and with an obscure guilt, a 'Gothic and barbarous legacy'. By the act of writing a 'Little Fugue', Plath places herself in a double relation to this legacy, a relation that is both repetition and revision. The 'Gothic' yew/finger/father/phallus transmits to the daughter messages which cannot be properly translated and 'orders' which she cannot perform. Mourning and inheritance are seen as inseparable; if the speaker cannot carry through this double work, still less can she abandon it. The yew tree, the 'black and leafy' voice of the father, and the 'tumult of keys' which constitutes Beethoven's music are superimposed upon each other by the poem's cryptographic surrealism. These talismanic images are, at the same time, invested with the burden of an oracular, teutonic Romanticism ('the big noises, the yew hedge of the Grosse Fuge'), whose oppressive effects are both psychic and historical. The 'yew hedge' becomes a crypt, from which 'dead men' cry. If, however, the father is the representative of an all-embracing, totemic, castrating power, he is at the same time himself figured as castrated and blinded; trauma contaminates the paternal image at all levels. This obscure rhetorical work is brought home, in the final stanza, to the Oedipal family:

> I survive the while,
> Arranging my morning.
> These are my fingers, this my baby.
> The clouds are a marriage dress, of that pallor.

While the speaker arranges her 'morning', the poem arranges her 'mourning'; mourning and housekeeping are figured as coterminous, as an *oikonomia*. She inscribes herself within an Oedipal symbolic, as 'guilty of nothing' (stanza seven), re-enacting a fatalistic Freudian script of femininity as castration, and phallic lack. The passage from daughter to wife and mother is associated with the white cloud/sheet/marriage dress; in a manuscript draft of 'Little Fugue', the clouds are described as 'these fool-white motherly clouds', and as 'mute'.[37] This fetishistic figuration of femininity as a veil of appearance is, of course, a privileged trope of modernist irony, signalling a crisis of representation. In her annotated copy of Nietzsche's *Thus Spoke Zarathustra*, Plath marked the lines: 'Woman has to obey and find a depth for her surface. Woman's nature is surface; a changeable, stormy film upon shallow waters. But a man's nature is deep, its torrent roars in subterranean caves: a woman senses its power but does not comprehend it.'[38] While 'Little Fugue' retains the outlines of what Plath calls 'the old father worship subject' (*J* 313) it also hints at the parodic possibilities of the Freudian/Nietzschean motif of the feminine as the scene of vaporous negativity, duplicity, and unstable appearance.[39]

DOUBLES, MASKS, AND FEMMES FATALES

> Cold glass, how you insert yourself
> Between myself and myself:
>
> > 'The Other'

For Plath, as we have seen, the poetic 'I' is inscribed as the product of polarized paternal and maternal legacies of writing, which can enter into dialogue with each other only through the trope of the return of the repressed. The construction of the speaker must therefore increasingly appear as the effect of a prior splitting or doubling. This process is often signalled by mirror imagery, as in some lines from the manuscript drafts of 'Elm' (3c), where the speaker appears as a Narcissus figure:

> In pools, I am beautiful.
> Is the soul of oneself so inaccessible?
> I scratch on the glass: the eyes within avert themselves.

Plath's undergraduate dissertation, 'The Magic Mirror', is an analysis of the double in Dostoyevsky, which refers to psychoanalytic and anthropological studies by Freud, Otto Rank, and Frazer. In particular, it cites Freud's view in 'The "Uncanny"' of the double as the product of a split between the critical agency or conscience and the rest of the ego; the surmounted narcissism of the primitive returns in the self-aware man as the feeling of the uncanny. Plath's summary of the recurring motifs of Golyadkin's breakdown in *The Double* might apply equally to her own poetry: 'the repetition of mirror imagery, identification with animals, and a simultaneous fear of murder and desire for death'.[40] Golyadkin's insistence that he is being confused with his *doppelgänger* finds an echo in one of Plath's Yaddo poems, 'The Burnt-Out Spa':

> Leaning over, I encounter one
> Blue and improbable person
>
> Framed in a basketwork of cat-tails.
> O she is gracious and austere,
> Seated beneath the toneless water!
> It is not I, it is not I.
>
> No animal spoils on her green doorstep.

The statement, 'it is not I, it is not I,' announces a split between a corporeal, objectified self—'animal spoils'—and an idealized, specular self-image 'one / Blue and improbable person'. Whereas the ruins of the spa machinery, a man-made attempt to harness the curative waters of the spring, testify to a general law of mortality and decay, the 'gracious and austere figure' reflected in the water is located beyond the realm of bodily corruption, 'where the durable ones keep house', as a later line suggests. She is likened to a good housekeeper, for 'no animal spoils on her green doorstep.' Yet there is also something faintly sinister about her, a gorgon-like resonance hinted at by the 'basketwork of cattails'. In 'An Appearance', the double is more clearly a persecutory figure. The image of the mechanized woman, conjured out of the landscape of domesticity, sharply refutes the Romantic nostalgia for an organic or 'natural' femininity. Her body is 'a Swiss watch, jewelled in the hinges', and 'from her lips ampersands and percent signs / Exit like kisses.' She is an allegorical cypher of femininity, reducible to the domestic appliances she operates and the repetitive functions she performs, a peculiarly willed, deliberate, and *written* construction. In manuscript, this poem was entitled 'The Methodical Woman', and a list of words written at the side of the page: 'index, file, order, tidy, symmetrical, system, discipline, rank, neat, systematic'.[41] The figure of the organized, 'efficient' housewife is at once a manipulable mask and a *doppelgänger* who threatens to usurp the speaker.

If the mask of the methodical woman is mere reified 'appearance', it none the less possesses a solidity and coherence that the self as linguistic performer entirely lacks. 'An Appearance' signals an increasing tendency in Plath's poems towards the construction of the speaker around an implied or named 'other' or 'rival'. The theatricalism which infects this discourse makes it impossible to distinguish between self and mask, original and copy. The speaker becomes a poet-impresario ('I wear white cuffs, I bow'). She disappears into rhetorical gesture: question, exclamation, apostrophe. At the same time, this ironic textual performance is seen as the product of a certain psychic violence. The speaker sews 'little dresses and coats' to 'cover a dynasty'; her reference to the 'red material / Issuing from the steel needle that flies so blindingly' turns an image of domestic labour into the Dickinsonian conceit of a regal costume manufactured from the 'material' of suffering.

Plath's conversion of the psycho-literary trope of the double into a rhetorical strategy erodes classical notions of mimesis and opens the way for a notion of poetic discourse as conjuration. Lyric subjectivity becomes riddled with a theatricalized, unstable irony, or mimicry. As Kenneth Burke argues, 'the irony of the monologue that makes everything in its image would be in this ratio: the greater the *absolutism* of the statements, the greater the *subjectivity* and *relativity* in the position of the agent making the statements'.[42] In 'The Rhetoric of Temporality', Paul de Man links the trope of irony with the Baudelairean concept of *dédoublement*, of self-duplication or self-multiplication. Irony is rooted, he argues, in 'the activity of a consciousness by which a man differentiates himself from the non-human world'.[43] De Man uses the metaphor of a physical fall or tripping up, drawn from Baudelaire's essay on comedy, 'De l'essence du rire', to explicate this ironic double consciousness. The moment in which a man falls, and laughs at himself falling, returns to him a sense of the facticity of his empirical self. It is therefore the capacity, through language, to see oneself as an object that defines, for de Man, the ironic gesture: 'The ironic language splits the self into an empirical self that exists in a state of inauthenticity and a self that exists only in the form of a language that asserts the knowledge of this inauthenticity' (*RT* 214).

In Plath's earlier poetry, I would argue, the drama of *dédoublement* is more or less contained by an elegiac code of decorum. However, as de Man points out, irony 'contains within itself the power to become hyperbole'. The concept of *vertigo de l'hyperbole*, 'dizziness to the point of madness', 'irony to the second power', or 'absolute irony', designates an exacerbated and corrosive sense of the theatricality of existence:

> When we speak, then, of irony originating at the cost of the empirical self, the statement has to be taken seriously enough to be carried to the extreme: absolute irony is a consciousness of madness, itself the end of all consciousness; it is a consciousness of non-consciousness, a reflection on madness from the inside of madness itself. But this reflection is made possible only by the double structure of ironic language: the ironist invents a form

of himself that is 'mad' but that does not know its own madness; he then proceeds to reflect on his madness thus objectified. (*RT* 216)

Far from being naïvely expressive, Plath's later poems are structured by an unstable and theatricalized irony that manifests itself as hyperbole. Not only Electra, Clytemnestra, and the other obvious *dramatis personae*, but all of Plath's speakers participate in a pantomime of what Paul de Man calls 'conscious inauthenticity'. This play of masks is the product of Plath's engagement with the legacy of modernism, as an ironic 'counterdiscourse' of the aesthetic, of which Baudelaire and Poe are often seen as the inaugurators.[44] In her edition of Baudelaire's *Les Fleurs du mal* (1857), Plath starred the final stanza of 'L'Héautontimoroumenos':

Ne suis-je pas un faux accord
Dans la divine symphonie,
Grace à la vorace Ironie
Qui me secoue et qui me mord?[45]

The Baudelairean dandy presents himself as the victim of a punitive internalized agency ('Ironie') which 'mauls and savages' him; he thereby acquires the status of a 'dissonant chord' in the 'divine symphony'. The prototype of this Baudelairean 'absolute irony' is the 'antic disposition' or 'feigned madness' of Hamlet, which turns his discourse into a ludic puzzle for his interlocutors. The rhetoric of 'Hamletism' recuperates loss for erotic, aesthetic, and cultural ends. It is predicated on the melancholic splitting of subjectivity described by Freud's essay 'Mourning and Melancholia', in which 'one part of the ego sets itself over against the other, judges it critically, and, as it were, takes it as its object'.[46] The melancholic's ostentatious display of loss deflects attention from the loss itself to the subject of loss, making it difficult to separate the affect from its display: does Hamlet feign madness, or does he madden in feigning madness?

Plath's later poems echo and parody the Baudelairean poet's self-lacerating irony and histrionic enjoyment of suffering. The theatricalism of her lyric discourse is fuelled by an internalized violence. However, the ironic doubleness of consciousness at work in these poems cannot be seen in the purely existential terms of de Man's 'The Rhetoric of Temporality'. That class, ethnic, or sexual difference might inform the construction of poetic voice is not considered by de Man, who, in this early essay, himself writes as a 'gracious and austere' ironist beyond the reach of such 'spoiling' empirical matters. But the fall into self-knowledge might be thought to have already taken place, as soon as the subject is conceived of as having a personal, sexual, and social history. Baudelaire's concept of *le comique absolu* can be read along a psychoanalytic and historical as well as an existential axis of disjunction, in terms of the return of the repressed. The ambiguous 'inherent violence' (*RT* 216) which de Man identifies in relationships between human beings, the excess that prevents consciousness from coinciding with itself, corresponds to the 'other scene' of the psychic. It is therefore inflected not only by sexual difference, but by the historically variable power structures attendant upon it.

Post-Romantic irony, as defined by de Man, is implicitly masculine, a tortured struggle for individuation and separation from the brute matrix of the empirical. In his Baudelairean fable, the ironic, twofold, or self-reflexive subject can emerge only at the expense of the abject, engendered self. As a passing comment in Plath's journals puts it, 'irony' is 'the mature stance which covers up the maudlin ladies' magazine blurt of tears' (*J* 228). The irony of her later poems is indeed Baudelairean in so far as it inscribes a resistance to the domestic, maternal, and 'sentimental'; but such an ironic stance can only be, for a poet who is also a self-professed 'housewife' and mother, self-negating in a quite different sense from that proposed by de Man in 'The Rhetoric of Temporality'.

The extent to which Plath's 'absolute irony' is fuelled by psychic violence is strikingly exemplified in 'Daddy'. Lyric subjectivity becomes an arena for the operation of a demonic self-reflexivity which harnesses the most regressive aspects of form and language for its effects. The relation between the punitively strict form of the poem and the extremity of its sentiments is, as has often been noted, a blasphemous one. Its nursery rhyme rhythms license an oscillation between a bullying superego and infantile rage, between willed incantation and compulsive repetition. The elements of caricature, parody, and hyperbole in 'Daddy' are so blatant that only a very determined misreading could identify the speaker with the biographical Sylvia Plath. Her own description of the poem as a dramatic monologue explicitly invokes the concept of a psychoanalytic *mise-en-scène*: 'Here is a poem spoken by a girl with an Electra complex. Her father died while she thought he was God. Her case is complicated by the fact that her father was also a Nazi and her mother very possibly part Jewish. In the daughter the two strains marry and paralyze each other—she has to *act out the awful little allegory* [emphasis added] once over before she is free of it' (*CP* 293 n.). Although the poem does indeed invent a 'dramatic' speaker, whose utterance reveals a state of psychic disintegration, it does away, at the same time, with the dramatic monologue's contextual framework, and therefore with the ethical basis of judgement which that form traditionally offers its readers. In its place, 'Daddy' generates a graphically schematized, phantasmagoric world of doubles and puppet-like projections. Since both oppressor and victim are *allegorical* figures, the tools of the father-oppressor are above all linguistic. Daddy's sign ('Ich') is the allegorical form that kills the force, the 'barbed wire' which traps and hurts the poet's 'tongue'. Daddy is also, of course, the representative of canonical literary tradition, invoked through echoes of, amongst other modernist texts, *The Waste Land*:

> The snows of the Tyrol, the clear beer of Vienna
> Are not very pure or true.
> With my gipsy ancestress and my weird luck
> And my tarot pack and my tarot pack
> I may be a bit of a Jew.

Eliot's lament for the decline of patrimony has some claim to being *the* patriarchal precursor poem of the century. For Plath, the nostalgic pre–First World War ideal of imperial Europe, already distinctly tarnished in *The Waste Land*, looks doubly ironic from a post-Holocaust perspective. And Eliot's Madame Sosostris, that bogus prophet of suspect Asiatic origins, is a fitting mask for a poet who deals out flashy icons of global American kitsch like playing cards. The reflex knowingness of the poem constructs a pastiche Europe, like the photo-collage made by Plath in 1960, which includes images of Eisenhower, Nixon, a bomber, a satellite, and a woman in a bathing suit.[47] Those critics who psychoanalyse the speaker in terms of the Oedipus Complex have, of course, already been beaten to it by the poem's own flippant Freudianism. Like the Nazi–Jew analogy, the family romance is one of the recycled and culturally overdetermined emblems which make up the bricolage vernacular of the late poems. When the speaker professes to be a Jew, she is as much and as little in earnest as she is when she claims that every woman adores a Fascist. Both are overweeningly, provocatively ironic and theatricalized statements. By putting the audience in the place of the addressee, the poem entangles the reader within the 'madness' of its ironic language.

If melancholia is traditionally connected with various kinds of ironic imitating, feigning, deception, and role-playing, it is also, as Juliana Schiesari has pointed out, marked as a cultural prerogative for male subjectivity.[48] The melancholic is typically obsessed by feminine duplicity, impurity, and predatory sexuality. He sees the masquerade of femininity as dangerous and evil; it is structurally necessary to the rhetoric of Hamletism not only that the woman should signify aesthetic appearance, but also that she should remain forever inadequate to the poet's desires, part carnal snare, part spiritual ideal. Yet in his fetishizing of loss he himself, of course, appropriates a certain femininity. What estranges the rhetoric of Hamletism from within is the excess or otherness it contains: the hysterical ghost of Ophelia.

Plath's construction of an ironic 'double consciousness' appropriates many of the rhetorical and iconographic clichés of Hamletism; she arrogates to herself an ironic and theatricalized display of psychic loss which canonical literary tradition has enshrined as a masculine cultural privilege. At the same time, the play of masks exploits and parodies the melancholic's preoccupation with feminine duplicity. In 'Stopped Dead', a vengeful and possibly insane speaker plots an unspecified act of foul play against her male companion in a car accident:

> You are sunk in your seven chins, still as a ham.
> Who do you think I am,
> Uncle, uncle?
> Sad Hamlet, with a knife?
> Where do you stash your life?
>
> Is it a penny, a pearl—
> Your soul, your soul?
> I'll carry it off like a rich pretty girl,
> Simply open the door and step out of the car,
> And live in Gibraltar on air, on air.

Here, the irony pivots, with a Hamlet-like performative opacity, on questions of genealogy, inheritance, and rivalry which are inscribed within an Oedipal symbolic.[49] The last line echoes Hamlet's response to Claudius's greeting, 'How fares our cousin Hamlet?' in Act III, Scene ii, lines 92–4: 'Excellent, i'faith, of the chameleon's dish. I eat the air, promise-crammed'. The play of this wit acts out a femininity which at once conceals and advertises a threat. In threatening to carry off his 'life' (rhymed with the phallic 'knife') or 'soul' ('stashed' away like hidden treasure) the speaker casts this 'sad Hamlet' as a fetishist to whose castration anxiety she mockingly 'plays up'. Yet at the same time she is herself a 'sad Hamlet with a knife', a cross-dressed Hamlet. In its scenario of phallus-theft, 'Stopped Dead' walks a thin line between the 'male' scenario of fetishism and its complement, the 'female' scenario of the masquerade. The poem's entry into the fetishistic imaginary of *Hamlet* precipitates a black comedy of sexual relations which tends to undo gender identifications.

In a much-cited essay, 'Womanliness as Masquerade' (1929), Joan Riviere argues that the Oedipal assignation of sexual difference not only casts the woman as castrated, but often results in her acting out her 'castration' in order to appease the powers-that-be, and to mask her identification with a 'masculine' intellectual or creative power.[50] Women with intellectual or professional ambitions, who participate in public discourse, may have a wish for masculinity which they dissimulate in order to avert punishment from their masculine rivals. Exaggeratedly feminine behaviour is a display of guiltlessness, an act of restitution to the father whose phallic power the woman desires. Riviere concludes that the distinction between 'authentic' femininity and the masquerade of femininity is therefore a tenuous and uncertain one. As Stephen Heath puts it in his commentary on Riviere, 'alienation quickly becomes a *structural* condition of being a woman (overlying the alienation which for Lacan is a structural condition of subjectivity in general, the subject's division in the symbolic) ... alienation is playing the game which is the act of womanliness and the act is her identity'.[51] From a psychoanalytic point of view, a certain *dédoublement* could be seen as integral to the construction of feminine identity. Femininity becomes a mask 'behind which man suspects some hidden danger'.[52]

The masquerade has often been seen as central to the mythology of 1950s femininity, especially in the area of film, where it 'generates images and stories of a doubled female subject which may be retold from the position of the curious, suspicious, fascinated, masculine subject'.[53] It is enmeshed in a network of competitive identifications, not only between men and women but also between women. In one of Plath's 'slick' stories, 'Day of Success', the housewife protagonist attempts to regain her husband from the clutches of the 'other woman' by donning a 'royal blue silk Japanese jacket ... an exquisite whispery, sapphire-sheened piece of finery that seemed to have no business whatsoever in her commonplace world' (*JP* 196). The seamlessness of the story's marriage plot, in which the husband turns out to prefer 'the wife and mother type' to the 'career girl', depends on the expulsion of the professional 'other woman', the protagonist's double and imagined rival.

Plath's textual masquerade is not merely a symptom of her well-documented attempts to reconcile the vocations of married domesticity and professional authorship, of her desire to be 'a triple-threat woman: wife, writer and teacher', or of her fear of becoming a housewifely 'drudge'.[54] The rhetorically volatile voice of the late poems, by turns elegiac, embittered, and defiant, generates scenarios of feminine aggression and rebellion, whose effect is to satirize the discourses and images of femininity. In the pseudo-dramatic monologue of 'Lesbos', addressed to a female interlocutor, the target of Plath's irony is, as in Baudelaire's 'Femmes damnées', the Sapphic vision of an island dedicated to female love and friendship.[55] The poem also contains a number of parodic echoes of that latter-day Hamlet figure and Baudelairean dandy, T. S. Eliot's J. Alfred Prufrock. Its speaker is a neurotic and narcissistic figure, who declares herself, at the outset, 'a pathological liar'; her discourse is a tissue of staged inauthenticity, invoking every kind of cliché from pop psychology to pop mysticism. This rhetoric of degraded femininity—a highly unstable compound of 'viciousness', hypochondria and erotic frustration—can be attributed neither to the 'I' nor to the 'you' of the poem. It is, rather, the product of an ironic, Prufrock-like zone of doubled consciousness. The figurative current of electricity which runs through the poem is the sign of a crackling nervous energy, which unites, divides, and blurs the identities of the two female protagonists, rendering the male figures in the poem mere inadequate conduits ('an old pole for the lightning'). This electricity is inseparable from the marketing (and self-marketing) of women as images, which pits them against each other as 'rivals', but also perversely eroticizes the hatred between them. The poem's landscape is the detritus of a female subjectivity that wants *to be exchanged*, to be a Hollywood starlet, a mermaid, or a *femme fatale*: 'I should sit on a rock off Cornwall and comb my hair. I should wear tiger pants, I should have an affair.' It is difficult not to be reminded of J. Alfred Prufrock's seaside reflections on his peach-eating, sartorially adventurous *doppelgänger*. Elsewhere in the poem, his confession 'I have heard the mermaids singing, each to each, / I do not think that they will sing to me' and his vision of them 'riding seaward on the waves / Combing the white hair of the waves blown back / When the wind blows the water white and black' also finds a mocking echo:[56]

> O vase of acid,
> It is love you are full of. You know who you hate.
> He is hugging his ball and chain down by the gate
> That opens to the sea
> Where it drives in, white and black,
> Then spews it back.
> Every day you fill him with soul-stuff, like a pitcher.
> You are so exhausted.

The comparison of the woman with a 'vase of acid' and a 'pitcher' filled with 'soul-stuff' parodies the Baudelairean fantasy of woman as a vehicle for imaginative release and oblivion.[57] The delicately nostalgic, evasive atmosphere of 'Prufrock', distilled from the exterior and interior settings through which he moves, turns 'acidic' in 'Lesbos'. It is filled with the 'stink of fat and baby crap', the 'smog of cooking', lit by 'the fluorescent light wincing on and off like a terrible migraine'. The frustrated housewife's fantasies inevitably circle back to the enclosures and prisons that generate them—the hell-like kitchen, the 'cement well' which immures pet kittens, the 'cute decor' which closes in at the end of the poem in an image of devouring female sexuality: 'like the fist of a baby / Or an anemone, that sea sweetheart, that kleptomaniac.'

'Lesbos' is a rewriting of an early, unpublished poem, 'marcia', addressed to Marcia Brown, a female college friend. Structured around a parallel series of domestic and seaside landscapes, 'marcia' is an ode to female friendship as nostalgic idyll, permeated with adolescent sensuality. 'Lesbos' is its surrealistic, embittered inversion, a parody love song, which presents its female protagonists, now housewives and mothers rather than college students, as 'venomous opposites'. On receiving a letter from her friend Marcia while teaching at Smith College in 1958, Plath reads in it signs of concealed 'resentment' and 'envy'; she sums up an apparently flattering remark as 'acid baths', plans a retaliatory attack, and describes herself as wearing a 'mask' of innocence. Here, the beloved friend becomes a rival figure who 'markets and cooks with no more savoir faire than I, I wife my husband, work my classes and "write"' (*J* 186–7). In the 1961 poem 'The Babysitters', the speaker elegiacally recalls the 'Marcia' figure and herself as 'little put-upon sisters' babysitting for rich families at the seaside. 'O what has come over us, my sister!' she exclaims. The ambivalence of 'sisterhood' in these texts is inseparable from the uneasy accommodations of domesticity with professional aspiration which constituted a shared destiny for middle-class, educated women in the 1950s.

In Plath's later poetry, the drama of *dédoublement* is transformed into a revenge plot starring the figure of the fatal woman or vampire. This revenge plot inverts the earlier victimization plot of Gothic romance; its most well-known moments are the scapegoating of 'Daddy', the daemonic apparition at the close of 'Lady Lazarus' who 'eats men like air', and the flight of the queen bee of 'Stings', who is 'more terrible than she ever was'. Far from being reducible to an aspect of biography or self-fulfillment, however, it brings into play a thematic of artifice and perversity, a dizzying circulation of inherited texts and images. The *fin-de-siècle* theme of femininity as appearance brings together a crisis of mimetic notions of representation with a crisis in the social meanings of femininity. In 'Purdah', the speaker adopts the mask of a veiled Oriental woman, ideally submissive and feminine, only to shatter it and reveal the apparition of the fatal woman:

> I gleam like a mirror.
> At this facet the bridegroom arrives
> Lord of the mirrors!
> It is himself he guides
> In among these silk
> Screens, these rustling appurtenances.

The speaker's ironic representation of herself as a 'valuable' object, a carved and faceted gemstone whose sole purpose is to mirror the male psyche, is achieved through a highly aestheticist and theatrical elaboration of the isolated detail. Here, style constitutes a commentary not only on the male fetishizing of the 'appurtenances' of femininity—jewels, cosmetics, fragrance, clothing—but also on their privileged status in symbolist and modernist poetic tradition as tropes of the aesthetic. The carved and 'faceted' gemstone serves as the model for the poem's formal organization, which spatializes temporal sequence ('at this facet'), at the same time as it achieves, through enjambment, the effect of a suspended or concealed threat. 'Purdah' is poised in the moment preceding the denouement of its own narrative: the breaking of purdah, the unleashing of revenge, the shattering of the illusion created by language, and the abrogation of formal control. The speaker announces her intention to 'unloose— / From the small jewelled / Doll he guards like a heart— / The lioness / The shriek in the bath / The cloak of holes'. The male-created images and representations which imprisoned the speaker in a state of 'purdah' are converted into a form of symbolic revenge, culminating in the invocation of the husband-murderer Clytemnestra, borrowed from Aeschylus' *Agamemnon*.[58]

The theatrical possibilities of suspense and deferral are also exploited in 'A Birthday Present', which turns on the metaphor of an 'annunciation' or encounter with an overwhelming, transcendent truth:

> What is this, behind this veil, is it ugly, is it beautiful?
> It is shimmering, has it breasts, has it edges?
>
> I am sure, it is unique, I am sure it is just what I want.
> When I am quiet at my cooking I feel it looking, I feel it thinking
>
> 'Is this the one I am to appear for,
> Is this the elect one, the one with black eye-pits and a scar?
>
> Measuring the flour, cutting off the surplus,
> Adhering to rules, to rules, to rules.
>
>
> Is this the one for the annunciation?
> My god, what a laugh!'

The birthday present is a phantasmatic, uncanny object, clothed in a fetishistic 'shimmer' and capable of being transmogrified into various shapes.

It estranges the *heimlich* in its literal sense of domesticity, appearing in the kitchen, the site of domestic labour. The image of a veiled and seductive but also reified female body, with 'breasts' and 'edges', recalls the mechanical woman/persecutory double of 'An Appearance' and 'The Applicant'. The 'veil' merges, in subsequent stanzas, with images of 'curtains' and 'babies' bedding'. As in 'Little Fugue' and 'An Appearance', the trappings and rituals of domesticity, of the 'methodical' woman, 'measuring the flour, cutting off the surplus', constitute a masquerade. The threat which lurks behind this masquerade unfolds as a parodic series of metaphoric substitutions: 'bones', a 'pearl button', a phallic 'tusk', a 'ghost-column'. These fetishistic images parody the annunciation or mystic marriage which the speaker ostensibly seeks. Although the poem's compulsive demand for 'truth' or 'revelation' has often been read in biographical terms (as a suicidal quest), the play of figurative veiling and unveiling suggests that the 'truth' itself may be less a goal than a series of false appearances of metaphoric substitutions. At a key moment, 'Poem for a Birthday' implicitly invokes Salome's dance as an analogy for its own procedures. A composite allusion superimposes the fate of John the Baptist on the encounter of Perseus and the Gorgon:

> I know why you will not give it to me,
> You are terrified
>
> The world will go up in a shriek, and your head with it,
> Bossed, brazen, an antique shield ...

The 'antique shield' which allowed Perseus to contemplate the monster Medusa while escaping the powers of her gaze, is, as Plath had written in an early poem, 'Perseus: The Triumph of Wit Over Suffering', 'a mirror to keep the snaky head / In safe perspective' and to 'outface the gorgon-grimace / Of human agony'. By contrast, 'A Birthday Present' enacts a estrangement of this 'safe perspective'.

The recurrent tropes of castration or decapitation in Plath's later poems invoke, either explicitly or implicitly, the figure of Salome, heroine of the Decadence. For male authors of the *fin de siècle*, such as Wilde and Huysmans, Salome served as the emblem of a definitively aesthetic combination of carnal sensuality and virginal purity. She is also, of course, a figure of transgressive female desire, the arch-masquerader whose dance, with its tantalizing sexual display, conceals a vengeful and castratory scenario directed against the male. Her blasphemous marriage with the severed head of John the Baptist pits a perversely sexualized female body against the Word and announces a regime of erotic empathy with the inorganic. The power of destruction wielded by

Salome has, since the *fin de siècle*, been linked with power of the visual image. Françoise Meltzer points out that she functions as 'an icon or *engine*, brought to life for the purpose of destroying the male'.[59] In Des Esseintes's description of Gustave Moreau's two paintings on the theme in Huysmans's *À rebours*, she is 'the Goddess of immortal Hysteria ... poisoning, like the Helen of ancient myth, *everything that sees her*, everything that she touches' [emphasis added].[60] The male artist's gaze is fetishistically riveted to an image of death-dealing femininity which it fears and loathes.

If Plath's textual masquerades can be seen as acts of symbolic revenge on male oppressor figures, they also encode an intense ambivalence towards the mother. In the Salome story, the daughter was often confused with her mother, Herodias, who was cast, in many versions of the story, as the instigator of the saint's beheading. Similarly, the dialectic of rivalry and reparation described by Riviere involves parental figures of both sexes; indeed, the burden of guarding oneself against maternal retribution was, she argued, much greater.[61] In 'Kindness', the speaker self-consciously aligns herself with a Decadent aesthetic, through an iconography of jewels, roses, fountains, and blood. She opposes the phallic 'blood jet of poetry' to the wisdom of 'Dame Kindness', maternal exemplar of the domestic and feminine virtues. The exotic, theatrical, and elusive substance of art is seen as nourished by despair and killed by the 'kindness' of domesticity: 'My Japanese silks, desperate butterflies, / May be pinned any moment, anaesthetised.' The scenario of 'Kindness' echoes the encounter in the first act of Mallarmé's dramatic poem 'Hérodiade' (1926) between the princess Hérodiade and her Nurse.[62] Mallarmé's Hérodiade, a mask for the Symbolist poet who desires the impossible ideal of 'pure' or absolute poetry, is the fiercely virginal, spiritually aspiring daughter of an absent warrior-king, who repels the attentions of the Nurse, and refuses to countenance the maternal doctrine of natural law which she represents. Only a mystic marriage with John the Baptist, representative of the knife-sharp, spiritual Word, will satisfy her.[63]

In Plath's poetry, the iconic figure of Salome presides over a revulsion against organicist views of language, and a movement towards a baroque somatology of fragmented part-objects. She announces a shift away from the preoccupation with aural embodiment and a willingness to exploit the 'inauthenticity' of visual experience. She also signals the extent to which Plath's experiments with psychic landscape and with lyric persona resist the tendency to read her poems as a psychobiographical narrative of self-discovery. The speaker is increasingly constructed through processes of doubling and estrangement which exploit the daemonic potential of rhetorical masks, and which implicate the reader, through structures of direct address, in the drama of *dédoublement*.

The hyperbole of the later poems tends to disjoin femininity from fixed and unchanging tropes of female 'nature' and to turn it into a thematic of artifice. Femininity becomes a rhetorical theatre, an ensemble of borrowed images and roles to be manipulated by the female ironist. It could be argued that this 'masquerade' colludes with that configuration of woman and modernity in which, as Jacques Derrida puts it in his commentary on Nietzsche, 'that which will not be pinned down by truth is, in truth-feminine'.[64] However, Plath does not fetishize a 'feminine' linguistic doubleness, difference, or undecidability for its own sake.[65] She rewrites the male-authored fantasy of the fatal woman as an ambiguous strategy of symbolic revenge, which, while it exploits the potential threat or aggression associated with female performance, constantly draws attention to the social production of such fantasies. Moreover, as I shall argue in the next chapter, Plath's ambivalent fascination with the spectacle of femininity forms part of a dialogue not only with male literary precursors such as T. S. Eliot, Baudelaire, and Mallarmé, but also with consumer culture; indeed, it becomes a means of undermining canonical oppositions between 'high' and 'low' forms of writing. Her ironic relation to images drawn from both 'high' and 'low' culture encodes a crisis in the social and literary meanings of femininity.

NOTES

1. Chris Baldick, 'Introduction', *The Oxford Book of Gothic Tales* (Oxford: Oxford University Press, 1992), p. xii.

2. Sigmund Freud, 'The "Uncanny"' (1919), *PFL* xiv. 335–76.

3. Mario Praz, *The Romantic Agony*, trans. Angus Davidson (Oxford: Oxford University Press, 1933).

4. M. H. Abrams, *The Mirror and the Lamp* (Oxford: Oxford University Press, 1953), 65.

5. Mary Jacobus, *Romanticism, Writing and Sexual Difference: Essays on 'The Prelude'* (Oxford: Clarendon Press, 1989), 206.

6. Plath MSS II, Box 9, f. 2, n.d., Lilly.

7. See Paul de Man, 'Anthropomorphism and Trope in the Lyric', in *The Rhetoric of Romanticism* (New York: Columbia University Press, 1984), 256, and 'Autobiography as Defacement', in *Rhetoric*, 67–81. See also Michel Riffaterre, 'Prosopopeia', in Peter Brooks et al. (eds.), *The Lesson of Paul de Man*, Yale French Studies, 69 (New Haven: Yale University Press, 1985), 107–23.

8. See Paul de Man, 'Tropes (Rilke)', in *Allegories of Reading* (New Haven: Yale University Press, 1979), 37.

9. Pierre Fontanier, *Les Figures du discours* (Paris: Flammarion, 1977), 404 (my trans.).

10. De Man, *Rhetoric*, 259.

11. Plath MSS, Sept. 1961, drafts 14a and b, Lilly.

12. Richard Marovich, *A Concordance to the Collected Poems of Sylvia Plath* (New York: Garland Publishing, 1986), 595.

13. See de Man, 'Autobiography as Defacement', in *Rhetoric*, 75–6.

14. Cited in Jonathan Culler, 'Apostrophe', in *The Pursuit of Signs* (London: Routledge and Kegan Paul, 1981), 138.

15. Culler, 'Apostrophe', 146.

16. Freud, 'The "Uncanny"', *PFL* xiv. 363.

17. Ted Hughes, 'Notes on Poems 1956–63', *CP* 292.

18. See Sigmund Freud, 'Medusa's Head', *SE* xviii. 273–4.

19. Ariel Poems MSS, 12–19 Apr. 1962, Smith. The thirteen manuscript drafts run to twenty densely corrected pages. Plath made three separate attempts at the poem, which she labelled 'a' (undated), 'b' (12 Apr. 1962), and 'c' (19 Apr. 1962). Further references to the drafts of 'Elm' will be by page number and letter, and will be incorporated in the text.

20. Sylvia Plath, BBC Interview (1962), rpt. in Peter Orr (ed.), *The Poet Speaks* (London: Routledge and Kegan Paul, 1966), 170.

21. Sigmund Freud, 'Mourning and Melancholia', *PFL* xi. 262.

22. Eve Kosofsky Sedgwick, *The Coherence of Gothic Conventions* (New York: Methuen, 1986), 12–13.

23. Plath MSS, draft 7, 21 Feb. 1962, Lilly.

24. Sedgwick, *The Coherence*, p. vi. See also Tanya Modleski, *Loving With a Vengeance: Mass-produced Stories for Women* (London: Methuen, 1984), and Mary Jacobus, *Reading Woman: Essays in Feminist Criticism* (New York: Columbia University Press, 1986). For a general survey of critical debate on 'Female Gothic', see Elaine Showalter, *Sister's Choice* (Oxford: Clarendon Press, 1991), 127–44.

25. See Sigmund Freud and Josef Breuer, *Studies on Hysteria*, *PFL* iii. 51–69.

26. For a discussion of the haunted house of Gothic romance as womb/tomb, emblem of the threatening or persecutory phallic mother of pre-Oedipal fantasy, see Norman N. Holland and Leona F. Sherman, 'Gothic Possibilities', in Elizabeth Flynn and Patrocinio Schweickart (eds.), *Gender and Reading: Essays on Readers, Texts and Contexts* (Baltimore: Johns Hopkins University Press, 1986), 217–27, and Claire Kahane, 'The Gothic Mirror', in Shirley Nelson Garner and Madelon Sprengnether (eds.), *The (M)other Tongue: Essays in Feminist Psychoanalytic Interpretation* (Ithaca, NY: Cornell University Press, 1985), 334–51.

27. Plath MSS, draft 2, 25 Feb. 1961, Lilly.

28. Plath MSS, draft 2, 21 Feb. 1962, Lilly.

29. Nicholas Abraham and Maria Torok, 'The Topography of Reality: Sketching a Metapsychology of Secrets', in *The Shell and the Kernel*, i, ed. and trans. Nicholas T. Rand (Chicago: University of Chicago Press, 1994), 159.

30. Hughes, 'Notes on Poems, 1956–63', *CP* 2911.

31. Geoffrey Hartman, in a discussion of Wordsworth's 'Yew Trees', calls the yew tree 'a totemic figure in literary discourse'. See Hartman, *The Unremarkable Wordsworth* (London: Methuen, 1987), 133.

32. William Wordsworth, *The Oxford Authors: William Wordsworth*, ed. Stephen Gill (Oxford: Oxford University Press, 1984), 334–5.

33. Alfred Tennyson, *Selected Poems*, ed. Christopher Ricks (Harlow, Essex: Longman, 1989), 346.

34. T. S. Eliot, *Collected Poems*, 1909–1962 (London: Faber and Faber, 1936), 104.

35. See Robert Graves, *The White Goddess* (London: Faber and Faber, 1961), 165, and Judith Kroll, *Chapters in a Mythology* (New York: Harper and Row, 1976), 111 ff.

36. Ariel Poems MSS, 2 Apr. 1962, Smith.

37. Ariel Poems MSS, draft 1, p. 4, Smith.

38. Friedrich Nietzsche, *Thus Spoke Zarathustra*, trans. R. J. Hollingdale (Harmondsworth: Penguin, 1961), 92. Plath's personal library, Smith.

39. On Nietzsche's view of femininity as, appearance, see *The Gay Science*, trans. Walter Kaufmann (New York: Vintage, 1974), 38; *Human, All Too Human*, trans. Walter Kaufmann (Cambridge: Cambridge University Press, 1986), 82, and *Beyond Good and Evil*, trans. R. J. Hollingdale (Harmondsworth: Penguin, 1973), 84.

40. 'The Magic Mirror: A Study of the Double in Two of Dostoyevsky's Novels.' Smith College Undergraduate Dissertation, 1955, Plath MSS, Box 11, f, 1, Lilly.

41. Ariel Poems MSS, 4 Apr. 1962, Smith.

42. Kenneth Burke, *A Grammar of Motives* (Berkeley: University of California Press, 1969), 512.

43. Paul de Man, 'The Rhetoric of Temporality', in *Blindness and Insight* (London: Methuen, 1983), 213. Further page references to this essay will be included in the text.

44. See Richard Terdiman, *Discourse and Counterdiscourse: The Theory and Practice of Symbolic Resistance in 19th Century France* (Ithaca, NY: Cornell University Press, 1985).

45. Charles Baudelaire, *The Complete Verse*, trans. Francis Scarfe (London: Anvil Press, 1986), i. 163. Plath's annotated copy of *Les Fleurs du mal*, personal library, Smith.

46. Freud, 'Mourning and Melancholia', 256.

47. Plath MSS, Smith.

48. Juliana Schiesari, *The Gendering of Melancholia* (Ithaca, NY: Cornell University Press, 1992), 75.

49. The manuscript of the poem contains, after 'Uncle, uncle', the line 'Have you made your will?'. Smith MSS, Draft 1, p. 1.

50. Joan Riviere, 'Womanliness as Masquerade', in Victor Burgin, James Donald, and Cora Kaplan (eds.), *Formations of Fantasy* (London and New York: Methuen, 1986), 35–44.

51. Stephen Heath, 'Joan Riviere and the Masquerade', in Burgin et al. (eds.), *Formations*, 54.

52. Riviere, 'Womanliness as Masquerade', 43.

53. John Fletcher, 'Versions of Masquerade', *Screen*, 29, 3 (Summer 1988), 57.

54. Quoted by Lois Ames, 'Notes Towards a Biography', in Charles Newman (ed.), *The Art of Sylvia Plath* (Bloomington, Ind.: Indiana University Press, 1970), 166.

55. Baudelaire, *Complete Verse*, i. 216–17.

56. Eliot, *Collected Poems*, 17.

57. See, for example, the 'Black Venus' cycle (*Poems* 22–39) of *Les Fleurs du mal*, in *Complete Verse*, i. 82–107.

58. Clytemnestra kills Agamemnon, in revenge for the sacrifice of their daughter Iphigeneia, by netting him in the folds of a cloak. Compare T. S. Eliot's lines in 'Sweeney Among the Nightingales', *Collected Poems*, 59–60: 'When Agamemnon cried aloud / And let their liquid siftings fall / To stain the stiff dishonoured shroud.'

59. Françoise Meltzer, *Salome and the Dance of Writing* (Chicago: Chicago University Press, 1987), 26. On the dancer in Symbolist aesthetics, see Frank Kermode, *Romantic Image* (London: Routledge and Kegan Paul, 1957); on Salome as Decadent heroine, see Elaine Showalter, *Sexual Anarchy: Gender and Culture at the Fin-de-Siècle* (London: Bloomsbury, 1991).

60. J.-K. Huysmans, *Against Nature*, trans. Robert Baldick (Harmondsworth: Penguin, 1959), 66.

61. See Riviere, 'Womanliness', 42.

62. For example, the line 'the mirrors are filling with smiles' echoes Hérodiade's words 'l'azur / Seraphique sourit dans les vitres profondes' ('the seraphic azure / Smiles in the deep windows'). See Stephane Mallarmé, *Selected Poems*, trans. C. F. MacIntyre (Berkeley: University of California Press, 1957), 38.

63. The Salome story is also suggested by an image of decapitation in the manuscript draft of 'Mystic' (composed on the same day as 'Kindness'): 'The sun rises on its red plate, the heart has not stopped'. See Ariel Poems MSS, 1 Feb. 1963, Smith.

64. Jacques Derrida, *Spurs: Nietzsche's Styles*, trans. Barbara Harlow (Chicago: University of Chicago Press, 1979), 55.

65. See Alice Jardine, *Gynesis: Configurations of Woman and Modernity* (Ithaca, NY: Cornell University Press, 1985).

TIM KENDALL

From the Bottom of the Pool:
Sylvia Plath's Last Poems

Sylvia Plath arranged her manuscript of *Ariel* so that it began with the word 'love' and ended with 'spring'. The collection, had it been published in that form, would therefore have pursued a message of affirmation: the poet had survived her harsh emotional winter, and could now look forward to the possibilities of regeneration. The theme of rebirth, explored in so many of *Ariel*'s poems, would have been enforced by the structure of the book.

Plath's carbon typescript of *Ariel* was found among her papers after her death. Also found, separately and on loose sheets, were the poems she had written since *The Colossus* but which were not incorporated into *Ariel*. These included most of her work from 1960 and 1961, as well as a few poems contemporary with *Ariel* and everything she wrote after 'Death & Co.', the last *Ariel* poem. Plath's reasons for including some poems in her *Ariel* manuscript and omitting others are not always obvious. Although value judgements must have played a significant part, it is also possible that poems which did not fit so comfortably into the scheme of rebirth were reserved for some more thematically appropriate future collection.

The absence from the manuscript of any poems written after mid-November ('Death & Co.', the last of her *Ariel* poems, is dated 14 November) also raises questions about her plans for poems as successful as 'Years', 'Mary's Song' and 'Winter Trees'. Whereas Ted Hughes suggests that Plath arranged

From *English* 49 (2000): pp. 23–38. © 2001 by The English Association.

Ariel 'some time around Christmas 1962',[1] Anne Stevenson's hypothesis that she ordered *Ariel* for the last time on or around 15 November (the day after 'Death & Co.') seems more probable,[2] especially as Plath reported, in a letter to her mother on 19 November, that she had 'finished a second book of poems'.[3] Plath always considered her latest work to be her best—for most of her career, with very good reason. However, having satisfied herself that she had finished a book, its title changed from *The Rival* to *The Birthday Present* to *Daddy* to *Ariel*, she felt confident enough to stop tampering. These were poems which, she told her mother, would make her name (*LH*. 468). Yet there is no indication that she tried to have *Ariel* published. The ruthlessly ambitious poet she had been for most of her writing life, so concerned with her own reputation and jealous of others', seems to have been replaced by someone assured of her achievement, and no longer dependent on external approval.

After the *Ariel* manuscript was completed, Plath's creative momentum kept her writing for another fortnight. In retrospect, there are signs that her inspiration was beginning to run down. By comparison with her October surge, six poems in fifteen days seems slow (though still prolific by any other standard); and a poem like 'Brasilia' is a rare and perhaps revealing failure, in that it recapitulates the themes and images already so powerfully explored in 'Mary's Song'. Plath may or may not have recognised that she was reaching the end of a fruitful creative phase, but at this stage domestic arrangements also intervened, to force the same result. Her move from Devon to London in December 1962 effectively halted her poetry for almost two months.

What happened when Plath began again, in the fortnight before her death, is curious and remarkable. On 28 January she revised 'Sheep in Fog', and wrote (if the manuscript dates are to be believed) three new poems. The next eight days produced eight poems—inviting comparisons with the productivity of the previous October. Then, in the six days leading up to her suicide, she wrote nothing which survives. The publication of a makeshift *Ariel* after Plath's death, including nine poems from 1963, has prevented readers and critics from appreciating the sea-change her style underwent in those last poems. For all its inevitable similarities with earlier work, that week of writing offered something radically different from Plath's earlier successes. She herself recognised the transformation: Hughes relates that he was shown only 'Totem' and 'The Munich Mannequins', which 'seemed to me, and to her too, even finer than the *Ariel* poems' (*WP*. 165). In the absence of the journals, Hughes provides only the most tantalising account of Plath's attitude to these new poems:

> She liked the different, cooler inspiration (as she described it) and
> the denser pattern, of the first of these, as they took shape. With

after-knowledge, one certainly looks at something else—though the premonitory note, except maybe in her very last poem, is hardly more insistent than it had seemed in many an earlier piece. (*WP*. 189)

Readers of these last poems inevitably find retrospective premonitions hard to avoid. 'Edge', in particular, seems to demolish distinctions between life and art. However, biographical information must not be allowed to overshadow a careful analysis of the nature of Plath's 'different, cooler inspiration' in her final poems. Paradoxically, the final crisis of her life coincided with a style and vision more detached than anything she had attempted in *Ariel*.

'Kindness', written on 1 February, provides one of Plath's most famous statements about her art: 'The blood jet is poetry, / There is no stopping it'. At first sight this sits oddly alongside Plath's reported insistence on her cooler inspiration. The poem's personified Dame Kindness busies herself tidying the speaker's house, making cups of tea, and applying her sugary sweetness as a poultice to all the hurts around her. The hurt of poetry, though, cannot be stanched: 'There is no stopping it'. Poetry exists in opposition to domestic life, as Plath had previously noted when telling her mother, amidst the onrush of her October work, that it seemed 'domesticity had choked [her]' (*LH*. 466). 'Kindness' represents poetry as violent, vital and uncontrollable, a sign of vibrant life but also the ebbing of that life: a blood jet which cannot be stopped leads eventually to death. Whereas 'Cut' could celebrate the thrill of cutting a thumb—and the exhilaration of that 'red plush'—Plath's late poems seem, as 'Contusion' puts it, 'washed out'. The blood jet has by now almost entirely drained the body.

As a result these poems are colder, and in one sense less urgent; the hope of rebirth has disappeared, to be replaced by resignation. *Ariel*, for all its emotional agony and toying with suicide, had been an uplifting collection. The poems offered an escape, through death, into the springtime of a new and better life. Plath described her Lady Lazarus, for example, as 'the Phoenix, the libertarian spirit [...] also just a good, plain, very resourceful woman':[4] the suicide is actually an exultant survivor, adapting to her situation and struggling to improve her lot. Plath's last poems are unable to find any such triumph or even consolation, as they create a new style from despair. Usually they lack *Ariel*'s relentless rhythmical energy, and dispense with the motor of rhyme: motion gives way to stasis, and the element of fatalism, culminating so overwhelmingly in 'Edge', deprives Plath's speakers of options. There is no place for resourcefulness now: destiny has become inescapable.

This shift is illustrated by one of Plath's finest poems, 'Sheep in Fog', written on 2 December and substantially revised almost two months later. As

Ted Hughes has pointed out, the poem therefore spans the different periods. Hughes's definitive reading of the manuscripts maps a swerve away from the relative uplift of the poem's original conclusion, to the ominous tone of the published version (*WP*. 191–211). Originally, in the version Plath abandoned before Christmas, the poem had ended,

> Patriarchs till now immobile
> In heavenly wools
> Row off as stones or clouds with the faces of babies.

In this form, 'Sheep in Fog' is tonally an *Ariel* poem. Admittedly, a hint of abandonment—the patriarchs are rowing off—does introduce some sense of anxiety. However, the babies imply new life, the switch from immobility to motion is almost always positive (as 'Ariel' indicates), and there seem to be at least hints of 'The Colossus' and 'Little Fugue' in the reference to the patriarchs rowing off 'as stones or clouds'. The metaphors are familiar, and the world of the poem recognisable to readers of Plath's earlier work.

Dissatisfied with this conclusion, Plath's revision of the final stanza two months later describes a much more terrifying eschatology:

> They threaten
> To let me through to a heaven
> Starless and fatherless, a dark water.

Death had been desirable in *Ariel* not only because it was the necessary precursor to rebirth, but because it allowed reunion with the father-figure. Even the earlier drafts of 'Sheep in Fog' had linked the father with the afterlife, by referring to the patriarchs in their 'heavenly wools'. Now the speaker's heaven is bewildering and isolated. The 'black lake' which Plath's speaker had crossed during her chthonic journey of death and rebirth in the April poems has become her final destination. Earlier in the poem, the speaker admits that 'People or stars / Regard me sadly, I disappoint them'. The implication must be that this disappointment will lead to the speaker being banished to a starless fatherless heaven, where the consolations of the *Ariel* mindscape are absent. The new concluding stanza contains one crucial detail: the speaker is 'threaten[ed]' with the prospect of being 'let [...] through to' this desolate heaven. No one forces her: the threat lies only in the possibility that she might be allowed, at last, to arrive where she wants to be. Whatever has been stopping her until now may not stop her for much longer.

The setting of 'Sheep in Fog', like the setting of 'Ariel', is the landscape around Plath's North Tawton home. In each case, her persona is riding a horse. Plath's introduction for BBC radio emphasises the obvious contrast:

> In this poem ['Sheep in Fog'], the speaker's horse is proceeding at a slow, cold walk down a hill of macadam to the stable at the bottom. It is December. It is foggy. In the fog there are sheep. (*CP.* 295)

The speaker of 'Ariel' hurtled suicidal towards an ecstatic extinction in the cauldron of morning. The difference from the 'slow, cold walk' of 'Sheep in Fog' could not be more marked. All passion, now, is spent. The horse is walking so slowly that the hooves sound like 'dolorous bells', as the journey back to the stable is accompanied by a death knell. Hughes convincingly uncovers references in the drafts to Phaethon, who was destroyed after taking and riding his father's sun-chariot. (All that remain in the finished poem are the word 'rust', which had originally referred to the 'scrapped chariot', and the line 'A flower left out', originally 'a dead man left out'.) Plath's movement from 'Ariel' to 'Sheep in Fog' is the movement from the red heat of Phaethon's life-affirming, self-destructive adventure to its wrecked and sombre aftermath, from a terrifying triumphalism to defeat and desolation.

This different tone is signalled even by the punctuation of the late poems. The *Ariel* work seems littered with exclamation marks emphasising moments of excitement or discovery, and question marks which indicate a speaker still searching and hopeful. (A quick tally on the basis of the October work reveals an average of two to three question marks, and as many exclamation marks, per poem.) The late poems are much more sparing of such punctuation, reflecting their cooler, more resigned tone. It would be wrong to argue that all the late work shares this emotional exhaustion. 'Balloons', for example, stands out from the pallor of many poems in the group because of its obvious delight in the brightness of the balloons' colours: 'Yellow cathead, blue fish', 'Globes of thin air, red, green'. However, even here an aftermath is being described; the balloons are leftovers from Christmas, and as they pop, they leave in their place 'a world clear as water'. 'Balloons' may be a celebration, but not an unambiguous one: to describe the world as 'clear as water' is at least to imply the possibility of drowning. This suspicion is reinforced by the number of supporting examples throughout Plath's last poems, most of which allude to water, pools and the sea: the newly-revised 'Sheep in Fog' warns of the 'dark water' of the speaker's heaven; 'Totem' mentions 'the beauty of drowned fields'; the child's eye in 'Child' is a 'pool', while 'Gigolo' ends with the speaker gazing at his own reflection in a watery 'eye'; the 'still waters' engulfing the paralytic cut him off from the world like 'A clear / Cellophane I cannot crack'; 'Mystic' ponders the benefits of 'walking beside still water', and wonders whether the sea 'Remember[s] the walker upon it'; in 'Contusion' the sea 'sucks' at a 'pit of rock', having regurgitated its dead victim; and 'Words' has water running over rock, before ending with 'fixed stars' at 'the bottom of the pool'.

These references are too numerous and insistent to be coincidental. Their effect is to give the impression of someone crossing between elements or between worlds, her (or in the case of 'Paralytic' and 'Gigolo', his) vision submerged and movements heavy and laboured. Earlier poetry associates the sea with a rich and strange afterlife, from which, in 'Full Fathom Five', the father might emerge, and to which Plath's persona is drawn: 'Father, this thick air is murderous. / I would breathe water'. However, a more recent source and inspiration for Plath's water imagery in her last poems is an autobiographical prose reminiscence, 'Ocean 1212-W', which she wrote in late 1962. In it she remembers how, as a baby, she once crawled straight towards the sea, and was 'just through the wall of green when [her mother] caught [her] heels'.[5] As she admits, 'I often wonder what would have happened if I had managed to pierce that looking-glass'. Plath's last poems seem to explore that possibility, stressing that crucial difference between a world 'clear as water' and a world clear as air.

To read 'Ocean 1212-W' alongside those last poems is to hear countless echoes and half-echoes. 'The stillness of hills stifles me like fat pillows' (*JPBD*. 122) evokes the 'hills' and 'stillness' of 'Sheep in Fog', while numerous details—a word like 'totem', for example, or the description of the tide as 'suck[ing]'—suggest that Plath's writing of the essay made accessible a source of images from her childhood which she was able to exploit in her late poems. The Munich mannequins, 'Intolerable, without mind', find an unlikely parallel in a starfish which Plath's speaker remembers flinging against a stone: 'Let it perish. It had no wit'. Earlier the speaker hears 'the lulling shoosh-shoosh of a full, mirrory pool; the pool turns the quartz grits at its rim idly and kindly, a lady brooding at jewellery' (*JPBD*. 117). The mirrory pool is a common trope in Plath: it appears, most obviously, in 'Mirror'. But it also points the way forward to the late poems, to 'Gigolo' and even 'Words', where the verb 'turns' reappears in a similar context. The quartz grits are turned 'idly and kindly', with the curiosity of that final adverb preempting 'Kindness', which also makes reference to a bejewelled lady. The late poems may represent a new direction, but that direction is at least obscurely signposted by 'Ocean 1212-W'.

Another way by which 'Ocean 1212-W' facilitates the creation of those poems is through its exploration of what Plath calls simply '*separateness*'—the separateness of the self from its environment. Whereas one of her early influences, Theodore Roethke, expresses exhilaration—'I saw the separateness of all things!'[6]—the same experience in 'Ocean 1212-W' provokes a cataclysmic disintegration. After her brother is born, Plath's speaker no longer finds herself 'the centre of a tender universe' (*JPBD*. 120). Her place is usurped by the baby. This causes a symbolic fall from an Edenic unity to division and distinction:

> As from a star I saw, coldly and soberly, the *separateness* of everything. I felt the wall of my skin: I am I. That stone is a stone. My beautiful fusion with the things of this world was over.

Later in the essay, however, the sea throws up a 'totem' in the form of a wooden monkey. The speaker takes this as a sign 'of election and specialness. A sign that I was not forever to be cast out'. Plath constantly replays this fall and recovery throughout her journals. It also informs the overarching metaphor of *The Bell Jar*—the entrapped separateness of the self under the jar, and the gradual, possibly temporary lifting of the jar as Esther heals: 'How did I know', she asks, that some day 'the bell jar, with its stifling distortions, wouldn't descend again?'.[7] 'Stifling' prefigures the description in 'Ocean 1212-W' of stifling hills. The passage also stresses how, in her self-dramatising myth, Plath portrays her fall into division not as a single, irreparable moment, but as a recurring process, as her life vacillates between blissful unity (which sometimes in the *Ariel* poems necessitates rather than precludes suicide) and terrifying isolation.

The effects of Plath's 'separateness' can be felt throughout the late poems. 'Edge' pushes the detachment to its furthest possibilities, as the self splits and the cold-blooded voice of the poem describes its own demise. 'Edge' had originally begun with the phrase 'Down there', and this clinical examination of the terrible scene of suicide and infanticide below is shocking because of its distance. Describing contemporary Northern Irish poetry, Seamus Heaney quotes Anthony Storr to draw an analogy with Jungian psychoanalysis—an analogy which may also help explain Plath's procedures in 'Edge' and other late poems:

> Jung describes how some of his patients, faced with what appeared to be an insoluble conflict, solved it by 'outgrowing' it, by developing a 'new level of consciousness' [...] 'One certainly does feel the affect and is shaken and tormented by it, yet at the same time one is aware of a higher consciousness looking on which prevents one from becoming identical with the affect, a

consciousness which regards the affect as an object, and can say
'I know that I suffer'.'[8]

Plath's 'higher consciousness' is her poetic imagination, pitilessly charting her
own inevitable demise. The insoluble conflict can now be escaped, in Plath's
case, only during the act of writing, which allows a temporary detachment
from, or outgrowing of, the self and the Jungian 'affect'. Whereas the speaker
of most of the *Ariel* poems is also the poem's protagonist, 'Edge' separates
voice from subject.

    This change is reflected in Plath's dramatic monologues. Although she
carefully distances herself from the speakers of 'Daddy' and 'Lady Lazarus',
those poems, along with other contemporary pieces like 'Medusa' and
'Purdah', tease the reader with the biographical readings which the poet
herself scrupulously discourages in her introductions for BBC radio. Such
poems thrive on ambiguity, on the likelihood which is never quite a certainty
that the speakers are identifiable with the poet. (Many readers do not
recognise that there is any slippage between poet and persona: for example,
several reviewers of Linda Wagner-Martin's biography expressed surprise
that Otto Plath was not, after all, a Nazi.) However, Plath's late dramatic
monologues seem more resistant to biographical appropriation. The gigolo
and the paralytic are distanced by gender, while the indeterminable sex of
the mystic only adds to an impression of anonymity; lacking the kind of
biographical prompt evident in 'Daddy' ('I was ten when they buried you'),
the mystic could be almost anyone.

    Yet these poems, too, anatomise Plath's higher consciousness. Their
more tangential engagement with the poet's biography reflects their 'cooler
inspiration', as they superficially resist simple parallels between art and life.
The misogynistic speaker of 'Gigolo', for example, invites identification
with the brutal males of other poems—the surgeon, the rabbit catcher, the
father figure, or the jailer. 'Gigolo' does, undeniably, convey a disgust at male
exploitation of women, although that exploitation is not merely one-way: the
'smiles of women' are described as 'bright fish hooks', suddenly reversing
the relationship between hunter and hunted. This complicates one obvious
interpretation of the poem as a self-betraying monologue of man's inhumanity
to woman. More importantly, though, 'Gigolo' embodies a concern with
discretion—not just secrecy, but discretion of the self, where repeated sexual
union only emphasises the speaker's inability to appreciate what Plath calls a
'beautiful fusion with the things of this world'. There is no place for 'family
photographs' or any kind of emotional relationship. Admittedly this is often
true of the *Ariel* poems as well: Plath's moments of 'beautiful fusion', in her
prose as in her poetry, rarely accommodate other people. Nevertheless,

the gigolo's inability to range beyond the barriers of the self does clearly distinguish him from Plath's *Ariel* personae. Interpreted in this light, the speaker of 'Gigolo' is revealed as the creation of Plath's higher consciousness, exploring one aspect of her postlapsarian separateness from the world around her. It might be argued that the gigolo is no less (and no more) the poet than the speaker of 'Sheep in Fog' or the girl with the Electra complex in 'Daddy'.

The water imagery of the poem, after the autobiographical explorations of 'Ocean 1212-W', certainly reinforces this identification. Initially portrayed as a lizard hiding in crevices, the gigolo is soon transformed into a sea creature: he 'Mill[s] a litter of breasts like jellyfish', and his diet includes fish and squid, among other aphrodisiacs. By the end of the poem, the submerging of his vision is total:

> I shall never grow old. New oysters
> Shriek in the sea and I
> Glitter like Fontainebleau
>
> Gratified,
> All the fall of water an eye
> Over whose pool I tenderly
> Lean and see me.

Here Plath employs a homophonic rhyme: I/eye. However, the poem's most conspicuous rhyme is saved until the conclusion, as the reflection of sound copies the visual reflection. Echo has pined away into a one-syllable rhyme, and the sexual gratification of this gigolo-Narcissus, having been aided by the aphrodisiac oysters, is expressed as a fountain ('Fontainebleau'). With a final splitting of identity, and in an enactment of Plath's desire to penetrate the sea's 'looking-glass', the gigolo creates a higher consciousness by admiring himself underwater.

Separateness from the world finds its most extreme embodiment in 'Paralytic', apparently written the same day as 'Gigolo'. Now paralysis prohibits engagement with surroundings: the speaker cannot 'touch' the world around him, cannot speak, cannot cling to the 'rock' of his mind, and cannot pierce the 'Cellophane' of 'Still waters' which 'Wrap my lips, // Eyes, nose and ears'. This underwater existence makes the paralytic akin to the gigolo, and it becomes clear that his inability to connect, as 'the day outside glides by like ticker tape', is something more than merely physical. Unlike the gigolo, he is not safe from family photographs, which visit him in the form of his wife and daughters. This conspicuously replays 'Tulips', turning, like the earlier poem, on the conflict between the desire for peaceful effacement and the pulls of the outside world: 'My husband and child smiling out of the family photo; / Their smiles catch onto my skin, little smiling hooks' ('Tulips'). Yet the wife and daughters of 'Paralytic' remain two-dimensional and distant, failing to challenge the speaker's detachment as he contentedly finds 'all / Wants, desire, / Falling from me like rings'. The poem's last stanza celebrates such self-sufficiency:

> The claw
> Of the magnolia,
> Drunk on its own scents,
> Asks nothing of life.

Plath's tulips in her earlier poem are vivid, bright and noisy, using up oxygen and demanding attention 'like an awful baby'. They succeed in drawing the speaker back towards the responsibilities of life and away from her wish to 'lie with my hands turned up and be utterly empty'. The magnolia of 'Paralytic' has no such ambition. It not only allows the paralytic his one desire—which is to be free from desire altogether—it even offers itself as exemplar.

Stylistically, too, these poems announce their shift away from the hopeful world of *Ariel*. The most important difference between the late poems and their predecessors is, as Plath noted, a difference of tone, and this new tone is created partly through an emphasis on the condensing of metaphor and simile. 'Tulips' is representative of the transitional poems of 1961, in the verbosity of its images. Some of the similes, when they finally arrive, have been so long expected that they appear redundant and repetitive: 'It is what the dead close on, finally; I imagine them/ Shutting their mouths on it, like a Communion tablet'; 'I could hear [the tulips] breathe / Lightly, through their white swaddlings, like an awful baby'; 'The tulips should be behind bars like dangerous animals'. In each case there have been enough clues to render the elaboration of the final simile unnecessary. The *Ariel* poems rarely make this mistake, but their extraordinary power often stems from a delighted indulgence in their own free-wheeling metaphorical ingenuity: one of the best examples, the cut thumb in 'Cut', is simultaneously a scalped pilgrim, a saboteur, a Kamikaze man, a member of the Ku Klux Khan who wears his head-covering Babushka style, a trepanned veteran, a dirty girl, and, finally, a plain 'Thumb stump'. By contrast the last poems work analogically, so that whereas in 'Cut' the cut thumb unites the metaphors, now images beget fresh images, sometimes leaving behind their original subject.

Just as bewildering, the metaphors are often whittled down to, or even beyond, their bare essentials. 'Totem', for example, contains the line,

'Dawn gilds the farmers like pigs'. Here a simile and a metaphor fight for dominance. To 'gild' is to cover partially or entirely with a thin layer of gold, so that the reader understands from the phrase 'Dawn gilds the farmers' how the low morning sun creates a bright aura around the farmers' outlines. The simile, 'like pigs', therefore seems curious: even if the same phenomenon can be observed around pigs, it still does not explain why they, in particular, should be chosen for the comparison. In fact the simile pulls the verb 'gilds' in a different direction—'gilds' being a variant spelling of 'gelds'. To bolster this reading, within four lines the poem describes the mercilessness of 'the glitter of cleavers, / The butcher's guillotine'. (There is also a memory of 'Little Fugue', where lopped sausages transmogrify nightmarishly into the 'cut throats' of humans.) This illustrates, in miniature, the extreme economy of Plath's late poems: 'Dawn gilds the farmers like pigs' forcefully compacts the metaphor of gilding with the simile of gelding.

The title of 'Totem', like the title of 'Words', suggests that the poem consciously seeks to explore its own methods of production. Many similar examples can be found throughout these late poems. Plath described 'Totem' as 'a pile of interconnected images, like a totem pole' (*CP*. 295). The description might equally be applied to 'The Munich Mannequins', where the figurative shorthand serves as an alienation effect, enacting Plath's cooler inspiration, and rendering the familiar obscure and unnatural:

> Perfection is terrible, it cannot have children.
> Cold as snow breath, it tamps the womb
>
> Where the yew trees blow like hydras,
> The tree of life and the tree of life
>
> Unloosing their moons, month after month, to no purpose.

Passages as condensed as this, and as relentless in their metaphorical insistence, are rarely found outside these last poems. Their 'denser pattern', as Plath described it to Hughes, places enormous demands on the reader. The poem opens with an apparently factual statement, which brooks no contradiction, about an abstract 'Perfection': it cannot have children. Within two lines, reality has been replaced by metaphor: 'yew trees' substitute for Fallopian tubes, and blow not like themselves but 'like hydras', as simile is joined to metaphor. Similarly eggs become 'moons', embodying their lunar cycle. In this world the figurative provides the only reality. 'Childless Woman', written two months earlier, gestures towards the style of 'The Munich Mannequins': 'The womb / Rattles its pod, the moon / Discharges itself from the tree with nowhere to go'. Here, however, the pod and the tree, and the pea and the moon, do not belong comfortably together. By comparison 'The Munich Mannequins' seems more confident of its metaphors, and less willing to explain or recapitulate them. It also takes greater risks by disorientating the reader with its reversal of familiar symbols: the yew tree, emblematic of death and, in Plath's work, more specifically the dead father, is now mysteriously transformed into a 'tree of life'. The passage rewrites the imagery of 'The Moon and the Yew Tree' for an internalised landscape—a landscape too visceral for the mind, and to be located instead in the organs of reproduction.

Because of their 'denser pattern', the obscurity of 'The Munich Mannequins' and 'Totem' in particular cannot be overstated. It is difficult even to determine the subject of these poems. Their unrhymed couplets, although often enjambed, create the impression of separate but related units, piled up—as Plath says of 'Totem'—'like a totem pole'. 'The Munich Mannequins' offers more of a temporal narrative, as it moves from Plath's long-standing preoccupation with female barrenness to the hotels of Munich whose occupants are as anonymous as the mannequins: 'hands' open doors, and 'broad toes' will fit into newly-polished shoes, but it never becomes clear whose hands or whose toes. Possibly they belong to the 'thick Germans' who slumber in their 'bottomless Stolz'. Plath ends the poem by rewriting and redeploying familiar images from earlier work:

> And the black phones on hooks
>
> Glittering
> Glittering and digesting
>
> Voicelessness. The snow has no voice.

These images are similar to the 'bald glyphs' which Hughes detects in 'Sheep in Fog' (*WP*. 207), and which represent the tiny visible portion of an otherwise submerged psychodrama.

The depths of that psychodrama become apparent through the reader's appreciation of Plath's recurrent imagery. The concluding lines of 'The Munich Mannequins' reveal the consistency of Plath's imaginative drive, and indicate how far her work, for all its stylistic shifts and remakings, can be viewed as a unified whole. The 'hooks' appear throughout her poetry, for example in 'Blackberrying' ('A blackberry alley, going down in hooks'), 'Tulips' ('Their smiles catch onto my skin, little smiling hooks') or 'Ariel' ('Nigger-eye / Berries cast dark/ Hooks'); normally they represent restriction, as the stringencies of the world hold the speaker back from the longed-for release. 'Glittering' is also prominent in Plath's active vocabulary, and almost always implies some kind of deceit or threat: 'Bastard / Masturbating a glitter' in 'Death & Co.', the 'Gigolo' glittering 'like Fontainebleau', or the 'glitter of cleavers' in 'Totem'. 'Digesting' evokes Plath's pervasive eating imagery. The 'black phones' remember 'Words heard, by accident, over the phone', and more particularly the 'black telephones' of 'Daddy', 'off at the root' so that 'The voices just can't worm through'. That last echo, coupled with the poem's apparently gratuitous anti-German prejudice, may reveal the unspoken presence of the father, while also acknowledging the impossibility of communication between his world and the poet's. 'The Munich Mannequins' portrays a perfect and therefore dehumanised society of bland prettiness:

> O the domesticity of these windows,
> The baby lace, the green-leaved confectionery [...]

This perfection is 'terrible' (another favourite Plath word) in both senses: it is appalling, and it inspires terror. The society keeps its atrocities—in which the father is, as always, implicated—well hidden under its superficial appeal. As if mimicking this repression, Plath's glyphs only hint at the threat. Munich may be a 'morgue', but it remains undisturbed by voices of dissent. The 'Voicelessness' which the poem reports is an admission of defeat, an amnesia or oblivion which ensures that no one can or will speak for the dispossessed. 'The Munich Mannequins' reverses 'Daddy', and replaces rage with resignation: the voices which 'can't worm through' are now the voices of victims, not perpetrators. None of this should suggest that 'The Munich Mannequins' only reveals its significance to those readers prepared to track Plath's recurring imagery throughout the body of her work. Such a contextual reading exposes the depths of Plath's psychodrama, but it merely uncovers what is already subliminally present in the poem. Hughes has commented on the drafts of 'Sheep in Fog' that through them,

> We understand [the poem] far better, because we have learned the peculiar meaning of its hieroglyphs. These drafts are not an incidental adjunct to the poem, they are a complementary revelation, and a log-book of its real meanings. (*WP.* 206)

Hughes may be too eager to create a hierarchy of understanding, which only those who have been privileged to have viewed the poem's drafts can ascend, but a similar principle holds for contextual appreciation of a poem like 'The Munich Mannequins'. The consistency of Plath's imagery through her work ensures that the bald glyphs of her later style can be elaborated with reference to earlier poetry. However, much of the impact of these poems derives precisely from the images' absence of elaboration. Their starkness awards Plath's work a powerful authority; the need to explain and expand, which mars an otherwise successful poem like 'Tulips', has now given way to an absolute confidence in the rightness and the effectiveness of the later poems' metaphors.

Eeriness is another effect of this brevity. The mannequins in their 'sulfur loveliness', the anonymous dehumanised hands and feet, and the black telephones which never ring, all help create a sinister atmosphere in which the sense of threat is never quite definable. 'Totem', an even stranger poem than 'The Munich Mannequins' and written on the same day, shares this quality, although now the danger becomes much more explicit: the poem begins with an engine 'killing' and eating its track, and incorporates on its journey the gelding of farmers, pigs on their way to market and the abattoir, a hare being dressed, a cobra, and finally a spider trapping flies. Besides Plath's assertion that the poem is structured 'like a totem pole', this animal imagery gives another rationale for the title: a totem, the distinguishing emblem of a tribe, usually consists of an animal representation. Plath's interest in anthropology provides a further image, when she describes 'a stick that rattles and clicks, a counterfeit snake'.

As the poem piles up these 'interconnected images', any semblance of a sustained narrative is quickly dispensed with. 'Totem' portrays an hallucinatory world where, like Plath's religious explorations in *Ariel*, everything preys or preyed upon. The 'Fat haunches and blood on [the farmers] minds', as they send their pigs to market, show them motivated more by bloodlust than financial reward, and reflect a world which is 'blood-hot and personal // Dawn says, with its blood-flush'. The conspicuous repetition suggests that 'blood', with the poem's associated images of mutilation and death, is the central motif. 'Totem' ends, as it begins, with more killing and eating:

> I am mad, calls the spider, waving its many
> arms.
>
> And in truth it is terrible,
> Multiplied in the eyes of flies.
>
> They buzz like blue children
> In nets of the infinite,
>
> Roped in at the end by the one
> Death with its many sticks.

This is both horrific and bizarre. Spiders are normally described as having legs, and so the reference to 'arms' sounds freakish. Nor does this spider have exactly eight 'arms': 'many' is imprecise enough to allow for eight, while also sanctioning the possibility of more. The flies' myriad of lenses, in the next couplet, multiplies the number of predators and arms, as if to emphasise the inescapability of the flies' 'terrible' fate. The poem also seems to allude to some famous lines from *King Lear*: 'As flies to wanton boys, are we to the gods; / They kill us for their sport' (IV.i.36–7). This would help explain Plath's weird simile—'They buzz like blue children'—where blue is associated, as often in her work, with coldness and with death, but where children are curiously made to 'buzz'. In Plath's reworking of Shakespeare, flies and children alike become caught in the 'nets of the infinite', that is, in the traps set by some greater and irresistible power. The poem's final image ('Death with its many sticks') recalls the earlier reference to a 'stick that rattles and clicks', while also referring to the stickiness of the spider's web. There may be one further allusion, or at least a shared idea: Seneca's observation that 'a thousand doors open on to' death, borrowed by Webster, Beaumont and Fletcher, and Massinger amongst others, is a sentiment which Plath, especially with her passion for Jacobean drama, must have encountered. In Plath's poem death may employ 'sticks' rather than doors, but the implication remains the same: there are countless different ways for death to catch its victims in the 'nets of the infinite'.

Plath's achievement in 'Totem' should not be underestimated. The poem is rarely anthologised and even less frequently discussed, partly because it presents the reader of Plath's work with new challenges which cannot easily be resolved. Yet this reason for its neglect is also evidence of its importance. Even more visibly than other late poems, 'Totem' is the work of a poet who has revolutionised her style, having abandoned the method which had served her so well in the *Ariel* work. Plath's recognition of this fundamental creative shift finds expression in 'Words', written a week later on 4 February 1963. 'Words' is, among other things, an apology for poetry, or at least for her new style, over which she professes little control. Words are described as

> Axes
> After whose stroke the wood rings,
> And the echoes!
> Echoes traveling
> Off from the center like horses.

These words possess, through simile and metaphor, a transsubstantive power. By the end of the poem, they are not just 'like horses', they have become horses: 'Words dry and riderless, / The indefatigable hoof-taps'. Whereas 'Ariel' recounted the poet's exhilarating union with her horse ('God's lioness, / How one we grow'), and 'Sheep in Fog' marked a slower and more resigned ride, 'Words' indicates that the horses have abandoned the poet. Even when she 'Encounter[s]' them 'Years later', the verb suggests chance rather than prior arrangement. The sense of desolation, a keynote of so many of these later poems, is overpoweringly present here too.

The poem's metaphoric drive ensures that it can never be reined in by its author: words take on an existence beyond the reach of the poem's original making. The cut made by the axes in the opening stanza also transforms itself through simile:

> The sap
> Wells like tears, like the
> Water striving
> To re-establish its mirror
> Over the rock
>
> That drops and turns,
> A white skull,
> Eaten by weedy greens.

Like the horses, this travels a long distance, via sap, tears, water, a mirror, and a rock, before arriving at the 'white skull' covered (or rather, in a return to familiar imagery, 'eaten') by weed. The passage is therefore partly an exploration of metaphor, illustrating how it develops its own logic in Plath's later poems, taking over the creative act: metaphor, and not the poet, controls the course of the poem. This impression of the poem writing itself, as images come unbidden and beget fresh images, portrays Plath's inspiration as avacular, and enforces an overwhelming sense of fatalism. The words themselves are 'dry', even after they have conveyed the poem's water imagery. The poet, by contrast, does not evade that underwater world. Metaphor, despite all its transformations, still leads the poet inescapably to death, the 'white skull' dropping and turning through water. At the end of the poem, metamorphosis is replaced by fixity, and the white skull by fatal stars: 'From the bottom of the pool, fixed stars / Govern a life'. The poet's fate is settled: the freedom achieved through poetry is short-lived and illusory.

Plath wrote three later poems ('Contusion', 'Balloons', 'Edge'), but 'Words' consciously represents a conclusion. Unable to alter her destiny, the poet is finally and inevitably 'roped in' (as 'Totem' describes it) by 'Death with its many sticks'. 'Words' therefore offers both a commentary on the working of metaphor in Plath's late work, and a compelling account of helpless resignation before a malign and implacable fate. That fate finds expression most famously in 'Edge', possibly the last poem Plath wrote, and in 'Contusion', where finally the underwater world of Plath's late poetry claims its drowned victim:

> Color floods to the spot, dull purple.
> The rest of the body is all washed out,
> The color of pearl.

This evokes *The Tempest* only to emphasise the absence of any sea-change. The drab repetition of 'color' indicates that nothing magical or transformative has happened on this occasion. Death, here as in other late poems, has now become an ending associated with defeat, rather than the necessary route to glorious rebirth.

'Edge' shares this finality: 'Her bare // Feet seem to be saying: / We have come so far, it is over'. The poem shares with other late poems, too, a sense of the inevitability, of death. Although the 'illusion of a Greek necessity' may be only an illusion, it is a persuasive one: the allusions to Medea and the moon's role as overseer ensure it. 'Edge' also embodies the pallor and eeriness of the late poems: only odours 'bleed', whereas references to the moon, bone, the toga, the children as 'white serpent[s]', and milk, effectively blanch the site of suicide and infanticide. In addition the poem's opening line, 'The woman is perfected', remembers the beginning of 'The Munich Mannequins', with its emphasis on coldness and snow. By contrast the moon's 'blacks crackle and drag'—a line which may envisage the night sky as a black cloak dragged along the ground by the hooded moon. 'Edge' therefore portrays a world drained of colour, leaving the moon as the bone-white, black-clad illuminator of the scene she observes impassively.

Cooler in its inspiration than any of Plath's previous poems, 'Edge' is for that reason also the most shocking. For more than chronological reasons it is the culmination of Plath's late style—a style of heightened detachment and resignation in the face of an intractable destiny. The poem allows itself only one brief moment of indulgence, as it reports that the dead woman 'wears the smile of accomplishment'. Yet this 'accomplishment' necessitates the killing of her children, and the 'folding' of them back into her body, in order that the mother's identity is reconstituted and what 'Ocean 1212-W' had called the 'beautiful fusion with the things of this world' may be permanently achieved in death. The final and unanswerable mystery which Plath leaves is how to read the woman's achievement. As its title suggests, the poem exists on the border—between life and death, art and life, artefact and prophesy, the lyric and the dramatic, poetry and morality. Yet 'Edge' does not fit comfortably into these accepted terms of reference. Hugh Kenner has disapprovingly observed of Plath's poetry in general that,

> Like Aurelia Plath reading Sivvy's letters home, we are continually outflanked by someone who knows what we'll approve and how we'll categorize, and is herself ready with the taxonomic words before we can get them out.[9]

Kenner draws attention to Plath as a manipulator of readers, noting for example of 'Daddy' that 'Parlor psychiatry is forestalled' because the Oedipus complex is consciously sketched. However limited an account of Plath's best work this may be, it seems especially inappropriate when applied to her late poems, which may be aware of, but are also indifferent to, 'what we'll approve and how we'll categorize'. 'Edge', especially, is poetry which has ceased trying to please. It provides no 'taxonomic words' because it defies existing categories. We are still learning how to read Plath's later work. Poetry offers few more challenging and unsettling experiences.

NOTES

1. Hughes, T. *Winter Pollen: Occasional Prose* ed. William Scammell (London: Faber, 1994), p. 172. Hereafter abbreviated in the text to *WP*.

2. Stevenson, A. *Bitter Fame: A Lye of Sylvia Plath* (London: Viking, 1989), p. 277.

3. Plath, S. *Letters Home: Correspondence 1950–1963* ed. Aurelia Schober Plath (London: Faber, 1975), p. 480. Hereafter abbreviated in the text to *LH*.

4. Plath, S. *Selected Poems* ed. Ted Hughes (London: Faber, 1981) p. 294. Hereafter abbreviated in the text to *CP*.

5. Plath, S. *Johnny Panic and the Bible of Dreams* ed. Ted Hughes, 2nd edition (London: Faber, 1979), p. 117. Hereafter abbreviated in the text to *JPBD*.

6. Roethke, T. *Collected Poems* (New York: Doubleday, 1966), p. 63.

7. Plath, S. *The Bell Jar* (London: Heinemann, 1963), p. 254.

8. Heaney, S. *Place and Displacement: Recent Poetry from Northern Ireland* (Dove Cottage: Trustees of Dove Cottage, 1985), p. 1.

9. Kenner, H. 'Sincerity kills', in Gary Lane (ed.) *Sylvia Plath: New Views on the Poetry* (Baltimore: Johns Hopkins, 1979), p. 34.

SUSAN GUBAR

Prosopopoeia and Holocaust Poetry in English:
Sylvia Plath and Her Contemporaries

Exploitation, larceny, masochism, sensationalism: the terms of opprobrium hurled against Sylvia Plath's use of Holocaust material generally accord with George Steiner's distress at any writer boasting "the right to put on this death-rig."[1] In 1962, the same year Plath wrote "Daddy" and "Lady Lazarus," Adorno qualified his famous injunction against the barbarism of composing poetry after Auschwitz.[2] Nevertheless, her appropriation of the voices of Holocaust victims still seems outrageous to those who reject any reasonable affinity or parallelism between Plath's individual suffering and mass murder. These readers wonder: how dare she presume to imagine herself as one of the victims, to arrogate the Otherness of the deceased through a projection that might be said to profane the memory of people exterminated by the Nazis? To honor the dead, Elie Wiesel has cautioned, the living must comprehend that "no one has the right to speak on their behalf."[3] To some, Plath's non-Jewishness, and her lack of a personal stake in the disaster, makes her speaking on behalf of the victims appear like a desecration. However, Plath's adoption of the voices of the imagined, absent dead—her deployment of the rhetorical figure of prosopopoeia—is hardly anomalous. The same rhetorical device surfaces in some of the most powerful poems about the Shoah, poems composed by literary women and men with quite divergent relationships to the calamity. The impersonation of an absent

From *The Yale Journal of Criticism* 14, no. 1 (Spring 2001): pp. 191–215. © 2001 by Yale University and The Johns Hopkins University Press.

speaker or a personification—prosopopoeia—allows those poets searching to find a language for the staggering horror of what had happened to speak as, for, with, and about the casualties in verse. This enabling device has been either ignored or disparaged for too long.

In "Posthumous Rehabilitation," Tadeusz Rozewicz supposes that the dead, who "see our snouts," "read our books," and "scrutinize our lectures" cannot, or will not, exonerate the guilt of the living—"the dead will not rehabilitate us," he insists.[4] As if to counter this lack of rehabilitation, post-war poets who have confronted Western civilization's guilt over the catastrophic genocide of the Final Solution sometimes attempt an admittedly nugatory, but nevertheless shocking, *rehabilitation of the dead*. Because the victims of the Holocaust did not have a cemetery, such writers ground their art in exactly the conviction that Elie Wiesel deduces from this fact, namely that the living must be their cemeteries. In the hard want of the bodies and of graves to mark their demise, the poet writes from the perspective of "corpses [deprived of] coffins," either directly before or directly after they were murdered, speaking words eerily evocative of the epitaphs carved on ancient gravestones.[5] Such a shocking reanimation of the dead cannot be equated with the traditional elegiac attempt to bring a particularly cherished person back into living *memory*, to assert the dead person's immortality, or to envision some union with the dead in a place elsewhere.[6] Nor does it form the only (or even the major) poetic response to the Shoah. Numerous writers have produced autobiographical meditations, historical analyses, ecphrastic portraits, liturgical reinventions of the *Kaddish*, and documentary verse.[7] But prosopopoeia allows the authors who manipulate it to summon the posthumous voice, to conceive of subjectivity enduring beyond the concentration camp, and thereby to suggest that the anguish of the Shoah does not, and will not, dissipate. Perhaps the inexorable vacancy, the vacuity, of the anonymous and numerous victims made this project urgent, licensed it, despite its unnerving presumption; or perhaps historical proximity to irreparable and stunning slaughter plunged some writers into an awareness of the impotence of the normative languages at their disposal.

So many of "the testimonies which bore the traces of *here*'s and *now*'s" were destroyed, Jean-François Lyotard once explained, that "the monopoly over history granted to the cognitive regimen of phrases" has been broken by the Shoah. The poet may therefore feel the need to step in (where Lyotard would have the historian venture forth) "by lending his or her ear to what is not presentable under the rules of knowledge."[8] Massive in its proportions, yet concealed at the time and denied later, the wrong suffered by millions of defenseless non-combatants marked for persecution and extirpation cannot be signified in extant words. Therefore "idioms which do not yet exist" need to be forged to prove that "the silence imposed on knowledge does not impose the silence of forgetting" but instead "a feeling" or a constellation of feelings (13, 56). In *The Differend*, Lyotard outlines the sinister logic of a revisionist who would sanction amnesia:

> in order for a place to be identified as a gas chamber, the only eyewitness I will accept would be a victim of this gas chamber; now ... there is no victim that is not dead; otherwise, this gas chamber would not be what he or she claims it to be. There is, therefore, no gas chamber. (3–4)

Grappling with the consequences of what Dori Laub has described as an atrocity perpetrated without witnesses, Lyotard's effort to combat repression issues from his belief that "[t]he shades of those to whom had been refused not only life but the expression of the wrong done them by the Final Solution continue to wander in their indeterminacy" (56).[9] A retort to Holocaust deniers, the adopted voices of the dead in poetry—deployed through the trope of prosopopoeia—express the wrong done to one-third of the world's Jewish population. Several decades before Terrence Des Pres' 1988 defense of Holocaust poetry, Sylvia Plath substantiated his assertion that the imagination confronted by negation "automatically starts asserting itself"; along with such contemporaries as Irena Klepfisz, Anthony Hecht, Randall Jarrell, Charles Simic, Jerome Rothenberg, Adrienne Rich, and Michael Hamburger, Plath implicitly agreed with Des Pres that "[w]e cannot *not* imagine."[10]

Whether spoken in the past tense by the dead or in the present by those condemned to a life-in-death, the imaginatively conceived voices of the victims shape the eerie dramatic monologues of Jewish and non-Jewish poets, seeking "to smuggle language / from mouths of the dying / and the dead."[11] For, as Anne Michaels puts it in "What The Light Teaches,"

> What was left but to cut out one's tongue,
> or cleave it with new language,
> or try to hear a language of the dead,
> who were thrown into pits, into lakes—.

In the aftermath of civilized savagery, the poetic employment of a dramatized first-person tends to slide toward "posthumous rehabilitation," even when the voice is supposedly issuing from someone alive, because readers implicitly recognize the doom hanging over the scapegoats of Nazi brutality. Many of the dehumanized prisoners lived the half-lives associated with the word "*Muselmann*," condemned to the "double dying" Alvin Rosenfeld has studied.[12]

If immediacy must be forfeited by verse meditations on photographs and by poetic responses to testimonials that constitute modes of proxy-witnessing, poems composed in the cadences of the dead and dying emanate an unnerving, invented proximity.[13] At the risk of usurping those killed in the Holocaust, British and American writers who summon up the audacity to write in English from the perspective of the immolated tap the techniques of some of the most important poems composed in Yiddish, German, Hebrew, and Russian. With its chorus of prisoners ingesting "black milk" ("we drink it and drink it"), Paul Celan's "Death Fugue" can stand for a number of unsettling works that have definitively entered the Holocaust canon (*TL* 222).[14]

In the less frequently taught Holocaust verse written in English, prosopopoeia has been put to a range of purposes characterized by varying degrees of distance between poets and their vulnerable personae. At one extreme, the trope generates a haunting surrogate figure embroiled in the fate to which writers suspect they would have been consigned if they had been born at the wrong place, in the wrong time. For a middle group of poets, who present their speakers as distinctively distanced characters, prosopopoeia issues an invitation to living readers to be morally and historically instructed by overhearing the voices of the dead or dying. At the other extreme, it results in a critique of the ruse of that luring rhetorical offer by exposing as spurious the very mechanism of identification that drives this aesthetic maneuver. Sylvia Plath's most famous works occupy both ends of this spectrum, yet her project of "posthumous rehabilitation" has met with disparagement from critics who argue that the equation she constructed—between her own traumatized womanhood and Jewish vulnerability in the Shoah—is an impudent analogy that reduces Jewish suffering to instrumentality. Such derogations depend upon reading Jewishness as the mere figure of verse "really" about womanhood; however, a reversal of the usual interpretive approach can attend to the uses to which Plath's poems put femininity as a figure of verse "really" about the psychological repercussions of Auschwitz on literature and Jewish identity.

I propose this shift not in order to supplant psychosexual approaches to Plath's three most sustained deployments of Holocaust matter, but to supplement them by contextualizing these poems within a literary tradition that has, thus far, gone disregarded. In other words, her transposition makes sense, and resembles the sense of personal connection to events not experienced firsthand articulated by many of her contemporaries—their visceral, but also aesthetic, reaction to what Marianne Hirsch has called "post-memory."[15] Like a number of poets in her generation, and not unlike Adorno, Plath viewed the Shoah as a test case for poetry and, indeed, for the imagination as a vehicle for conveying what it means for the incomprehensible to occur.

Using Holocaust imagery, "Getting There" expresses Plath's horrified compassion for captive shades being hurtled by the on-rushing fatality of history toward an irrevocable, incomprehensible death sentence—a sentence that later observers will know only as a hiatus where evidence ought to exist.

"How far is it? / How far is it now?" the poem begins, locating its speaker in a train traveling through Russia. The proud "gods" of the willful steel engine Krupp know its destination, while this anonymous prisoner drags her body "through the straw of the boxcars," thinking of bribery, of a letter, of a fire, of bread. At the end of this first stanza, which is dedicated to an inexorable driving propulsion toward what the speaker dreads, the train stops where nurses and the wounded appear:

> Legs, arms, piled outside
> The tend of unending cries—
> A hospital of dolls.
> And the men, what is left of the men
> Pumped ahead by these pistons, this blood
> Into the next mile,
> The next hour—
> Dynasty of broken arrows![16]

The train pumping ahead on its pistons, the blood pumped ahead in its pistons, the plummeting forward of the poem's short lines and their multiple gerunds issue only in a furor of a future. The poem evokes the furious pace of the Nazis, recalled by eye-witnesses: "'Out! Out! Everyone! Fast! Fast!' *The Germans were always in such a hurry.*"[17] This is not the autobiographical Plath writing in *The Bell Jar* about women being reduced to the passive place from which phallic arrows shoot off, nor is it the Plath of "Ariel," who speaks about her personal desire to become an arrow flying suicidally into the red eye of morning.[18] However, the poet's persistent identification does seep into the "I" of this poem, perceiving the collective emasculation of a "Dynasty of broken arrows" and "dragging my body" through the Russia that "I have to get across."

In the second stanza, which also begins "How far is it?," the horror of the boxcar has been supplanted by the horror of a forced march. With red, thick mud slipping on her feet, the speaker experiences the earth as "Adam's side," out of which she rises in agony. Steaming, breathing, "its teeth / Ready to roll, like a devil's," the train metamorphoses into a screaming animal, as Plath-Eve confronts a series of "obstacles" amid the thunder and fire of guns, including "The body of this woman," whose "charred skirts and deathmask" might signify her own "double dying" (249). Simultaneously at the trainstop,

on the march, in the cattle car, Plath's persona seeks some silent stasis, but
her wish to bury the wounded and to count the dead remains stymied in the
subjunctive. The end of the poem, sometimes read as a hopeful attempt to
imagine rebirth, sounds more disturbing in the context of the Shoah:

> The carriages rock, they are cradles.
> And I, stepping from this skin
> Of old bandages, boredoms, old faces
>
> Step to you from the black car of Lethe,
> Pure as a baby.[19]

At the conclusion to which the poem flies, Plath-Eve arrives at Hades, where
forgetfulness flows. Unable to retain a sense of herself or her past—she is
stripped of her possessions, her clothing, her previous life, her identity—she
too enters the "tent of unending cries." The Final Solution, toward which all
events rush, transforms Plath's victim into a being as innocent, but also as naked
and defenseless, as an infant. Unlike Whitman's "Out of the Cradle Endlessly
Rocking," where the endlessly rocking cradle of waves and of poetic meters
consoles by weaving death into life, the rocking cradles of the train's carriages
plunge toward the inconceivable "[t]here"—not of birth but of oblivion.

Blatantly disturbing in its revision of the "rocking cradles" of Yeats's
"Second Coming" as well, Plath's "Getting There" sutures the gap between
poet and persona through the same sort of empathy that motivates Irena
Klepfisz's project as a "keeper of accounts"—a bookkeeper of the casualties of
anti-Semitism who "can be revived again" in her verse when they "awaken in
me."[20] From its shocking opening lines—"when they took us to the shower
i saw / the rebitsin"—to its conclusion—"my smoke / was distinct i rose
quiet left her / beneath" (*AFW* 47)—Klepfisz's "death camp" reminds us how
ordinary but also how unknown many of the victims of the Shoah were then
and remain now. But it also refutes Lyotard's Holocaust denier by providing
eyewitness testimony that the gas chamber was used to murder:

> when they turned   on the gas   i smelled
> it   first   coming at me   pressed myself
> hard to the wall   crying   rebitsin   rebitsin
> i am here with you   and the advice you gave me
> i screamed   into the wall   as the blood burst from
> my lungs   cracking   her nails in women's flesh   i watched
> her capsize   beneath me   my blood in her mouth   i screamed
> (*AFW*, 47).

Besides visually marking a kind of stammer in speech that cannot communicate the experience described, the pauses punctuating Klepfisz's lines (here and elsewhere in her oeuvre) recall the theologian Arthur Cohen's interpretation of the Holocaust as caesura.[21] These stammers raise questions about the Christian and Jewish concept of God and marking the necessity of recognizing the human capacity for evil. There is no way to piece together the lost context of interactions to which Klepfisz's nameless persona alludes: she remembers the advice of the rabbi's wife, but whether the speaker has heeded or hated that advice, what that advice might have been, remains a mystery. As we read of the victim's recollection of her body being burned, of her feeling the weight of the rebitsin's corpse flung on top of her, the idea that her smoke "was distinct" at the end, or that she has triumphed by leaving the rebitsin "beneath," becomes a hollow victory. The common fate the two women share occludes any grudges, or difference, that might have existed between them in life.

As "death camp" demonstrates, another warrant—beyond Des Pres' "We cannot *not* imagine"—for attempting "posthumous rehabilitation" derives from the blatantly unrealistic rhetoric of prosopopoeia: readers of Klepfisz's poem *know* that the author has merely simulated the personification of the dead. For even those poets who strenuously decrease their distance from the "deathmask" disclose an awareness of the inescapable inauthenticity at the core of their undertaking. Bestowing presence onto the absent dead is inherently oxymoronic. "*Prosopon-poiein*," Paul de Man explains, "means to *give* a face and therefore implies that the original face can be missing or nonexistent"; this optative fabrication stresses its own illusory nature.[22] The disjunction between "deathmask" and ventriloquist bears witness to contemporary poets' efforts to confront the flimsy insubstantiality of the visionary company they keep. In addition, of course, the English language itself marks not merely British and American writers' remoteness from the catastrophe, but also the fictionality of their impersonations. English was one of the few Western languages not generally spoken by prisoners inside the boxcars, camps, gas chambers, and mass graves that supply the settings of Holocaust verse. Klepfisz—whose meditations on forced immigration communicated to Adrienne Rich what it means to feel "rooted among ... those who were turned to smoke,"[23]—felt haunted by absent, foreign ancestors. This motivated her translation-work, particularly her translation of her most resonant Yiddish precursor, Kadia Molodowsky. Molodowsky, in her often-quoted poem "*Froyen lider*" (Women poems), writes of Jewish women who appear to her in dreams:

Es veln di froyen fun undzer mishpokhe
bay nakht in klaloymes mir kumen un zogn ...

(The women in our family will come to me in my
dreams at night and say ...).[24]

Klepfisz quotes these lines at the end of her collection of essays, *Dreams of
an Insomniac*, connecting her own sleepless nights and her own ghosts with
Molodowsky's, suggesting that her verse commemorates "*undzer mishpokhe*
(our family) the Jewish people"—both her own dead family members *and*
the nameless dead of the Jewish people.[25] When the past tense of "death
camp" modulates in other poems by Klepfisz into the present tense, spectral
representatives of "*undzer mishpokhe*" express pain in the midst of the
surrealistic disruption of their lives.[26] In "herr captain," the poet intertwines
events from various pasts in a palimpsest of sexual abuses. The first speaker,
a Jewish prisoner, whispers to a Nazi captain "i'm not over / used," then
metamorphoses into her own (or the poet's) grandmother, who revenges
herself against "her cossack lover" by slashing his hands with a butcher knife.
Violent details remain unexplained, so that the reader cannot sort out which
rape story is being told: the sentences "i was pierced / in two" and "my mother
floats in well water zeide in mourning tears his red hair" fuse defilement in the
camp and in the shtetl, making it difficult to understand what has happened
to whom. The hallucinogenic registers of the poem converge again at the
end, when the speaker bleakly accepts the man who "brings me soap / his
boots are shiny / not like the others who arrive from the fields / crusted over"
(45–46).

Whereas Plath's "Getting There" and Klepfisz's "death camp," and "herr
captain," provisionally elide the gap between the poet's personal self and the
posthumous voice, the works of Anthony Hecht, Randall Jarrell, and Charles
Simic stress the chasm between the "there" of the casualties and the "here" of
the author, the "then" of the Shoah and the "now" of the reader. Putting the
same rhetorical figure to different use, Hecht, Jarrell and Simic do evoke the
voices of the dead, but at the same time, they figure the linguistic discontinuity
between Auschwitz and poetry—between victim and poet—by emphasizing
either the complex and fleeting nature of identification (as Hecht does) or
by choosing child-speakers quite obviously hampered by their linguistic
and cognitive immaturity (as Jarrell and Simic do). That the dead and dying
speak in these poems contradict de Man proposal's (about prosopopoeia) that
living readers must be encased in a deadly silence.[27] For these writers, the
figure of prosopopoeia holds out the promise of "heteropathic memory,"
an "identification-at-a-distance" that Kaja Silverman defines as a method of
aligning (without interiorizing) the "not-me" with the "me."[28] At an epiphanic
moment in Hecht's ambitious sequence of poems, "Rites and Ceremonies,"
heteropathic memory moves from compassion ("when I pray, / I am there,

I am there") to the adoption of the posthumous stance: "We are crowded in here naked, female and male. / An old man is saying a prayer. / And now we start / To panic, to claw at each other, to wail / As the rubber-edged door closes on chance and choice."[29] But the momentary conflation of "there" and "here" will not be—cannot be and perhaps ought not be—sustained.

Hecht's most ambitious response to the Shoah—which invokes the words of Job, the Psalmists, Isaiah, Matthew, Herbert, Hopkins, and Eliot—questions both the durability of his identification with the dead, as well as poetry's efficacy as lamentation and supplication:

> Lord, who, governing cloud and waterspout,
>   o my King,
> held me alive till this my forty-third year—
>   *in whom we doubt*—
> Who was that child of whom they tell
>   in holy lauds and threnes?
> whose holy name all shall pronounce
>   Emmanuel,
> which being interpreted means,
>   *"Gott mit uns?"* (38)

The interruption of italicized doubt, the German translation of Emmanuel, and the question mark that follows it all undercut the most noble biblical and literary languages. Similarly, Hecht's fragmentary refrain "Out of hearing" (42–3) punctuates the lines he quotes from Herbert: "O that thou shouldst give dust a tongue / To crie to thee, / And then not heare it crying!" Since *"Gott mit uns"* was inscribed on the belts of some Nazi soldiers, the line *"in whom we doubt—"* takes on profound bitterness. "It is as if," Peter Sachs explains, "this insistent and unassimilably 'broken verse' were the timeless voice of poetry itself lamenting the limits of its efficacy."[30] Such "broken verse" links Hecht's unheeded prayer with the unheard voices of the dead when "the rubber-edged door closes on chance and choice." His sardonic reflection that "the little children were suffered to come along, too" inflects two disturbing deployments of prosopopoeia in the Holocaust context.

Possibly influenced by Nelly Sachs, whose "Dead Child Speaks" about "the knife of parting" from the mother (*HP* 67), Jarrell and Simic let imagined representatives of the one million Jewish children murdered by the Third Reich talk directly to the readers of their verse. So, in "The Death of the Ball Turret Gunner," Jarrell uses prosopopoeia to conflate eradication with a forced evacuation from the womb: "hunched" upside down in the "belly" of a plane, the aborted speaker declares, "When I died they washed me out of the turret with a hose."[31] Jarrell similarly uses prosopopoeia in "Protocols." Prefaced with the parenthetical words "Birkenau, Odessa; the children speak alternately," this poem consists of the voices of two children antiphonally describing their entrance into alienating, annihilating experiences: one being squashed in a train that arrives at a factory with a smokestack, the other traveling in a barge into deep water. The child who comes to the factory is told by his mother not to be afraid and feels water "in a pipe—like rain, but hot," until he is "washed and dried." The other is held by his mother in a place that "*is no more Odessa*" and where "*the water drank me.*" The poem's sardonic title derides the militarism by which both children arrive at a common fate: "*And that is how you die. And that is how you die.*" Whether washed and dried by the mother or held up by her, the children's experiences make a mockery of any solace that would embrace death as what Wallace Stevens called "the mother of beauty."[32]

Moving from Plath's and Jarrell's uncanny present tense to a definitively posthumous modality, Simic also conflates the trauma of the Shoah with the shock of separation from the mother, death with birth: "My mother was a braid of black smoke." As if meditating on Paul Celan's "graves in the air" in "Death Fugue" as well as Plath's stepping out of the "cradles" of the train in "Getting There," Simic creates a shocking speech act *after* the crematorium:

> My mother was a braid of black smoke.
> She bore me swaddled over the burning cities.
>   The sky was a vast and windy place for a child
> to play.
>   We met many others who were just like us.
> They were trying to put on their overcoats with
> arms made of smoke.
>   The high heavens were full of little shrunken
> deaf ears instead of stars.[33]

Like Hecht and Jarrell, Simic represents a consciousness quite distinct from that of the adult poet. The words "bore" and "swaddled" identify the child's death with his birth into another realm where he abides in his delusion of reunion with his mother and with his playmates. Evanescent smoke floating across the sky—all that remains of the remains of child, mother, and many others—troubles normative ideas about the spirituality and the corporality of the dead.

Like Blake's *Songs of Innocence and Experience*, Simic's verse imagines the child's naivete—for instance, his contemplating a "braid of black smoke" as the umbilical cord—to emphasize how inconceivable this experience is to the innocent. The child's ferocious desire for presence paradoxically propels both his image-making, his efforts to make substantial the silence of the heavens ("full of little shrunken deaf ears instead of stars") and his own dissipating insubstantiality after the crematorium. As has the Jewish star, celestial stars—images of steadfast eternity, purity, integrity—have been demeaned or extinguished. Yet powerful as the speaker's quest for meaning is, it hardly serves as an antidote to his fate.[34] The trope of wind as an inspirational breath of divinity—as an ideal of transcendence in this "vast and windy place"—is rendered inefficacious, as is the principle of meaning-making as a survival strategy.[35] Since amid and after institutionalized sadism *The World Doesn't End* (the title of the volume in which Simic's poem appears), Simic and Jarrell use posthumous voices to conceptualize subjectivity beyond death, thereby intimating that suffering does not end or fade away like smoke, even though bodies do. Similarly, although in "Mary's Song" Plath writes that the "thick palls" of Jews "float / Over the cicatrix of Poland, burnt-out / Germany," she emphatically concludes, "They do not die" (257).

Less the result of a compulsive haunting, the adoption of the voices of the dead in Hecht's, Jarrell's, and Simic's verse appears to be driven by a moral duty not to forget those very experiences one could never have personally apprehended. Jerome Rothenberg's effort to produce "poetry as the language of the dead" throughout *Khurbn* relies on a quotation from Hijikata about this responsibility: "To make the gestures of the dead, to die again, to make the dead enact their deaths again, this is what I want to feel. The dead are my teachers & live inside me."[36] Rothenberg's "*Di Toyte Kloles*" ("The Maledictions") begins with a curse that could also be understood as the sort of plea to which Hecht, Jarrell, and Simic responded: "Let the dead man call out in you because he is a dead man" (33). At the conclusion of *Eastern War Time*, Adrienne Rich's sequence about the deportation, resistance, and extermination of the Jews, she reconstitutes Hecht's voices "blown away on the winter wind" in an ensemble of speakers who serve as her teachers:

> I'm a man-child praising God he's a man
> I'm a woman bargaining for a chicken
> I'm a woman who sells for a boat ticket
> I'm a family dispersed between night and fog.[37]

These witnesses need to testify because mimesis cannot provide an adequate reflection of the inexplicably grotesque and undocumented suffering endured by so many. Yet the last lines that conclude her Whitmanesque catalogue of subjectivities—"I am standing here in your poem unsatisfied / lifting my smoky mirror"—attests to the poet's awareness of the insufficiency of the very trope of prosopopoeia she exploits.

The presence of living speakers in Rich's chorus demonstrates that when poets reproduce the voices of the dead *before* their demise, the impact of dramatic monologues seems less scandalous. Their admonitions to keep unrecorded but ghastly historical events in mind seem more pedagogical. This is the case, even though such admonitions and recollections echo against our awareness of their impending mortality and the impossibility of their testifying about their personal responses to it. In *Night of the Broken Glass*, Emily Borenstein mourns for her family—lost "in the mass graves of Poland / and in the flames of the Warsaw Ghetto." In many of the poems in this collection, she hears the voices of civilians on their way to death, crying out to her. So, at the conclusion of "Round-Up": "We are ordered to tear up grass / with our teeth. / Routed with giant dogs / we are beaten, driven half-clothed / through the streets / while we dream, dream of a piece of wet bread / or another potato."[38] Beyond its inclusion of one poem created by the resistance fighter who is its central character, Ruth Whitman's *The Testing of Hanna Senesh* consists of a sequence of invented poems composed in Senesh's persona and recounting her training in espionage, her parachuting into enemy territory, the torments of torture she endured until her death: "I watch myself like a person in a dream / while they invent devices to break me down."[39] Similarly, Stephen Berg adopts the perspective of the French poet Robert Desnos at Buchenwald in "Desnos Reading the Palms of Men on Their Way to the Gas Chamber": "I stumble through the prisoners to hold them, / needing to touch as many as I can / before I go" (*TR* 274). William Heyen's "Passover: The Injections" is spoken by someone awaiting the approach of malevolent soldiers: "We lie down in the fields, / thousands of us, / never mind the rain" (*HP* 60).

Yet according to Michael Hamburger—whose verses about historical victims analyze the link between the posthumous perspective and the critique of humanism brought into being by the Holocaust—the trope of prosopopoeia dramatizes precisely the sorts of empathetic identification that the Shoah itself called into question.[40] For if empathy or identification were such powerful psychic forces, how could National Socialism's killing campaign have occurred? Hamburger takes this up in his poem, "Between the Lines." The poem is written from the point of view of a prisoner, E. A. Rheinhardt. Rheinhard, as he "[blunders] into death," feels a hideously unsuitable concern for his torturer (114); and then is filled with mordant self-derision at his own capacity for an ill-fated compassion. This self-mockery unmasks identification as nothing but the pathetic delusion of projection. An epigraph about Rheinhardt's "terrible gaffe" involves a revealing case of mistaken identity: when an elegant but tormented man speaking cultivated French came out of an interrogation room, Rheinhardt expressed his concern, only later to be informed that he had been sympathizing with "a Gestapo man." Although this quotation from Rheinhardt's 1944 prison diary gestures toward the more modest documentary mode, in "Between the Lines" Hamburger invents the subsequent reactions of its author. Back in the cell he shares with three other men, Rheinhardt's soliloquy records how deeply the incident has changed him. Never before had he laughed in that prison where, even after a food parcel arrived, he drifted away from companionship with the others. But now the other inmates seem "close to me," for the error has demonstrated that the knowledge upon which Rheinhardt prided himself has made him no less feeble—maybe more feeble—than they.

Indeed, when Hamburger's Rheinhardt cries "To the killer who cracks my joints: '*Je te comprends, / mon ami ...*','" he discovers how his cosmopolitan education has conspired against him, has deluded him into assuming that a civilized person could not possibly be a Gestapo man. Ridiculing his own impotent pretensions, Hamburger's persona understands "how one I could not believe in / allows me to blaze like his martyrs" and "how the soul / Anatomists cannot locate even now will rise up" when his "turn comes to blunder again." Skeptical agnosticism notwithstanding, Rheinhardt's faith in humanism has blinded him to the human, even humane face brutality frequently wears. If the gallows humor that Hamburger reads "Between the Lines" of Rheinhardt's diary makes his dramatic monologue evocative of Robert Browning's, it is a Browning portrait filtered through the lens of Baudelaire's and T.S. Eliot's doomed doubling with a "hypocrite reader."[41] Hamburger's Rheinhardt, laughing that the joke is on himself, damns his own humanism as a foolish self-delusion that renders him far more vulnerable than the others with whom he shares "the thick stench / From the bucket" as well as "our common attrition by hunger and filth." At the same time, Rheinhardt's hapless projection of his own interiority onto the Gestapo man thematizes and qualifies the identification inciting the formal production of the posthumous voice by Hamburger's contemporaries. As in Rheinhardt's gaffe, the "'*Je te comprends*'" informing prosopopoeia devolves into a flaccid delusion.

But, surprisingly, no poet has been more scathingly critical of the figure of prosopopoeia than Sylvia Plath. Even as she exploited the trope in the Holocaust context, Plath emphasized her awareness that imaginative identification with the victims could constitute either a life-threatening trap for the poet or a sinister trip for the poet's readers, as "Daddy" and "Lady Lazarus" demonstrate. In "Daddy," Plath considers what her identification might mean, rather than simply assuming that identification: "I think I *may well be* a Jew" (emphasis mine). In this, Plath's self-conscious method sustains this distance in a more sustained way than Anne Sexton does in the (probably) influential line from "My Friend, My Friend": "I think it would be better to be a Jew."[42] Plath's line echoes Sexton's, but with a difference: Plath maintains a definitively post-war perspective on her own deployment of the voice of the victims. Similarly, Plath's is a more self-consciously fictive and qualified identification than John Berryman's effort to see himself as an "imaginary Jew."[43] Plath illuminates not merely the psychological scenarios which most critics examine but also offers brilliant insights into a debilitating sexual politics at work in fascist anti-Semitism. From this perspective, "Daddy" reads less like a confessional elegy about Plath's grief and anger at the loss of her father, more like a depiction of Jewish melancholia—the primitive, suicidal grieving Freud associated with loss over a love object perceived as part of the self[44]—and thus a meditation on an attachment to Germany in particular, and to Western civilization in general, that many European Jews found not only inevitable but galling as well.

Although numerous readers have noted that Plath anathematizes Naziism as patriarchalism pure and simple, they have failed to understand how the dependencies of a damaged and damaging femininity shape her analysis of genocide. A "bag full of God," a "Ghastly statue," an "Aryan" blue-eyed "Panzer-man" with a "neat mustache," Daddy deploys all the regalia of the fascist father against those robbed of selfhood, citizenship, and language, for the speaker's stuttering tongue is "stuck in a barb wire snare. / Ich, ich, ich, ich, / I could hardly speak." The daughter confronts a symbolic order in which the relationship between the fragile "ich" and the overpowering national and linguistic authority of Daddy frustrates any autonomous self-definition. That, as Jacqueline Rose points out, the English "you do not do" can be heard as the German "you *du* not *du*" (226) heightens awareness of a confluence between the daughter's vulnerable and blurred ego boundaries, her ardent responsiveness to the lethally proximate society that constructed her, and the European Jew's conflicted but nevertheless adoring address. Standing "at the blackboard," the fascist represents the irrational power of rationality, of the arts and the sciences, of culture in the Fatherland. According to Plath, the Jews chuffed off "to Dachau, Auschwitz, Belsen" suffered the horror of impending extermination along with a crippling consciousness of complicity, if only the collusion of those doomed by a long history of intimacy to love and respect a force dead set against them.

For, through a rhetorical strategy itself implicated in the calculus of colonization, the poem dares to confront the daughter-speaker's induction into revering Daddy and his charismatic power: "Every woman adores a Fascist, / The boot in the face, the brute / Brute heart of a brute like you"

(223). The daughter's subsequent decision to make and marry "a model" of Daddy (224) suggests how difficult it may be for a consciousness captivated by the inimical source which shaped it to escape self-destructive forms of thralldom that refigure bonds saturated with the only pattern of attachment known—lexicons of emotion devised by the dead Daddy. Vampiric, the phantom father and his constructed surrogate, the husband who loves "the rack and the screw," have drained the speaker of her creative talents, her currency, her autonomy. Depleted, the daughter rages against her appalled feelings of radical insufficiency, which bespeak a blurring of boundaries between Jewishness and Germanness that many German-Jews lamented before, during, and after the Shoah. Since this tiny percentage of the German population played a relatively important role in business, finance, journalism, medicine, law, and the arts in the twenties and thirties, many German-Jews felt shocked at the betrayal of a culture to which they had vowed what Saul Friedlander calls "ever-renewed and ever-unrequited love."[45] When Leo Baeck, the famous Berlin Rabbi, sat down to pay his electric bill moments before the SS dragged him off to Theresienstadt, Hyam Maccoby thinks his act exemplified not passivity but instead many Jews' inability to believe that "this Germany, *which they loved, felt obligations toward ..., felt gratitude toward*" could have dedicated itself to their annihilation (emphasis mine).[46] The forfeiture of a beloved language and a revered homeland, the loss of a citizenship that had signified and certified professional status and security: such grief reeks of the narcissistic wound Plath's daughterly speaker suffers after she tries to commit suicide, only to find herself instead "pulled ... out of the sack" and stuck together "with glue."

As the Mother Goose rhymes on "you," "*du*," "Jew," "glue," "screw," "gobbledygoo," "shoe" accumulate, the poem goose steps toward the concluding "I'm finally through" that proclaims a victory over the spectral afterlife of the fascist, but only at the cost of the daughter's own life. At the very moment Plath declares she is "through" with her father, the final line intimates that she herself is also and thereby "through." No longer supported by the fragile hyphen between German and Jew, the outraged daughter knows her "gipsy ancestress" and her "Taroc pack" only confirm her status as a pariah, even decades after the catastrophic engagement with Daddy. Plath's scandalizing feminization of Europe's Jews suggests just how appalling, how shameful would seem, *would be*, the emasculation of often intensely patriarchal communities. Just as Plath's speaker asks herself who she can possibly be without Daddy, European Jewish men and women might well have asked themselves who they could possibly be after the Shoah definitively estranged them from their fathers' lands, their mother tongue, their neighbors' customs, their compatriots' heritage or so the ghastly number of post-war suicides of survivors-who-did-not-survive intimates. Without in any way conflating the different motives and circumstances of Walter Benjamin, Paul Celan, Primo Levi, Peter Szondi, Jean Amery, Bruno Bettelheim, Jerzy Kosinsky, Piotr Rawicz, Tadeusz Boroswki, and Andrzej Munk, this frightful list of suicides attests to the devastating ongoingness of the Shoah.[47]

If identification with the victims who could not disidentify with their tormentors constitutes the trap of prosopopoeia in "Daddy," the trope functions as a trip in "Lady Lazarus." What does it mean to think of the imperilled Jews as—to borrow a phrase Maurice Blanchot used to approach the complex subject of Holocaust-related suicides—fetishized "masters of un-mastery"?[48] The wronged speaker here can only liberate herself from "Herr Doktor" or "Herr Enemy" by wresting the power of persecution from him and turning it against herself. We know that the ongoingness of the torments of the Shoah perpetuated postwar suicides, but did those casualties mutate into mystic scapegoats whose envied status as paradigmatic victims would in turn generate ersatz survivor-celebrities?[49] This is one way to grasp the shock of "Lady Lazarus," for the narcissistic and masochistic speaker has become obsessed with dying, relates to it as "a call." With her skin "Bright as a Nazi lampshade," her foot "A paperweight," and her face "featureless, fine / Jew linen," Lady Lazarus puts her damage on theatrical display through her scandalous suicide artistry (244). Have Jews been made to perform the *Trauerspiel* for a "peanut-crunching crowd" at the movies and on TV, like the striptease entertainer through whom Plath speaks? Does Lady Lazarus's "charge" at making death feel "real" and at "the theatrical // Comeback" anticipate a contemporary theatricalization of the Holocaust? Certainly, her vengeful warning that "there is a charge / For the hearing of my heart" evokes the charge—the cheap thrill and the financial price and the emotional cost—of installations, novels, testimonials, college courses, critical essays, and museums dedicated to the six million.

The commodification of Lady Lazarus's exhibitionism issues in spectators paying "For a word or a touch / Or a bit of blood // Or a piece of my hair or my clothes"; she brags about her expertise at the art of dying: "I do it so it feels *like* hell. / I do it so it *feels* real" (245, emphasis mine). The spectacular quality of Plath's figure adumbrates the notorious celebrity of a writer like Benjamin Wilkomirski, whose gruesome bestseller *Fragments* (about a child's experiences in the camps) was praised as "free of literary artifice of any kind" before it was judged to be a fraud.[50] In remarks that gloss Plath's suicide-performer's pandering to her audience, Daniel Ganzfried argued that Wilkomirski's suicide would be read as an authentication of his identity as a victim: "These people talking about suicide will *suggest* it to him.... Some of his supporters would love him dead because then it looks like proof that he's

Wilkomirski."[51] Plath's poetry broods upon—just as Ganzfried's argument reiterates—the contamination of the very idea of the genuine. As Blanchot cautions, "If there is, among all words, one that is inauthentic, then surely it is the word 'authentic.'"[52] To the extent that the impresario of Plath's stage, "Herr God"/"Herr Lucifer," has reduced Lady Lazarus from a person to an "opus" or a "valuable," the poem hints that even reverential post-Shoah remembrances may be always-already defiled by the Nazi perpetrators—that prosopopoeia will not enable the poet to transcend the tarnished uses to which the past has been, can be, will be put. In the voice of a denizen of disaster, Plath mocks the frisson stimulated by the cultural industry she herself helped to spawn.[53]

Revolted by her own dehumanization, Lady Lazarus then imagines triumphing over the murderous Nazis by turning vengeful herself, if only in the incendiary afterlife conferred by the oven:

Ash, ash—
You poke and stir.
Flesh, bone, there is nothing there—

A cake of soap,
A wedding ring,
A gold filling.

Herr God. Herr Lucifer
Beware
Beware.

Out of the ash
I rise with my red hair
And I eat men like air.

As it feeds on "men like air"—predatory psychic dictators but also perhaps men turned to smoke—the red rage that rises out of the ashes only fuels self-combustion, debunking the idea of transcendence or rebirth at the end of the poem. With its ironic echo of the conclusion of Coleridge's "Kubla Kahn"—"Beware, beware, his flashing eyes, his floating hair"—"Lady Lazarus" repudiates Romantic wonder at the power of the artist, replacing the magical "pleasure dome" of his artifice with the detritus to which the Jewish people were reduced.[54] The poem's speech act amounts to a caustic assessment of the aesthetic sell-out, the disaster-imposter luminary: "there is nothing there—." That no consensus exists among contemporary historians over whether the Nazis made cakes of soap out of their victims (though they certainly did "manufacture" hair and skin, rings and fillings and bones) drives home the bitter irony that propels the poem, namely that imaginative approaches to the Shoah may distort, rather than safeguard, the dreadful but shredded historical record. Reenactments of the calamity, including her own, are indicted, even as Plath issues a warning that they will take their toll.

Will the figure of prosopopoeia, so seductive for poets from Jarrell and Plath to Simic and Rich, outlive its functions as the Holocaust and its atrocities recede into a past to which no one alive can provide firsthand testimony? Or will the imperatives of "post-memory" imbue this rhetorical strategy—which insists on returning to the unbearable rupture of suffering—with newfound resonance once the Shoah can no longer be personally recalled? Given the passage of time as well as the flood of depictions of the catastrophe, the very vacuity of the desecrated (buried alive, incinerated, unburied, dismembered) bodies that licensed the personifications of prosopopoeia may make verse epitaphs seem shoddily inadequate.[55] Plath's taunting sneer—"I turn and burn. / Do not think I underestimate your great concern" (246)—chronologically preceded the highly profitable entertainment industry the Holocaust business has so recently become. However, besides forecasting it, "Lady Lazarus" offers up a chilling warning about the fetishization of suffering with which the figure of prosopopoeia flirts. Indeed, Plath's verse uncannily stages the bases for accusations of exploitation, larceny, masochism, and sensationalism that would increasingly accrue around Holocaust remembrance. In addition, her impersonation of the real victims invariably generates awareness of the spurious representation put in the place of the absence of evidence. Calling attention to what Geoffrey Hartman and Jean Baudrillard term our propensity to adopt a "necrospective," poems deploying prosopopoeia draw us closer to an event that is, simultaneously, distanced by their debased status as merely simulated and recycled image-substitutions.[56]

Today, in accord with scholars who stress the exceptionality of the Shoah, creative writers may choose to emphasize the opacity of the disaster, as Jorie Graham does, rather than to freight it with voices of their own devising.[57] For we have become exceptionally sensitive to the political and moral problems posed by a trope like prosopopoeia—quandaries articulated by one of the poets who has employed it herself: "The living, writers especially, are terrible projectionists," Adrienne Rich has declared, "I hate the way they use the dead."[58] Anne Michaels calls the effort "to smuggle language / from the mouths of the dying / and the dead" a "suicide mission" because what is rescued cannot be "the old language at all; / only the alphabet the same" and because "language of a victim only reveals / the one who named him."[59] Yet, addressing the aetiology and ethics of prosopopoeia in earlier Holocaust verse, Graham's "Annunciation With A Bullet In It" exposes both the injuries and the urgencies of using the voices of the dead. There, she returns to Lyotard's central issue, splicing her poem with eye-witness testimony taken from Isabella Leitner's *Fragments of Isabella, a Memoir of Auschwitz*. As forecast by its title and its occasional setting (someone has shot the poet's dying dog, with whom she sits throughout the night), the poem concentrates on shocking moments of inexplicable violence.

In particular, sections 5 through 12 of "Annunciation With A Bullet In It" include reprinted passages from Leitner's account of her deportation ("Anyone not up at four a.m. will get a *Kugel*"), the strength she gains in the camps from her three sisters ("*Cipi, Chicha, Rachel, Isabella*. We seem to be alive"), their touching of a newborn baby ("before she is wrapped in / the piece of paper / and handed over to the Blockelteste—"), her fear of carrying a dead body ("the *Oberscharffurhrer* will choose me, I know he will"). All these quotations, sprinkled with foreign words and prefaced by the phrases "Then, she said," resemble the more modestly documentary works of such poets as Charles Reznikoff and Barbara Helfcott Hyett more than they resemble the language employed by Plath.[60] Both Reznikoff and Hyett limited themselves to affixing line breaks to (and deleting what they viewed as extraneous details from) the oral testimonials they recorded and then published. Still, in Graham's poem, the documentary source is immediately followed by another quotation ("Said the angel")—this one expressing the sinister logic of the cynic Lyotard paraphrased in *The Differend*, a revisionist who has "analyzed thousands of documents" and "tirelessly pursued specialists":

> I have tried in vain to find a single former deportee
>
> capable of proving to me that he had really seen
>   with his own eyes
> a gas chamber
>   TIRELESSLY
> (wingprint in dust) (smoke) the
>
> only acceptable proof that it was used to kill
>   is that one died from it—
> (tirelessly)—
>   but if one is dead one cannot testify
> that it is
>   on account of such a chamber—
>
> There is, therefore, no gas, chamber (72–3)[61]

When history consists of "a rip where evidence exists" or a "stammer between invisibles, / The soft jingling of a chain" (75, 73), can any documentation be found to meet the perverse objections raised by Lyotard's Holocaust denier?[62] To Graham's consternation, what cannot be "seen" in her complex meditation threatens to degenerate into the equivocations of the word "*seem*," turning the "plaintiff" into a "victim" who cannot find the means to prove the damages incurred (75, 73).[63] Although Isabella Leitner's incorporated testimony focuses, like Walter Benjamin's Angel of History, on a single catastrophe rather than the "chain of events" we observe from a distance, the words of her Auschwitz memoir jingle against those of Lyotard's malignant "angel."[64] "Annunciation With A Bullet In It" recalls Graham's earlier definition of history as "*the creature, the x*," a beast "on a chain, licking its bone": "it is on a chain // that hisses as it moves with the moving x, / link by link with the turning x / (the gnawing now Europe burning)."[65]

A retort to Lyotard's revisionist, the adopted voice of one of Leitner's family members at the conclusion of the poem—whose emphatic lie ("I really really am not hungry" [77]) bespeaks her loving offer of a piece of bread—testifies to her survival in Leitner's and Graham's memory, but only as "A stammer between invisibles." In fact, we know nothing of her fate, nor that of the other two sisters in the concentration camp with her. Indeed, in *Fragments of Isabella*, Leitner herself has no definitive knowledge of one sister's destiny ("Cipi, Cipi, where are you?"); she may have been compelled to undertake the death march to Bergen-Belsen, or possibly she survived the British liberation.[66] That "Annunciation," with its promise of an emancipating enunciation, has been riddled by such absences accords with Cynthia Ozick's protest against any "search for spots of goodness, for redemptive meaning" in the Shoah.[67] At the same time, Graham's poem explains why some of her precursors felt compelled to go beyond testimonial evidence, to occupy the "rip where evidence exists," to communicate a "stammer between invisibles." Despite the indubitable fact that the inanimate dead cannot possibly attest to what or who murdered them, imaginatively inhabiting the genocidal hole in annunciation means disproving the logic of revisionists. Bloodless, even the words of survivors or photographs of the victims only generate after-the-fact narratives that "*the creature, the x*" gnaws, "making stories like small smacking // sounds, / whole long stories which are its gentle gnawing."[68] "How," Graham asks in another poem, "can the scream rise up out of its grave of matter?":

> The war is gone. The reason gone. The body gone. Its
> reason gone. The name the face the personal
>   identity and yet here
> is a pain that will not diminish ...[69]

As if inspired by Walter Benjamin's Angel of History, Graham and others among Plath's peers "would like to stay, awaken the dead"[70]—though their stutters and caesuras, their foreignisms and fragments prove that they know full well that the not-said, the unheard, and the unsayable have all been buffeted in the storm of time, irresistibly propelling them away from the pile of debris growing skyward. Through their invention of the voices of the dead and dying as well as their sometimes explicit, sometimes implicit, acknowledgment of the futility of their task, American and British writers provide images that testify to the feelings of an event as well as its incomprehensibility. "The past can be seized only as an image which flashes up at the instant when it can be recognized and is never seen again," Benjamin declared; "every image of the past that is not recognized by the present as one of its own concerns threatens to disappear irretrievably."[71] By generating unreal images of a past partially obliterated from history, the figure of prosopopoeia enabled poets of Plath's generation to fulfill Benjamin's definition of the most adroit historian: "Only that historian will have the gift of fanning the spark of hope in the past who is firmly convinced that *even the dead* will not be safe from the enemy if he wins. And this enemy has not ceased to be victorious."

NOTES

This essay could not have been written without the support of a Rockefeller Fellowship in the spring of 1999 and the staff as well as the other Fellows at the Virginia Foundation for the Humanities. Early and late in the formulation of this subject, the generous help of Jahan Ramazani shaped my thinking. I am also grateful for the critical insights of Linda Charnes, Donald Gray, Geoffrey Hartman, Anna Meek, Nancy K. Miller, and Alvin Rosenfeld.

1. George Steiner, "In Extremis," *The Cambridge Mind*, ed. Eric Homberger, William Janeway, and Simon Schama (London: Jonathan Cape, 1969), p. 305. Needless to say, this one quote does not do justice to Steiner's complex attitudes toward Plath or toward who could write about the Shoah, which changed over time. Irving Howe argues that "it is decidedly unlikely" that the condition of the Jews in the camps "was duplicated in a middle-class family living in Wellesley, Massachusetts, even if it had a very bad daddy indeed" in his Letter to the Editor, *Commentary* (October 1974), 12. More even-handed, Sidra DeKoven Ezrahi nevertheless believes that Plath's use of Holocaust imagery "represents a kind of devaluation of the particularity as well as the monstrosity of the historical experience" (*By Words Alone: The Holocaust in Literature* [Chicago: The University of Chicago Press, 1980], p. 214). Recent exceptions to the attacks on Plath's use of Holocaust material are James Young in "The Holocaust Confessions of Sylvia Plath," *Writing and Rewriting the Holocaust: Narrative and the Consequences of Interpretation* (Bloomington: Indiana University Press, 1988), pp. 118, 133. Young wants "to shift the emphasis away from the poet's 'right' to Holocaust imagery" and toward an examination of "how the Holocaust has mattered" in imaginative literature. Similarly, Jacqueline Rose, in *The Haunting of Sylvia Plath* (Cambridge: Harvard University Press, 1992), argues

that "the critique of Plath merely underlines the fact that the Holocaust is the historical event which puts under greatest pressure—or is most readily available to put under such pressure—the concept of linguistic figuration" (207).

2. Theodor W. Adorno's "Commitment" (1962) in *The Essential Frankfurt School Reader*, ed. Andrew Arato and Eike Gebhardt, introduction by Paul Ricoeur (New York: Continuum, 1982) includes the sentence "I have no wish to soften the saying that to write lyric poetry after Auschwitz is barbaric"; however, he goes on to explain that "it is now virtually in art alone that suffering can still find its own voice, consolation, without immediately being betrayed by it" (312).

3. Elie Wiesel, *From the Kingdom of Memory: Reminiscences* (New York: Summit Books, 1990), p. 194.

4. Tadeus Rozewicz, "Posthumous Rehabilitation," in *Holocaust Poetry*, ed. Hilda Schiff (New York: St. Martin's, 1995), p. 170.

5. The phrase "corpses without coffins" comes from Wiesel's "A Plea for the Dead," reprinted in *Art from the Ashes*, ed. Lawrence L. Langer (New York: Oxford University Press, 1995), p. 141. For critical and creative background on prosopopoeia, see: William Wordsworth, "Essay upon Epitaphs" in *The Prose of William Wordsworth*, ed. W.J.B. Owen and Jane Worthington Smyser, Vol. II (Oxford: The Clarendon Press, 1974), pp. 49–62; and Edgar Lee Masters, *Spoon River Anthology* (New York: Macmillan, 1962). Although in *On the Margins of Discourse* (Chicago: University of Chicago Press, 1978) Barbara Herrnstein Smith views all lyrical poems as fictional representations of personal utterances, the speakers of the poems under discussion articulate utterances in implausible, if not impossible speech acts (142).

6. A number of critics examine laments composed by a bereft friend or relative grieving over loss and seeking (sometimes hopelessly) consolation; therefore even those elegies skeptical about solace are formally different from poems exploiting prosopopoeia. See Celeste Schenck, *Mourning and Panegyric: The Poetics of Pastoral Ceremony* (University Park: The Pennsylvania State University Press, 1988); Peter M. Sachs, *English Elegy: Readings in the Genre from Spenser to Yeats* (Baltimore: Johns Hopkins University Press, 1985); and Jahan Ramazani, *Poetry of Mourning: The Modern Elegy from Hardy to Heaney* (Chicago: The University of Chicago Press, 1994).

7. Such poems, many composed in the English language, have been anthologized in Steward J. Florsheim, *Ghosts of the Holocaust: An Anthology of Poetry by the Second Generation* (Detroit: Wayne State University Press, 1989); Charles Fishman, *Blood to Remember: American Poets on the Holocaust* (Lubbock: Texas Tech University Press, 1991); Milton Teichman and Sharon Leder's *Truth and Lamentations: Stories and Poems on the Holocaust* (Urbana: University of Illinois Press, 1994); Schiff, *Holocaust Poetry*; and Marguerite M. Strair, *Beyond Lament: Poets of the World Bearing Witness to the Holocaust* (Evanston: Northwestern University Press, 1998). For some of the poems cited here (and for all of the translated verse), I have used the initials of these volumes and page references will follow in parentheses.

8. Jean-François Lyotard, *The Differend: Phrases in Dispute*, trans. Georges Van Den Abbeele (Minneapolis: University of Minnesota Press, 1988), p. 57. All citations from *The Differend* will be to this edition; page references will follow in parentheses.

9. Shoshana Felman and Dori Laub, *Testimony: Crises of Witnessing in Literature, Psychoanalysis, and History* (New York: Routledge, 1992), p. 80. Felman and Laub offer other related meditations on the "silence imposed on knowledge."

10. Terrence Des Pres, *Praises & Dispraises: Poetry and Politics, the Twentieth Century* (New York: Viking, 1988), p. 228. Because I am implicitly questioning the assumptions

behind identity politics (the idea that only a Jew can write about Jewish experience), I refrain in this essay from categorizing the poets discussed; however, Klepfisz, Hecht, Rothenberg, and Hamburger describe themselves as Jewish writers, whereas Rich and Graham define their ancestry as part-Jewish. My sense of Plath's generation remains a fluid one, containing Jarrell (1913–1965), Hecht (1923–), Hamburger (1924–), Rich (1929–), Plath herself (1932–1963), Simic (1938–), and Klepfisz (1941–). Certainly the writer with whom I conclude, Graham (1951–), produced her work at a greater remove from the Shoah, and has been fully schooled in the verse produced by her predecessors.

11. This quote and the next come from Anne Michaels, *The Weight of Oranges / Miner's Pond* (Toronto: McClelland University Stewart, 1997), pp. 115–6.

12. In her "Lager Lexicon," Isabella Leitner defines "*Muselmann*" as a "totally emaciated, skeletonized prisoner (ready for the crematorium)" (in *Fragments of Isabella: A Memoir of Auschwitz* [New York: Dell, 1979], p. 128). See Alvin Rosenfeld, *A Double Dying: Reflections on Holocaust Literature* (Bloomington: Indiana University Press, 1980).

13. I derive the word "proxy-witnessing" from Robert Jay Lifton's idea of "survivors by proxy" in "An Interview," *Trauma: Explorations in Memory*, ed. Cathy Caruth (Baltimore: The Johns Hopkins Press, 1995), p. 145; and from Dominick LaCapra's idea of the "secondary witness" or witness of witnesses in "Lanzamann's *Shoah*: 'Here There Is No Why,'" *Critical Inquiry* 23, no. 2 (Winter 1997), 267.

14. Consider Jacob Glatstein's "I Have Never Been Here Before," Sachs' "A Dead Child Speaks," Dan Pagis's "Written in Pencil in the Sealed Railway-Car" and his "Testimony" as well as Yevgeny Yevtushenko's "Babii Yar" (*AA*, p. 659 and *HP*, pp. 67, 180, 43, and 94).

15. Marianne Hirsch, "Family Pictures: *Maus*, Mourning, and Post-Memory," *Discourse* 15, no. 2 (Winter 1992–93), 8. On "post-memory," see also Andrea Liss, *Trespassing Through Shadows: Memory, Photography and the Holocaust* (Minneapolis: University of Minnesota Press, 1998), p. 86; as well as Hirsch's subsequent book on this subject, *Family Frames: Photography, Narrative, and Postmemory* (Cambridge: Harvard University Press, 1997). The effort to read Plath's poems as statements about the Shoah also makes sense in light of her letters which "clearly show that, for her, such a simple boundary between internal and external worlds did not exist. Political concerns and historical imagery are not simply used as enabling structures or metaphors through which to explore her own experience ..., but are a framework of emotional and political history from which personal experience cannot escape": Al Strangeways, *Sylvia Plath: The Shaping of Shadows* (Cranbury, N.J.: Associated University Presses, 1998), p. 95.

16. Sylvia Plath, "Getting There," *The Collected Poems*, ed. Ted Hughes (New York: Harper & Row, 1981), p. 248. All citations from Plath's verse will be to this edition; page references will follow in parentheses.

17. Leitner, *Fragments of Isabella*, p. 30.

18. On Plath's use of the arrow in fiction and verse, see Sandra M. Gilbert, "A Fine, White Flying Myth: The Life/Work of Sylvia Plath," *Shakespeare's Sisters: Feminist Essays on Women Poets*, ed. Sandra M. Gilbert and Susan Gubar (Bloomington: Indiana University Press, 1979), p. 251.

19. According to Linda Bundtzen, "The train's carriages are transformed into the mother's cradles, rocking the dead and wounded toward resurrection" (250) as the speaker becomes "a mother-god, raising the dead, her body the divine vehicle for human salvation from history" (*Plath's Incarnations: Woman and the Creative Process* [Ann Arbor: The University of Michigan, 1983], p. 251).

20. Irena Klepfisz, *"Bashert,"* in *A Few Words in the Mother Tongue: Poems Selected and New (1971–1990)* (Portland: Eighth Mountain, 1990), p. 200. All citations from Klepfisz's verse will be to this edition; page references will follow in parentheses.

21. Arthur Cohen, *The Tremendum: A Theological Interpretation of the Holocaust* (New York: Crossroad, 1982), p. 58.

22. Paul de Man, *The Rhetoric of Romanticism* (New York: Columbia University Press, 1984), p. 57. See Jonathan Culler's and Barbara Johnson's related points about apostrophe and animation in, respectively, *The Pursuit of Signs: Semiotics, Literature, Deconstruction* (Ithaca: Cornell University Press, 1981), p. 146, and "Apostrophe, Animation, and Abortion," in *A World of Difference* (Baltimore: The Johns Hopkins University Press, 1987), pp. 184–99.

23. Adrienne Rich, *Sources* in *Adrienne Rich's Poetry and Prose*, ed. Barbara Charlesworth Gelpi and Albert Gelpi (New York: W.W. Norton Critical Edition, 1993), p. 18. Rich composed a perceptive and complementary introduction to Klepfisz's collected poems, paying special attention to Klepfisz's verse about the Holocaust and transplantation.

24. Kathryn Hellerstein analyzes Molodowsky's poems as evidence of the "ambivalent spiritual exile of a Yiddish woman poet" in "In Exile in the Mother Tongue: Yiddish and the Woman Poet," *Borders, Boundaries, and Frames: Cultural Criticism and Cultural Studies*, ed. Mae Henderson (New York: Routledge, 1995), pp. 67–68. Klepfisz, who spoke Polish (not Yiddish) as a child, views the loss of Yiddish as a linguistic casualty of the Shoah in several of the essays in *Dreams of an Insomniac: Jewish Feminist Essays, Speeches, and Diatribes* (Portland: Eighth Mountain, 1990) and thus experiments with bilingual Yiddish/English poetry in a number of works.

25. Klepfisz, *Dreams of an Insomniac*, pp. 208–9.

26. The past tense here recalls Emily Dickinson's as well as Christina Rossetti's mortuary verse.

27. I am disagreeing with de Man's proposition: "by making the dead speak, the symmetrical structure of the trope implies, by the same token, that the living are struck dumb, frozen in their own death" (*The Rhetoric of Romanticism*, p. 78). I also disagree with de Man's conclusion, "Death is a displaced name for a linguistic predicament" (81), since, as Eric L. Santner points out, this proposition "precludes the possibility of distinguishing one victim from other. Furthermore, the historical victim … is overshadowed here by an impersonal and apathetic 'dismemberment' at the violent hands of the signifier" (*Stranded Objects: Mourning, Memory, and Film in Postwar Germany* [Ithaca: Cornell University Press, 1990], p. 29). On "the discontinuity between the personal self and the voice that speaks in the poetry [of Verlaine] from the other bank of the river, beyond death," see de Man, *Blindness and Insight: Essays in the Rhetoric of Contemporary Criticism*, 2nd edition (Minneapolis: University of Minnesota Press, 1983), p. 181.

28. Kaja Silverman, *Threshold of the Visible World* (New York: Routledge, 1995), p. 185. Also resonant is the discussion of "empathic unsettlement" (699) by which "one puts oneself in the other's position while recognizing the difference of that position and hence not taking the other's place" (722) in Dominick LaCapra, "Trauma, Absence, Loss," *Critical Inquiry* 25, no. 4 (Summer 1999): 696–727.

29. Anthony Hecht, *Collected Poems* (New York: Alfred A. Knopf, 1990), p. 39. All citations from Hecht's verse will be to this edition; page references will follow in parentheses.

30. Peter Sachs, "Anthony Hecht's 'Rites and Ceremonies': Reading *The Hard Hours*," in *The Burdens of Formality: Essays on the Poetry of Anthony Hecht*, ed. Sydney Lea (Athens: The University of Georgia Press, 1989), p. 86.

31. Randall Jarell, "The Death of the Ball Turret Gunner" and "Protocols" in *The Complete Poems* (NY: Farrar, Strauss, and Giroux, 1969), pp. 144, 193.

32. Wallace Stevens, *The Collected Poems* (New York: Vintage-Random House, 1982), p. 69.

33. Charles Simic, *The World Doesn't End: Prose Poems* (New York: Harcourt Brace Jovanovich, 1989), p. 3.

34. Simic is questioning such thinkers as Victor Frankl whose *Man's Search for Meaning: An Introduction to Logotherapy*, trans. Ilse Lasch (Boston: Beacon Press, 1962) posits the idea that meaning-making furnishes a key to survival. The psychological process of "creating meaningful images" may be "at the heart" of what Robert Jay Lifton and Eric Olson call "*symbolic immortality*" (75), but it furnishes little solace here: see their *Living and Dying* (New York: Praeger, 1974).

35. Simic's poem addresses an issue described by Sidra DeKoven Ezrahi in *Booking Passage: Exile and Homecoming in the Modern Jewish Imagination* (Berkeley: University of California Press, 2000), p. 145: "Because human flesh has been metamorphosed into smoke," she has explained, "the temptation of the post-Holocaust imagination is to reground and literalize that which has become abstracted out of existence."

36. Jerome Rothenberg, *Khurbn and Other Poems* (New York: New Directions, 1989), pp. 3, 27. Subsequent citations from Rothenberg's verse will be to this edition; page references will follow in parentheses.

37. Adrienne Rich, *An Atlas of the Difficult World: Poems 1988–1991* (New York: W.W. Norton, 1991), pp. 44, 45.

38. Emily Borenstein, *Night of the Broken Glass: Poems of the Holocaust* (Mason, Texas: Timberline Press, 1981), pp. 2 and 23.

39. Ruth Whitman, *The Testing of Hanna Senesh* (Detroit: Wayne State University Press, 1986), p. 57.

40. See Michael Hamburger, "In A Cold Season" in *Collected Poems, 1941–1994* (Oxford: Anvil Press Poetry, 1995), pp. 109–112. All citations from Hamburger's verse will be to this edition; page references will follow in parentheses. On the repercussions for survivors of the failure of empathy, see Dori Laub and Nanette C. Auerhahn, "Failed Empathy—A Central Theme in the Survivor's Holocaust Experience," *Psychoanalytic Psychology* 6, no. 5 (1989): 377–400.

41. The conclusion of the first section of *The Waste Land*, where Eliot writes "You! Hypocrite lecteur!—*mon semblable—mon frère!*," alludes to Baudelaire's preface to *Fleurs du Mal*.

42. The critic who found the Sexton quote and brought it to the attention of Plath's readers was Heather Cam in "'Daddy': Sylvia Plath's Debt to Anne Sexton," *Sexton: Selected Criticism*, ed. Diana Hume George (Urbana: University of Illinois Press, 1988), pp. 223–6.

43. On Berryman, see Hilene Flanzbaum, "The Imaginary Jew and the American Poet," in *The Americanization of the Holocaust*, ed. Flanzbaum (Baltimore: The Johns Hopkins Press, 1999), pp. 18–32. For an excellent approach to "Daddy" and "Lady Lazarus" in terms of Plath's "agonistic mourning" (263), see Ramazani (276–82, 285–88).

44. Sigmund Freud, *Mourning and Melancholia* in *The Standard Edition of the Complete Psychological Works of Sigmund Freud*, ed. James Strachey, Vol. XIV (1914–1916) (London: The Hogarth Press, 1957), pp. 243–58.

45. Saul Friedlander, *Nazi Germany and the Jews*, Vol. 1 of *The Persecution , 1933–1939* (New York: HarperCollins, 1997), p. 78. Writing about the centrality of Jews in German culture, one young intellectual explained, "We Jews administer the spiritual possessions of a people that denies us the right and the capability of doing so" (quoted in Friedlander, 78).

46. Ron Rosenbaum, *Explaining Hitler: The Search for the Origins of Evil* (New York: HarperCollins, 1999), p. 335.

47. Holocaust-related suicides are an important subject. See Maurice Blanchot's elliptical analysis in *The Writing of the Disaster*, trans. Ann Smock (Lincoln: University of Nebraska Press, 1995), p. 70; Mary Lowenthal Felstiner, who examines the incidents of suicide in the family of Charlotte Salomon in *To Paint Her Life: Charlotte Salomon in the Nazi Era* (New York: Harper Collins, 1994); Victor Frankl, who explains "The thought of suicide was entertained by nearly everyone" in the camps (16); and a number of documentary books demonstrating that "Epidemics of suicides usually synchronized with waves of exportation or similar acts of oppression" (Jacob Apenszlak, *The Black Book of Polish Jewry: An Account of the Martyrdom of Polish Jewry Under the Nazi Occupation*, co-edited with Jacob Kenner, Dr. Isaac Lewsin, Dr. Moses Polakiewicz [New York: Howard Fertig, 1982], p. 189). A friend of Plath's, A. Alvarez testified, "I personally have known half-a-dozen suicides or near suicides; and each has prefaced his act with a fierce immersion in the literature of the camps" (*Beyond All This Fiddle: Essays 1955–1967* [New York: Random House, 1968], p. 28). In *Poetics* (Cambridge: Harvard University Press, 1992), Charles Bernstein has claimed that "To acknowledge the Second War means to risk suicide and in the process to politicize philosophy; and if we desire to avoid death and evade politics, repression is inevitable" (196). The "cultural question whether after Auschwitz you can go on living" troubled Adorno, too: "mere survival calls for the coldness, the basic principle of bourgeois subjectivity, without which there could have been no Auschwitz" ("Meditations on Metaphysics" in *Negative Dialectics*, trans. E.B. Ashton [New York: Continuum, 1973], p. 363).

48. Blanchot, *The Writing of the Disaster*, p. 70.

49. In *The Archivist* (Boston: Little, Brown and Company, 1998), the novelist Martha Cooley presents a portrait of a woman unhinged by her absorbed reading about the Holocaust and her identification with the victims.

50. The quote comes from a blurb on the book by Jonathan Kozol, but many other reviewers could be quoted in their praise of the authenticity of *Fragments*. In "The Memory Thief," *The New Yorker*, June 14, 1999, 48–68. Philip Gourevitch also discusses Jerzy Kosinski as an imposter.

51. Gourevitch, "The Memory Thief," 66.

52. Blanchot, *The Writing of the Disaster*, p. 60.

53. See Saul Friedlander, who views the "frisson" of the Holocaust entertainment industry as a product of "the meeting of kitsch and death" in *Reflections of Nazism: An Essay on Kitsch and Death*, trans. Thomas Weyr (Bloomington: Indiana University Press, 1993), p. 25.

54. See the discussion in Sandra M. Gilbert and Susan Gubar of Plath's use of a ghostly iambic pentameter in this closing allusion to Coleridge: *Letters from the Front*, Vol. 3 of *No Man's Land: The Place of the Woman Writer in the Twentieth Century* (New Haven: Yale University Press, 1994), p. 290.

55. In *Reading the Holocaust* (Cambridge: Cambridge University Press, 1999), Inga Clendinnen describes an "inversion effect": the matter of the Shoah "is so potent in itself that when art seeks to command it, it is art which is rendered vacuous and drained of authority" (164–5).

56. Because we live in an unreal present of endless image substitutions, Geoffrey Hartman writes, quoting Baudrillard, we "'want to prove we died between 1940 and 1945,'" a period associated with "'real history'" (*The Longest Shadow: In the Aftermath of the Holocaust* [Bloomington: Indiana University Press, 1996], p. 45).

57. See Claude Lanzmann's influential attack on efforts to explain the Holocaust or understand the perpetrators in "The Obscenity of Understanding," *Trauma: Explorations in Memory*, ed. Cathy Caruth (Baltimore: The Johns Hopkins University Press, 1995), pp. 200–20; many agree with him that, as Saul Friedlander puts it in *Memory, History, and the Extermination of the Jews of Europe* (Bloomington: Indiana University Press, 1993), "the 'Final Solution,' as a result of its apparent historical exceptionality, could well be inaccessible to all attempts at a significant representation and interpretation" (113).

58. Adrienne Rich, *Sources* in *Adrienne Rich's Poetry and Prose*, p. 113.

59. Michaels, *The Weight of Oranges / Miner's Pond*, p. 115.

60. Jorie Graham, *Materialism* (Hopewell, N.J.: The Ecco Press, 1993), pp. 66–77. All citations to this work will be to this edition; page references will follow in parentheses. Charles Reznikoff's *Holocaust* (Los Angeles: Black Sparrow Press, 1975) is based on Nazi war crime trials, Barbara Helfgott Hyett's *In Evidence* (Pittsburgh: University of Pittsburgh Press, 1986) on interviews conducted with members of the United States Armed Services.

61. Lyotard's words in *The Differend* also contextualize the concerns of Graham's "History" and "From the New World" (see *DUF*, pp. 40–41, 106–109).

62. Recently, the British revisionist David Irving has claimed, "'there were never any gas chambers at Auschwitz'": see D. D. Guttenplan, "Is a Holocaust Skeptic Fit to Be a Historian?" *The New York Times*, 26 June, 1999, B 1, 11.

63. In *The Given and the Made: Strategies of Poetic Redefinition* (Cambridge: Harvard University Press, 1995), Helen Vendler has analyzed the "formal consequences, for Graham's verse, of the insusceptibility of matter to dependable interpretation" (110).

64. The phrase "chain of events" comes from a passage from Walter Benjamin's description of the angel of history that Graham quotes in "On Description," *Materialism*, p. 55.

65. The creature x appears in Jorie Graham, "History," *The Dream of the Unified Field: Selected Poems 1974–1994* (Hopewell, N.J.: The Ecco Press, 1995), pp. 145, 147.

66. Leitner, *Fragments of Isabella*, p. 84.

67. Cynthia Ozick, Comments in "Round Table Discussion," in *Writing and the Holocaust*, ed. Berel Lang (New York: Homes and Meier, 1988), p. 279.

68. Graham, *The Dream of the Unified Field*, p. 146.

69. Graham, *Materialism*, pp. 100–2.

70. Graham, *Materialism*, p. 55.

71. This and the next quote from Walter Benjamin come from "Theses on the Philosophy of History," *Illuminations*, ed. Hannah Arendt (New York: Schocken, 1969), p. 255.

LINDA WAGNER-MARTIN

Plath's Triumphant Women Poems

Sylvia Plath would have been the first to admit that there were multiple roles for women during the 1960s besides mothering or not mothering. In the age of professionalism, of incipient careerism, a woman would have been expected to have identities other than her status as a bearer of children. Just as so many of Plath's journal entries dealt with her future work, and the conundrum of which work a talented woman writer, artist, and teacher should take up, so many of her poems deal with the varieties of achieving women. It is also clear in her journals that she was intentionally searching for women writers to emulate. She regularly mentions Virginia Woolf, Emily Dickinson, Stevie Smith, Willa Cather, Lillian Hellman, Louise Bogan, Adrienne Cecile Rich (often with some asperity, since Rich was her contemporary and by having won the Yale Younger Poets competition, already headed toward an important career as poet).[1] In fact, Liz Yorke has concluded that the journal entries "make it clear that Plath made a self-conscious decision to study women. Her critique of the ideology of the feminine; her critical consciousness of women's emotional, erotic and economic loyalty and their subservience to men can be shown as developing continuously from this time [1958]."[2]

Unfortunately, by the time Plath had freed herself from her apprenticeship modes and was writing in what seemed to be her true voice, she was obsessed with rage at what she saw as the betrayal of their life

---

From *Sylvia Plath: A Literary Life*: pp. 106–118. © 1999, 2003 by Linda Wagner-Martin.

together—and her opportunity to become a good writer—by her husband. It was barely possible to scrape out time to write during these years with two very young children, yet Plath had. She had finished *The Bell Jar* and "Three Women," she had worked on several short stories that satisfied her, and many, many poems. Writing within a family household was possible, if difficult. But she was accustomed to difficulties. Plath was not so oblivious to how hard maintaining her writing schedule was, however, as to believe she could write effectively if there were no other adult in that household. The years had made her a pragmatist.

Just as we have seen that she created a mythic structure from her comparison of her own fertile womanhood with the barrenness of other more fashionable women, so it seems plausible that she would emblematize the realm of patriarchal power that not only minded babies but accepted poems, scheduled BBC readings, and wrote reviews as a man of a certain type. For the "old boy network" that was determining her fate as a writer, particularly in England where *she* had no connections except through her still-outsider husband, she had only anger and even contempt. Her quasi-flirtation with Al Alvarez was prompted at least in part by his power both to accept her work and to review it, and there was frequently a sexual element in her dealings with other established literary men on the British scene. In some ways, the fact that Hughes had begun an affair—while enraging on its own terms—also may have been catalytic in freeing her to express her deep-seated anger against the controlling and male-dominated literary world. Again, Yorke sees the male presence in so many of what can also be read as Plath's "strong woman" "poems as more indefinite than the figure of a disloyal husband: "Hatred against men begins to fuel the vitriolic stance of many poems."[3]

Two situations illustrate her frustration at being a woman writer in the British literary world. The first is the narrative of her meeting Alvarez in 1960. *Lupercal*, Hughes's second poem collection, had just appeared. Admiring it greatly, Alvarez phoned and suggested that he and Ted take their infants for a walk, thereby having a chance to talk about poetry. When he arrived at the flat, Alvarez recalled that Mrs. Hughes struck him as "briskly American: bright, clean, competent, like a young woman in a cookery advertisement, friendly and yet rather distant." He pays small attention to her. But as Hughes is getting the baby's carriage out, Plath turns to Alvarez,

> "I'm so glad you picked *that* poem," she said. "It's one of my favorites but no one else seemed to like it."
>
> For a moment I went completely blank; I didn't know what she was talking about.
>
> She noticed and helped me out.

"The one you put in *The Observer* a year ago. About the factory at night."

"For Christ's sake, Sylvia *Plath*." It was my turn to gush. "I'm sorry. It was a lovely poem."

"Lovely" wasn't the right word, but what else do you say to a bright young housewife? ...[4]

The apparent inability to equate "housewife" and "young mother"—not to mention, perhaps, "American"—with "poet" created little more than a minor social gaffe here, but Plath's life was filled with occasions when she was the quiet American to her husband's ever-growing reputation as one of England's brightest rising stars. At a Faber & Faber cocktail party, she is called out into the hall to witness Hughes's having his picture taken in the company of Stephen Spender, T. S. Eliot, Louis MacNeice, and W. H. Auden. There was no question that Auden would remember having a brief conference with the Smith coed Sylvia Plath, yet now he is standing only six feet from that girl's poet spouse. As the five men look into the camera, sherry glasses in hand, there is an air of self-congratulation that Plath would have found difficult to stomach.[5]

As he recounted that first meeting, Alvarez had the conscience to admit, "I was embarrassed not to have known who she was. She seemed embarrassed to have reminded me, and also depressed."[6]

Faced with the issue of role, Plath knew her place was to be the help-meet, the alert and sensitive supporter to her husband and his burgeoning career. One imagines that when the Hugheses are invited to T. S. Eliot's home for dinner, Plath is hardly a participant in the conversation; she would certainly not talk about how many poems she had recently published. Australian poet Charles (known as Mike) Doyle remembers being invited to Ted and Sylvia's Boston apartment for dinner the year before, and having no idea that Plath also wrote poetry. He recalled her cooking a chicken dinner and then clearing the table and washing dishes, while he and Ted sat for hours reading and commenting on their poems in manuscript. Charles Doyle remembers it as being a long evening of talk about specific poems—the men's poems. He concludes, "Nothing was said about her poetry."[7]

A second situation is the years-long period of interaction with Peter Davison, a poet and editor of Harvard University Press (and other presses subsequently) with whom she had had an affair during the summer of 1955, just before she sailed for her Fulbright year in England. Davison writes in his memoir that he felt "used" after Plath broke off the sexual relationship, and summarized their later contact, after he had become Poetry Editor of *The Atlantic*, by saying, "she sent me some of her last poems for *The Atlantic*."[8]

The truth of the statement is that Plath besieged that magazine, sending both her poems and Hughes's to it regularly. It was prominent and it paid well: poets who published there were known, and notable.

She had published in *The Atlantic* before Davison was connected with it, and seemed always to be treated a bit high-handedly. For instance, the magazine kept a large group of her poems for months and then, on April 18, 1955, sent her a check for $25 and told her to revise "Circus in Three Rings."[9] Perhaps they will include it if she can get the first or third stanzas up to the quality of the second, which someone wrote was "a perfect beauty," and then use as title either "The Tamer" or "Lion Tamer." Over Edward Weeks' unsigned but typed name, the quasi-acceptance cheered the Smith co-ed on: the letter concluded, "do a revision which will win us completely. I am confident that you can."

Plath replied politely and sent Weeks the revision and five new poems, saying she would not cash the $25 check until she heard from him. (*The Atlantic* printed "Circus" as it had been submitted originally, despite the revision Plath sent them.) The interchanges continue. In the spring of 1956 they accept "Pursuit," the poem she wrote about the possibility of meeting Hughes, although they comment that it seems too long. Then Weeks asks if he can see her poem "Two Lovers and a Beachcomber by the Real Sea," which was shown to him by a friend. Ironically, that poem had been included in the batch of work that had originally prompted the $25 check and the patronizing encouragement.

In September of that year, Plath hears from Davison, who has just joined the staff. Her reply to him is enthusiastic and overblown, and—even though she and Hughes have already married—she describes Hughes's work to him with the comment that she has become his "agent." She closes that she is eager to know the details about his job, and wants to keep in close touch with him while she remains at Newnham for the year. She also tells him that she and Ted will be married next summer in Wellesley.

Davison's reply is cordial, and he is encouraging about Hughes's poems. But Plath notices that, whereas she had already been published in *The Atlantic*, and although her poems were appearing in *Poetry*, *The Spectator*, *The Nation*, *London Magazine*, *Granta*, *Partisan Review*, *New Yorker*, *Harper's*, and a number of other good places, neither she nor Ted found ready acceptance at *The Atlantic* once Davison was there. She comments on this in letters home and in her journal; and there is a comic scene of Davison—now married to a former housemate of Plath's at Smith—taking her and Hughes out to dinner and talking throughout the meal about little except his own poetry. Finally, Plath submits their work directly to Edward Weeks, and acceptances begin again. In the autumn of 1960, her poem "The Manor Garden" appears, and in 1961, "Words for a Nursery."

Davison is right, Plath did send what she called "this rather alarming wad of new stuff"[10] to him November 16, 1962, telling him she was both eager to have his opinion and eager to have any payment. He returned most of the poems but kept six, and noted on her letter—as he passed the poems to Weeks—that "In the Bee Box" was his favorite. He replied to Plath on November 20, saying that the poems were "quite extraordinary," and that the bee poem hummed with "fright." Although the letter began 'Dear Sylvia,' his reply was addressed to "Mrs. Ted Hughes."[11] Even at the peak of her finest production, Plath could not gain recognition for herself, or for her work, on her own terms.

Plath would have smiled grimly at the set of editorial responses appended to a copy of Davison's letter in the *Atlantic* file. Although one reader commented on "Terrific vitality, color and originality," even that most enthusiastic responder went on to complain that the emotions in the poems seemed to be "contrived." The four readers could not figure out what was going on. One wrote, "I think she is overdoing these bees." Another noted, "She certainly is queer for bees. Too much buzz and not enough sting in most of these."[12] (*The Atlantic* did accept both "Bee Box" ["The Arrival of the Bee Box"] and "Wintering," eventually, and they saw print in April 1963.)

Considering these representative anecdotes from the six years that Plath served as 'agent' for Hughes's work—not to mention typist, arranger, and record keeper—simultaneous with her offering to do the same for Luke Myers,[13] while trying to develop as a writer herself (and serve as agent, typist and record keeper for her own work), Professor Yorke's assessment that in her late poems Plath was finally speaking out for her feminine/feminist rights is credible. Yorke insists that Plath's late work "presents us with the spectacle of femininity in crisis. It symbolizes the aggressive return of the repressed through a dramatic poetry of mythic formulas, plots and patterns—in which the stage is set for the poet/woman to introduce her shrieks, her suffering, her anguish, her murderous fury, her disruptive *disorder* into the well-regulated, gendered codes of conventional patriarchy."[14]

Plath's neatly-typed letters throughout her marriage are illustrative of that well-regulated behavior. Whether she was writing to Theodore Roethke about a possible teaching post for Hughes, even though it was Plath herself who was so moved by Roethke's poetry,[15] or to John Lehmann with submissions for both of them to *London Magazine*,[16] or to Brian Cox about *Critical Quarterly*,[17] she appeared to be the tidy and competent secretary she had so feared becoming. Unfortunately, as we have seen, some of her earlier poems gave off the same aura of starched neatness—

with any recognizable emotion kept at a distance. The truly dramatic changes between those college-era poems, like "Circus in Three Rings" and "Two Lovers and a Beachcomber by the Real Sea," and such late poems as "Applicant," "Purdah," and "Lady Lazarus," were both shocking and inexplicable. That comparatively few of the very late poems were accepted by the first magazine Plath submitted them to was partly because of this wide discrepancy between what a Plath poem had often been, and what editors were reading as Plath poems in the autumn of 1962.

All three of these later poems show the persona moving from her conventional state of social acceptance to the flourish of triumph, no matter how unconventional her behavior has become. In "Applicant," the woman appears to be applying for the job of marrying some man, any man; in "Purdah," she is a reluctant member of a man's harem; and in "Lady Lazarus," she is a woman who readily defies death to taunt the society that would contain, and constrain, her. The tone of the voice interrogating the applicant in that poem is clearly haughty, probably British, and condescending; if one is not "our sort of person,"[18] nothing can be done. Being "our sort of person" sets up sexual classes as well as economic ones. Calling the woman "sweetie," as did the aggressor in the Johnny Panic story, this voice insults her with regularity: an empty head, a naked body, a scenario right out of the Hallmark anniversary charts, this woman does not even merit the dignity of a feminine personal pronoun. Instead, she is an "it" in the lines near the conclusion: "It can sew, it can cook, / It can talk, talk, talk." These repetitive sentences balance with the repetition in the concluding line, "Will you marry it, marry it, marry it."

In "Purdah" the question is not of marriage, it is of the man's ownership of the woman, who smiles, enigmatic, watching the sun polish her shoulder. Yet the warning occurs early: even as she plays her usual role, the woman is changing, "shifting my clarities."[19] With unbelievable swiftness, the woman attacks her lover, unloosing "The lioness" (the power of her self), "The shriek in the bath" (reminiscent of that most famous of murders, Clytemnestra's of Agamemnon, which results in "The cloak of holes"). A poem of vengeance, "Purdah" adds a surreal chapter to the anguished punishment the persona metes out in "Burning the Letters," as she destroys her beloved's writing. A key metaphor in that poem is, "The dogs are tearing a fox. This is what it is like— / A red burst and a cry / That splits from its ripped bag and does not stop..."[20] To kill a fox, when one of Hughes's best-known early poems was "The Thought-Fox," speaks pointedly, even if metaphorically.

Polite anger is one stance; explosive rage that does not end is another. Plath's use of the word "shriek" throughout these poems, whether or not the persona is herself doing the shrieking, signals the reader that what she has to tell cannot be told in a normal pitch. Ideally, the poem is a means of voicing all kinds of states, yet it cannot express the volume of rage (or, it cannot express rage in the volume of sound) that the poet or her created persona would think appropriate.

Merely murdering the powerful man responsible for the female persona's state is not enough. (The reader will see the intricacy of a possible ritual death in the poem "Daddy.") Instead, in the brilliantly titled "Lady Lazarus," Plath uses the metaphor of Lazarus returning from the dead, changing him into a woman (and a woman of some social power) so as to reverse the gender of that miracle. Throughout the poem there is no mention whatever of the biblical origin, or of whatever god might have been responsible for Lazarus's resurrection. Instead, Plath's Lady Lazarus is under the command of her own superior will. Superior in all respects to the general population, and to her former beloved, the persona can even out-do her competition in killing herself. She does this with no personality change: "I am the same, identical woman."[21] Even as she is martyred by the male patriarchy—what can be more representative of that power but the German title "Herr" and the various manuscript designations of "Herr Professor," "Herr Doktor," "Herr God," "Herr Lucifer," and finally the direct name of "Enemy"?—the woman does not remain dead. From the pile of ash, she becomes the uncontained and mystic phoenix, rising from the carnage that men have created for her, and of her. Her final act, always phrased comically, is to "eat men [in the plural] like air."

Critic Susan Van Dyne, in her meticulous work with the many manuscript drafts of Plath's late poems, points out here that the audience for what she calls Lady Lazarus's *performance* is not a single adversary, but the world of men—a world for which the persona has only contempt ("the peanut-crunching crowd"). "What Lady Lazarus suffers is not male brutality but the gendered asymmetry of her relationship to power in which her role is always defined as dependent and defective: to male professor she is student; to executioner, criminal; to priest, sinner; to doctor, patient." And yet, by her addition of comedy to this shriek, Van Dyne notes, Plath sidesteps the trap of sentiment: "Her burlesque of suffering both confesses the damage of gender and uses it as a weapon ... The persistent double consciousness of 'Lady Lazarus' is not the split self of alienation that marks Plath's other poems of rage but a strategy for control."[22]

Who are the antagonists in Plath's late poems like "Lady Lazarus"? Sometimes her persona's own self, but more often men—husbands, fathers, power figures at large—or, as she begins to suggest here, filaments of airy stuff that have no substance. If even the physical strength of men, a strength they customarily vaunt over weaker women, is subterfuge, where does their superiority lie? In manuscripts for the poem, Plath includes lines that show the protagonist's ordinariness, and her recurring purity: "Yes, lady, I'm like you, / I have a child or two. // Yessir, yessir Though the doctors say it's rare/ Each time I rise, I rise a blooming [bloody] virgin." The mark of a woman's successful life—up to a point—being her virginity, there is a tonal difference between the two words Plath bracketed in the draft. While both might be slang, "blooming" reinforces the glowing incandescent skin this exuberance warrants, whereas "bloody" must have more sinister connotations.

Again, the woman persona can stand alone. Yet as long as she has to do battle with men, readers have been tempted to read these poems as autobiographical, as poems about the battles—literal and figurative—between Sylvia Plath and Ted Hughes. Realizing this, Plath turns to poems about women who separate themselves from such adversarial men—this is her route to "Ariel," and it is probably the reason she chose *Ariel* as the title for the collection she planned to publish from her late poems.

For in "Ariel," the woman persona is completely alone. Her mind is free from the canker of hatred for her husband; her spirit is coming into a newly fruitful phase as she leaves human discord behind. Fusing her human identity with the animal spirit is itself a kind of transcendence, and recalls Robert Graves's insistence in his *White Goddess* (a book that was a kind of Bible for Ted Hughes) that the spirit of that fiery female goddess often appears as a mare, tigress, owl, sow, serpent, she-wolf, female spider, snake, or queen bee.[23] (Of these, the serpent and the racehorse are holy animals, as is the lion.)[24] Reading Plath's poems retrospectively, from this vantage point, shows how thoroughly she was mining Graves's philosophy.

In "Ariel," the persona, and the reader, is on a ride into the unknown, into a world that may be natural or spirit, real or imaginary, physical or emotional. What is known only is that the persona and God's lioness, either as mythical or spiritual identity, are united, fused, into one. Reminiscent of a sexual image, here Plath denies the bodily detail: all the viewer sees is berries, shadows; all she hears is the child's cry in the morning dawn. What has happened is a transfiguration. Leaving behind "Dead hands, dead stringencies"[25] [and in draft, the phrase is "dead men"], finding herself empowered to move forward—perhaps for the first time, alone—the persona does not fear what may be ahead.

Literally, "Ariel" is said to be the name of Plath's horse, but surely we are made fools of if we read this evocative poem so simply. As the poem says, "Something else // Hauls me through air—" This poem is Plath at her metaphysical best; we are hesitant to recognize that theme because we have noticed it so seldom. (Our reading of Plath's poetry has been stymied because there have always been interesting ways to read her work—if not from the technical appreciation perspective, or the autobiographical, then from the feminist.) The literary associations with the name "Ariel," however, lead us to the metaphysical. Whether we are with Prospero in *The Tempest*, or with Prospero in W. H. Auden's *The Sea and the Mirror*, his verse commentary on Shakespeare's play, we must grant the excessive power that Ariel commands, even in the face of the whole British kingdom. Small and slight, gendered both sexes and neither, Ariel is the all-knowing—and achieving—sprite any writer would wish to be. Particularly a woman writer. Although the name Ariel sounds feminine, at least in contrast to the adversarial Caliban, it is not womanly: it is the best of the spirit world, the best of imaginative power.

In the gendered narrative of Shakespeare's play, the shaman Prospero, thinking he has been able to protect his innocent daughter Miranda, finally breaks his staff and rids himself of his "rough magic." As he does this, he frees Ariel from his control. With close attention to the way the shaman can relinquish his magic powers, Plath may be suggesting that the self-styled shaman in her life, her controlling husband—controlling in the province of art if less so in the domestic—no longer has power over her creative spirit, the Ariel in Plath.

Auden creates his dialogue between Prospero and Ariel so that wisdom is expressed throughout it. Prospero defines magic as "the power to enchant that comes from disillusion," and continues that the wise man is one who has learned to tell "the difference between moonshine and daylight." In her customary intertextual way, Plath may be assuming the mantle of one who has been disillusioned, and has now grown past that angry despair. Particularly apt is Prospero's farewell comment to Ariel. He blesses the spirit, saying "Ages to you of song and daring."

There is little question that Plath knew that her late poems, which she characteristically saw as songs or lyrics, were superior to any she had ever written; and that they were so clearly superior because of their great daring. Part of that daring was inherent in the poems—they would take on the subtle hints of meaning that had first surprised her when she wrote "Tulips" and parts of "Three Women." They would grow from the slightest suggestion of an image, forgetting to follow rational coherence, and they would take on new themes in the process of following those scatty images. Like "Cut,"[26] images and metaphors run out of gaps, cracks, flaps, and they do so unchecked because the poet, at last, is willing to be known as "Dirty girl." For it is, finally, the misbehaving no-longer-tidy Plath who has taken control of her art. The freedom to find this new voice has been given to her through her willingness to leave behind all the studies, all the knowledge, all the tutoring—by Hughes as well as by Kazin, Fisher, Krook, and countless other well-intentioned professionals—so that she might come to bedrock.

For Mary Kurtzman, and to some extent Timothy Materer in his book *Modernist Alchemy*, that bedrock is comprised in large part of Plath's Cabalistic beliefs that grew stronger with each month of the poet's last years. Luke Myers lends credence to Kurtzman's readings as he notes that Hughes had been well-versed in those elements for some time.[27] Kurtzman's reading of "Ariel" depends, line by line, on those beliefs as generated from Tarot card 14, Art or Temperance, on which a black-white woman is doing alchemical work over a cauldron, with a lion and an eagle at her feet. Associated with this iconography is the number 60, the Hebrew letter S, the sign Sagittarius, the God Jupiter, the Goddess Diana, the color blue, the horse, the Arrow, the hips and thighs, the Centaur, and the Path of union with one's Higher Self or Holy Guardian Angel, symbolized by the Sun. Considering how brief the poem "Ariel" is, the fact that so many of these symbols occur in it lends weight to this critic's detailed reading (see *Centennial Review*, 32, 1988). As she concludes, "Knowing the spiritual meaning of 'Ariel'—[the word as translated from the Hebrew means 'God's lioness']—helps one avoid some critical pitfalls."[28]

The speaker, says Kurtzman, "is Plath, a persona neither suicidal nor insane. She is a mystic using her own, always idiosyncratic, version of the ancient language of mysticism. Like H.D., she renames the patriarchal myths, reclaiming Ariel as feminine and declaring her independence from the 'hooks' of male definitions of woman. She becomes the Goddess of the cauldron of poetic inspiration—autonomous, creative, fertile, the very voice of the Angel Ariel."[29] Card 14 also, as Kurtzman notes, is the basis of the major ritual of the Golden Dawn, the mystic society that was so important to W. B. Yeats, and it is in Yeats' house that Plath lived the last few months of her life.

Originating from a number of complex sources, the late Plath voice is, truly, unique. There was no way she could have learned to use it by modeling her poems after those of other poets. There was no way she could have practiced finding it by writing poems on subjects her husband set out for her, as if she were a little tired monk, burrowing away in some chilly monastery. There was no way she could have released herself from the "oughts" and "shoulds" of her superior education, with its classist emphasis on taste, on what the right sort of people read and liked. What could have released the poet from the well-educated Wellesley girl was the right to experience unfeigned passion.

Naked (i.e., "White/Godiva, I unpeel"), visionary (surrounded with darkness yet capable of sight), and incredibly fast ("foam to wheat"), the poet persona has never experienced anything like this, loosening, this unburdening, this flying apart. In some perverse echo of Eliot's *The Waste Land*, Plath's "Ariel" shows the validity of shoring fragments against ruin. Here, her act of fragmenting saves her. She has known enough to take action, she has finally overcome Mrs. Willard's curse that she recounts in *The Bell Jar*, and she has herself become the arrow, complete with its vindicating speed and straightness, rather than remaining in the suitable? womanly space, the place from which the (male) arrow shoots off.

And why should she not? Isn't this the vision of a woman of enormous ambition? Where in her thirty years had Plath ever settled for less than a superior rating, a first prize, even a husband to beat out all former suitors? Why should she not aim for that complete transcendence as she becomes a part of the natural world, losing herself as she looses herself in the cauldron of morning? Reaching that kind of nirvana left no room for mourning.

"Ariel" also serves as a culmination for another set of themes Plath had worked with earlier, when she was first learning about Robert Graves' particularly feminized mythology. In 1958 she had written an intricate syllabic poem about a run-away horse named Sam; the elegant long lines of "Whiteness I Remember"[30] might appear very different from the terse shape of "Ariel" but the description of the rider's consummate power, her union with the powerful—and mythic—horse, foreshadows what Plath accomplishes in the later poem. "Whiteness I Remember" is one of the poet's first attempts to evoke the persona's sheer fright; it is a kind of ur-text for "Ariel," where the persona no longer fears either riding or going past the physicality of riding into some new metaphysical region. In the 1962 poem, the rider is in control throughout the ride because the human being fuses with the animal, and begins to understand the source of its power. There is another similarity between these two poems, and that is the speed at which Plath wrote them; she comments in her journal that "Whiteness" is a "book poem," but that she should have taken longer to write it. In her words, "I write my good poems too fast ..."[31] By 1962, she had learned not to question the way poems came.

As has been mentioned, Sandra Gilbert links the voice of many of Plath's late poems with the women's voices in *The Waves* (in connection with Plath's imagery of ascent she describes Rhoda's "ascending" images, for example, and that character's notion of becoming "incandescent"), but she finds a more significant correspondence between Plath's work and the late poems of Yeats, particularly his "To Dorothy Wellesley." There he writes of Wellesley being no "common" woman but rather one awaiting visitation of the "Proud Furies each with her torch on high." Gilbert also cites Yeats' poem "He and She" as a possible source for Plath's repeated phrase "I am I," quoting the lines

She sings as the moon sings:
"I am I, am I;

The greater grows my light
The further that I fly."[32]

The finishing lines of that sexain—"All creation shivers / With that sweet cry"—are in the poet-persona's voice rather than the woman's. The woman artist, so intent on extending her reach as she confirms her self identity, prompts the imagery of both ascent and light, and suggests some possible reinscription on Plath's part in her poem "Fever 103 ."

A pair poem to the riddle of mystery that, in its fragmentation, "Ariel" has been, in the blunt "Fever 103 " Plath creates a gloss on the notion of "dirty girl," the sexual and sexualizing naughty woman who will not stay decorously in her place. But rather than accept the barbs of jealous (and still male-dominated) society, the persona here declares her purity. Whether she is strangled like Isadora Duncan (or like Plath in the scene Paul Alexander recounts on the Spanish hillside during her honeymoon),[33] or killed by radiation, or wrung completely out of life by the raging fevers her body was subject to during this torturous and torturing autumn, the persona is so intent on her purpose and her direction that she succeeds. Wryly, she asks her tormentor, "Does not my heat astound you. And my light. / All by myself I am a huge camellia / Glowing and coming and going, flush on flush."[34] Sexual innuendoes aside, the persona insists, All by myself. *All by myself.* This combustible being, willing herself to rise in order to escape the dross of life, the boorishness of some parts of British life in particular, the crass weight that some human beings pile on to the fragile spirit, finally sings out in the triumph she has been working toward: "I / Am a pure acetylene / Virgin" and; as such, unattended and surprisingly cavalier about who or what is no longer necessary in her existence, the woman persona overcomes all odds. Amazingly, she rises—and "To Paradise."

Suitably, as the last stage in her metaphoric lift-off, she sees her "selves dissolving" and names them "old whore petticoats." The social forms disregarded, the petticoats, slips, and modest undergarments trashed, the entirely pure woman, alone, recognizes that the way she has whored her path through life has been to accept roles she did not ever want, only because society coerced her. Knowing herself, whether she follows that injunction from Emerson or from Confucius, has enabled the pure persona to reach her vision of Paradise. In that place she is reunited with the personae of those sister poems, "Lady Lazarus" and "Ariel." And these women protagonists now have no use for anything that remains of their earlier lives.

As this persona says clearly, in a voice that now cannot be mistaken, "I am too pure for you or anyone." It is, truly, the Plath voice.

NOTES

1. Sylvia Plath, *Journals*, pp. 32, 54–5, 152, 164, 186, 196, 211–12, 217, 310, 316–17, 321.

2. Liz Yorke, *Impertinent Voices, Subversive Strategies in Contemporary Women's Poetry*, 1991, p. 66.

3. Ibid.

4. A. Alvarez, *The Savage God*, p. 8.

5. See photo in Wagner-Martin, *Sylvia Plath*, photo section after p. 104.

6. Alvarez, *Savage God*, p. 8.

7. Charles Doyle, letter to Wagner-Martin, October 20, 1983.

8. Peter Davison, *Half-Remembered*, pp. 170–1.

9. Information that follows is drawn from the file of Plath letters at *The Atlantic*.

10. Sylvia Plath to Peter Davison, November 16, 1962 (*Atlantic* file).

11. Peter Davison to Sylvia Plath, November 20, 1962 (*Atlantic* file).

12. Editorial comments, *Atlantic* file.

13. Lucas Myers, Appendix I, Anne Stevenson, *Bitter Fame*, p. 314.

14. Liz Yorke, *Impertinent Voices*, p. 81.

15. Sylvia Plath, correspondence with Theodore Roethke, University of Washington, Library Rare Books Collection.

16. Sylvia Plath, correspondence with John Lehmann, *London Magazine*, The Harry Ransom Humanities Research Center, University of Texas, Austin.

17. Sylvia Plath, correspondence with Brian Cox, *Critical Quarterly*, University of Kansas, Kenneth Spencer Research Library.

18. Sylvia Plath, "The Applicant," *Collected Poems*, p. 221–2. As a gloss on that locution, Ted sometimes addressed Olwyn in his letters as "upper class English" (The Lilly Library, Indiana University).

19. Sylvia Plath, "Purdah," *Collected Poems*, p. 242–11.

20. Sylvia Plath, "Burning the Letters," *Collected Poems*, pp. 204–5; see Van Dyne, *Revising Life*.

21. Sylvia Plath, "Lady Lazarus," *Collected Poems*, p. 244–7 and manuscript versions at Smith College Rare Books Collection. In W. B. Yeats' *A Vision*, he uses Lazarus as a kind of double; he also writes that "virginity renews itself like the moon." (*A Vision*, 1961, p. 24.)

22. Susan Van Dyne, *Revising Life*, pp. 55, 57.

23. Robert Graves, *White Goddess*, 1948, p. 12.

24. Ibid., p. xi.

25. Sylvia Plath, "Ariel," *Collected Poems*, pp. 239–110 and manuscript drafts at Smith College Rare Book Room.

26. Sylvia Plath, "Cut," *Collected Poems*, pp. 235–6.

27. Luke Myers, Appendix I, Anne Stevenson, *Bitter Fame*, pp. 320–1.

28. Mary Kurtzman, "Plath's 'Ariel' and Tarot," *Centennial Review*, Summer 1988, pp. 286–95. See also Timothy Materer, *Modernist Alchemy: Poetry and the Occult*, 1995.

29. Ibid., p. 294.

30. Sylvia Plath, "Whiteness I Remember," *Collected Poems*, pp. 102–3.

31. Sylvia Plath, *Journals*, p. 248; she realized, thinking back to the way she had written "Mad Girl's Love Song" [not included in *Collected Poems* but published in *Smith Review*, Spring 1953, and *Mademoiselle*, August 1953] and "Pursuit" [*Collected Poems*, pp.

22–31 that fluid composition might be a way into her truly creative imagination (*Journals*, p. 131).

32. Sandra M. Gilbert, "In Yeats' House," *Critical Essays on Sylvia Plath*, pp. 204–22.

33. See Paul Alexander, *Rough Magic*, p. 194.

34. Sylvia Plath, "Fever 103 ," *Collected Poems*, pp. 231–2.

SUSAN BASSNETT

Poetry and Survival

Aconfessional poet, an extremist poet, a post-romantic poet, a pre-feminist poet, a suicidal poet—all these terms have been used (and are still being used) in attempts to define and explain Sylvia Plath's writing. Some critics have seen her as schizoid, carrier of a death wish that they perceive in everything she ever wrote. Others have seen her as the victim of male brutality, destroyed by a faithless husband, having been undermined by an ambitious mother, over compensating for her own inadequate marriage. There will no doubt be other equally extravagant 'explanations' of her writing in the future, since, like the works of Keats, with whom she shares the dubious honour of having died young, her writing does not slot easily into categories and headings.

Working on Sylvia Plath's poetry and prose for many years, reading the secondary source material, talking to people who knew her and, by no means least, writing my own poetry, I find it impossible to accept any of these glib definitions, these reductions and over simplifications of a complex personality and multifaceted writer. Her writing simply does not fit into these easy categories. Some of her poems do indeed appear to be written in the confessional mode but not many of them; some of them might have been written by someone well acquainted with the feminism of the late sixties but some of them decidedly not; some of them show a fascination with death, others equally show delight in life and in living. Nor do the poems show a

From *Sylvia Plath: An Introduction to the Poetry*, second edition: pp. 117–138. © 2005 by Susan Bassnett.

steady progress towards suicide. Read with hindsight, it can be seen that she
went through several stages of anger, despair, grief, quietness and longing for
an end to pain but those stages are not part of a steady movement towards
dying. In a note in *Encounter*, Ted Hughes wrote:

> It is impossible that anyone could have been more in love with
> life, or more capable of happiness, than she was.[1]

Other friends and acquaintances have expressed similar astonishment that
she could have taken her own life. Alvarez asserts his belief that she had never
intended to die at all:

> I am convinced by what I know of the facts that this time she
> did not intend to die. Her suicide attempt ten years before had
> been in every sense, deadly serious. She had carefully disguised
> the theft of the sleeping pills, left a misleading note to cover her
> tracks, and hidden herself in the darkest, most unused corner of a
> cellar, rearranging behind her the old firelogs she had disturbed,
> burying herself away like a skeleton in the nethermost family
> closet. Then she had swallowed a bottle of fifty sleeping pills. She
> was found late and by accident, and survived only by a miracle.
> The flow of life in her was too strong even for the violence she
> had done it. This, anyway, is her description of the act in *The Bell
> Jar*; there is no reason to believe it false. So she had learned the
> hard way the odds against successful suicide; she had learned that
> despair must be counterpoised by an almost obsessional attention
> to detail and disguise.

By these lights she seemed, in her last attempt, to be taking care not to succeed.[2]
Alvarez' distinction between the first suicide attempt and the second, successful
one seems important to bear in mind. A failed suicide attempt at 21, when
under enormous academic pressures, is not, after all, so unusual and certainly
does not indicate a lasting desire to die. When she killed herself in 1963,
ten years later, Sylvia Plath had been living under other kinds of enormous,
untenable pressures and it seems far more likely that those pressures were the
immediate cause of the depression that led her to take her own life, rather than
any romantic notion of the inevitability of self-induced death. Those readers
who study her work as a series of prefigurations of suicide will find plenty of
references to death, many to suicidal death. But it seems to me to be as absurd
to read the poems as death wishes as it is to read the poems as evidence of
mental illness. That she could have been judged to be mentally ill and unstable

is a sign of the failure of many readers—especially male ones—to understand the dilemmas about which she tried to write. The great outpouring of women's writing over the past twenty years has shown more clearly than anything else could that the problems with which Sylvia Plath wrestled are problems that are by no means unique. What was unique was the way in which she gave voice to those contradictions and fragmented aspects of her personality at a time when other women were still keeping silent. The most straightforward way to reject the writing-as-prelude-to-dying reading is to go back to the poems and prose and look again at them. *The Bell Jar* is a novel about a suicide attempt that fails; but it is also a novel about a woman who learns how to live with herself and how to come to terms with the world, that world of destruction and horror that is described in the first sentences of the book:

> It was a queer, sultry summer, the summer they electrocuted the Rosenbergs, and I didn't know what I was doing in New York. I'm stupid about executions. The idea of being electrocuted makes me sick, and that's all there was to read about in the papers—goggle-eyed headlines staring up at me on every street corner and at the fusty, peanut-smelling mouth of every subway. It had nothing to do with me, but I couldn't help wondering what it would be like, being burned alive all along your nerves.[3]

When she leaves the hospital at the end of the novel, Esther has no answers—'all I could see were question marks'—but she has looked into herself and seen the problem areas that she had been trying so hard to conceal—her relationships with men, her difficulties with her mother, the split between her sexual and intellectual lives, her obsession with marriage and social status. She has also learned enough to realise that she cannot erase the past, that the images of pain will never leave her because they are part of her history:

> I remembered everything.

> I remembered the cadavers and Doreen and the story of the fig-tree and Marco's diamond and the sailor on the Common and Doctor Gordon's wall-eyed nurse and the broken thermometers and the negro with his two kinds of beans and the twenty pounds I gained on insulin and the rook that bulged between sky and sea like a grey skull.

> Maybe forgetfulness, like a kind snow, should numb and cover them. But they were part of me. They were my landscape.[4]

Before *The Bell Jar*, she had written another breakdown story, 'Johnny Panic and the Bible of Dreams', completed in December 1958 but not published until ten years later. In his preface to her collected stories, Ted Hughes discusses her fears about putting her life into her writing and suggests that the Johnny Panic story had tapped 'the molten source of her poetry as none of her poems up to then had'. He sees this story as a turning point and suggests that the writing of stories, despite her intensely hard work and desire to succeed with them, was not her strongest point. The reason he gives is interesting:

> If a story is inevitably a fantasy, and if every fantasy leads eventually to the heart of the labyrinth, her problem was that she could not linger among the outer twists and turns and complications, where the world is still solidly itself and comparatively safe, however thrilling. She had an instant special pass to the centre and she had no choice but to use it. She could no more make up an objective ingenious narrative than she could connect up all the letters in her handwriting, where nearly every symbol seems to sit perched over a gulf. This lighting pass through all the walls of the maze was her real genius. Instant confrontation with the most central, unacceptable things.[5]

If 'Johnny Panic' marks a shift in her prose narrative style, it may be, as Hughes suggests, because it tackles the fearsome issues of madness, suicide and an uncaring world. At the end, when the I-speaker becomes a Christ figure ('the crown of wire' on her head, 'the wafer of forgetfulness' on her tongue) she experiences the horror of electric-shock treatment, the closest she can come to sharing the fate of the Rosenbergs. As someone who had undergone such treatment during her breakdown, Sylvia Plath could write about it 'from the centre', from having been there. It is a story full of bitterness and anguish but the final note is not one of despair and resignation, it is one of anger and anger, despite the references in the words to dying, fuels survival and desire for revenge:

> At the moment when I think I am most lost the face of Johnny Panic appears in a nimbus of arc lights on the ceiling overhead. I am shaken like a leaf in the teeth of glory. His beard is lightning. Lightning is in his eye. His Word changes and illumines the universe.

> The air crackles with his blue-tongued lightning-haloed angels. His love is the twenty-story leap, the rope at the throat, the knife at the heart.

> He forgets not his own.

Sylvia Plath writes her breakdown story and suicide attempt in prose; in poetry she writes other themes. A set of poems written in February–March 1961 arise out of her period in hospital, with her miscarriage and appendicitis. Again, though, this is not an exclusively Plathian preoccupation but one which recurs in the poetry of many twentieth-century women writers, from the Russians to the Americans. Hospital poetry seems to belong more to women writers than to men, partly because the experience of childbirth is often in a hospital context but partly also because the doctor–patient relationship is a very powerful one in female mythology. At its most disarming, it is the basis of the saccharine love stories of romantic fiction between doctors and nurses or doctors and patients; at its most terrifying it is the area in which male power over women's bodies can be most clearly demonstrated. The woman in the hands of the male surgeon experiences a double powerlessness, that of the sexual as well as the medical, and it is probably for this reason that hospital or medical poetry should keep recurring in the work of so many women writers.

'Tulips', dated 18 March 1962, is a poem built on the experience of being a patient in hospital where time seems to have another meaning and extremes of feeling are dulled by the daily routine. The poem is made up of nine seven-line stanzas, each one a separate unit, without the device of the run-on line between verses that Plath so often uses. The end-stopped verses reinforce the feeling of the packaging of time into distinct units of the hospital day. But within that packaging, the mind of the I-speaker ranges out beyond the limits imposed on her. The first line contrasts the stillness within with the desire for movement: 'The tulips are excitable, it is winter here'. The I-speaker has given herself up to the doctors, she has handed herself over:

> I am nobody; I have nothing to do with explosions.
> I have given my name and my day-clothes to the nurses
> And my history to the anaesthetist and my body to the surgeons.

This helplessness is described further in the second verse where the I-speaker has virtually been dismembered by the doctors and nurses—'They have propped my head between the pillow and the sheet-cuff'. In the third verse her body is compared to a pebble and the medical staff are like water running over it. She has lost all feeling and become a stone. What is more she does not need 'baggage'—the literal baggage of her overnight case and the emotional baggage of the photo of her husband and child.

The fourth verse moves onto another dimension. The I-speaker talks about herself as 'a thirty-year-old cargoboat' who has 'let things slip'. As the

rest of her life has slipped out of view, the metaphor of drowning is used—
'the water went over my head'. Purified by this absence she is 'a nun now'. In
the fifth verse, dazed with the medically induced peacefulness, she describes
freedom as a kind of total stasis:

> I didn't want any flowers, I only wanted
> To lie with my hands turned up and be utterly empty.

In this world of whiteness and motionlessness, the tulips are an intrusion,
symbols of the life of activity outside—'the tulips are too red in the first place,
they hurt me', 'the vivid tulips eat my oxygen', 'the tulips should be behind
bars like dangerous animals'. The redness of the tulips gradually forces the I-
speaker to leave her death-in-life state. They breathe at her 'through the gift
paper', they turn their faces to her and in the last two verses, as the pace of the
language speeds up and the number of images increases, the tulips become a
force for life, bearers of noise in verse 8 and warmth in verse 9, bringing the
I-speaker back up out of her drowning state into an awareness of life:

> And I am aware of my heart: it opens and closes
> Its bowl of red blooms out of sheer love of me.
> The water I taste is warm and salt, like the sea,
> And comes from a country far away as health.

'Fever 103 ' is a very different medical poem. Dated 20 October 1962, it
derives from a period of depression and high fever that is documented in
the letters home (it was on 21 October that Sylvia Plath wrote angrily to her
mother about the person out of Belsen needing to know that others have been
there and survived). 'Fever 103 ' is a poem about a descent into hell and is
full of images of hell. The first line asks the crucial question about eligibility
to enter: 'Pure? What does it mean?' and the reader is drawn in, past three-
headed Cerberus 'who wheezes at the gate', into the realm of sin, 'the tinder
cries' and 'the indelible smell / of a snuffed candle'. The next line after this
image, with the keyword 'snuffed', opens with the word 'love' repeated twice,
another example of Sylvia Plath's ability to set words alongside each other in
such a way that their fields of connotation open out in all kinds of directions.
The yellow sullen smokes that 'roll / from me' are presented as signs of the
ever-presence of hell and the reader proceeds through a range of images
of suffering ever deeper into the depths—Isadora Duncan, strangled with
her own scarf in the wheel of a car, after a lifetime of emotional desolation
following the deaths of her two children, 'the aged and the meek' choked to
death, the image of the dying baby contrasted with the 'ghastly orchid', the

leopard turned white and killed in just an hour by radiation poisoning and, finally, the ultimate horrors of both the speakers inner life and the world: unfaithfulness in marriage and the atomic bomb

> Greasing the bodies of adulterers
> Like Hiroshima ash and eating in.

The tenth verse opens with a direct address to 'darling'. For three days and nights (the time Dante spent in Hell) she has been unable to eat or drink, in great pain—'your body / hurts me as the world hurts God' and undergoes a series of metaphorical transformations—'I am a lantern.... All by myself I am a huge camellia....'

> The beads of hot metal fly, and I, love, I
> Am a pure acetylene
> Virgin
> Attended by roses

The bitter, jokey tone of the poem shifts in the last few lines to an enigmatic conclusion. The acetylene virgin ascends to heaven, out of the fires of hell, but alone without you or him, or any man. This last sentence is without a main verb; it is a deliberate syntactical shift that stresses linguistically the breaking down of the old self, glibly able to handle words with fluency and flair:

> Not you, nor him
> Not him, nor him
> (My selves dissolving, old whore petticoats)—
> To Paradise.

In a note for her BBC reading of this poem, Sylvia Plath said:

> it is about two kinds of fire—the fires of hell, which merely agonize, and the fires of heaven, which purify. During the poem, the first sort of fire suffers itself into the second.

Out of the hell of fever and pain, the woman rises up to paradise. She is a survivor. Between these two poems, Sylvia Plath wrote another kind of hospital poem, *Three Women*, a piece for BBC radio, broadcast on 19 August 1962. As the use of personae in her poetry shows, she had a strong sense of the dramatic and *Three Women* is a verse play for three female voices.[6] The First Voice is that of a woman who gives birth to a healthy male child:

Who is he, this blue furious boy,
Shiny and strange, as if he had hurtled from a star?
What did my fingers do before they held him?

The Second Voice is that of a woman who suffers a miscarriage and loses the child:

It is usual, they say, for such a thing to happen.
It is usual in my life, and the lives of others.
I am one in five, something like that. I am not hopeless.
I am beautiful as a statistic. Here is my lipstick.

The Third Voice is that of a young student who gives birth to a girl that is given away for adoption immediately:

The books I carry wedge into my side.
I had an old wound once, but it is healing.
I had a dream of an island, red with cries.
It was a dream, and did not mean a thing.

On the surface, the three women represent three different moments of the childbearing process—the satisfied first-time mother, the sorrowful woman who loses her baby, the immature woman who gives birth and then renounces the child and returns to her previous life. But what makes *Three Women* rise above the level of cliché is the constant variation of viewpoint throughout the piece. Each woman tells her story, giving her point of view, and there is no definitive ideological narrative voice that locates the women in any moral hierarchy: the First Voice begins to speak with authority and patience 'I am slow as the world ... I am calm. I am calm' but recognises that this is a calm that presages something very different. 'It is the calm before something awful'. Then comes the moment of the child's birth and all the calmness and stoicism vanish in the pain of the happening:

I am the centre of an atrocity.
What pains, what sorrows must I be mothering?

In the next verse, she links that pain with the pain of living in the world:

Can such innocence kill and kill? It milks my life.
The trees wither in the street. The rain is corrosive.

Childbirth has a political dimension; producing another human being is to expose that child to the horrors that wait for it in the world, to experience for a few moments the primal pain in which all is terror and chaos:

> My eyes are squeezed by this blackness.
> I see nothing.

But after the birth, that feeling of terror changes. The child born is one of many, brother to the rest of mankind:

> I see them showering like stars on to the world—
> On India, Africa, America, these miraculous ones,
> These pure, small images. They smell of milk.
> Their footsoles are untouched. They are walkers of air.

Faced with this absolute purity that she has to defend, the First Voice meditates on her role as protector: 'How long can I be wall, keeping the wind off?' Sooner or later, she fears, the darkness of life and the pain in the world will reach out and engulf him. But her monologue ends on a note of hopefulness; she has painted his nursery, made his small world as beautiful as possible and wishes for him a life of ordinariness:

> I do not will him to be exceptional ...
> I will him to be common,
> To love me as I love him,
> And to marry what he wants and where he will.

The Third Voice has a very different style and language. From her first speech she uses short, assertive statements, repeating the cry: 'I wasn't ready'. Later, in her final speech, she repeats another sentence, only this time it is a question: 'What is it that I miss?' Between that first cry of unwillingness and unreadiness and that final question, the Third Voice goes through a series of stages that leave her increasingly troubled and ill at ease. The birth is associated with horror—'It is a place of shrieks' and the cries of the child when born are like 'hooks that catch and grate like cats'. The cries pierce the mother's side 'like arrows'—and when she leaves her in the hospital she has to undo her fingers 'like bandages'. Leaving the child behind, walking out into the world again with 'the clothes of a fat woman I do not know', she is suddenly afraid:

> I am so vulnerable suddenly,
> I am a wound walking out of hospital.
> I am a wound that they are letting go.
> I leave my health behind. I leave someone would adhere to me ...

Once outside again, back at college, the wound starts to heal and she is left with the memory of something that has been lost, something that troubles her despite her insistence that 'it is so beautiful to have no attachments'. For the Third Voice, the world is outside the hospital; leaving the child, she leaves behind some part of herself in a place that has been unreal to her. This is in direct contrast with the First Voice for whom the hospital becomes the centre of the world and the source of all creation. The Third Voice is doomed to live with another kind of pain, the pain of loss. Both women learn about suffering through the birth of their children; once the actual pain of the birth itself is over, they are left to deal with the pain of living as mothers, one with the daily fears of what will happen to her child in the world as he grows, the other with the pain of having been briefly a mother but having renounced that role in order to grow in other ways. For neither woman does the future look whole and happy and the underlying significance of this emphasis on sorrow and motherhood is that woman's lot is seen to be a hard one. Men do not feature in their lives as sharers or as easers of their pain.

It is in the speeches of the Second Voice that men are mentioned most frequently. The Second Voice loses her child before birth, hence she does not pass through the gates of childbirth that are marked as an exclusively female rite of passage. Having lost her child, she has lost that special experience—'I see myself as a shadow, neither man nor woman'. In her first speech the Second Voice describes the first tell-tale sign of the miscarriage but goes on immediately in the next line to talk about the world she now cannot leave, the world of men. Significantly, it is a world of work, an office:

> When I first saw it, the small red seep, I did not believe it. I watched the men walk about me in the office. They were so flat!

That image of flatness, of two-dimensionality which she sees as typical of men, is an image that recurs throughout her monologue. In the next line of the first speech, she associates that flatness with inadequacy: 'There was something about them like cardboard and now I had caught it'. The Second Voice tells how she leaves the hospital looking as she did when she came in—'the mirror gives back a woman without deformity / the nurses give back my clothes, and an identity'. She puts on her make-up, 'the red mouth I put on with my identity,' and goes out. Her husband, she says, will understand

and will love her as if she had lost 'an eye, a leg, a tongue'. But behind this neat appearance there has been a massive change in her reality. 'How shyly she superimposes her neat self / on the inferno of African oranges, the heel-hung pigs'. She has experienced a kind of suffering that marks her within. At home, with her husband, quietly mending a silk slip she reflects that 'I think I have been healing'. She holds the pain inside, waiting.

The Second Voice concludes the piece, with the image of herself and her husband sitting quietly together in silence, she with her outward calm and control and inner turmoil, he oblivious, turning the pages of a book. The husband is seen as distant and although she talks about his love and understanding, she also says that he cannot share in what she is feeling. 'I am a wife', she says almost at the end of her monologue and the placing of that four-word statement stresses its ambiguity. What does it mean to be a wife, she seems to be asking, if she is denied a child. The next words return to her pain—'The city waits and aches'. In the previous verse, the subject of the verbs *ache* and *wait* had been *I*. Now it is the city, the whole world, reality itself that shares her pain with her. Reality, that is, as a woman experiences it not as a man does.

The verse play ends with an image of hope: 'The little grasses / crack through stone, and they are green with life'. It is an image of beginning, of promise; the city of stone comes alive again and the woman too, in time, will heal and perhaps will succeed in giving birth. The little grasses of the last lines recall the image of the opening speech by the First Voice, when she describes herself as attended by 'leaves and petals'. The woman denied the fulfillment of childbirth waits and hopes for some future moment of fruition.

Unquestionably this is a work that glorifies motherhood as a uniquely female experience. The woman who renounces her child cannot, nevertheless, renounce the experience she has undergone, which has marked her forever in a very special way, just as the woman who loses the child mourns the loss of participating in that specialness. But the First Voice, the one who gives birth to a wanted child, is not held up to the others as an ideal. Her happiness is tempered by anxiety and the source of that worry is living in the world that creeps in through all kinds of channels. Throughout the poem there are references to the vastness of the world, in comparison to the boundaries within which the women move; Africa reaches out even through the fruit in the shop windows, the shadow of war and the nuclear bomb, of the thalidomide children, touches the new mother and her child. The Second Voice makes the gap between the world of women and the world of men explicit throughout her monologue:

> And then there were other faces. The faces of nations,
> Governments, parliaments, societies,
> The faceless faces of important men.

It is these men I mind:
They are so jealous of anything that is not flat! They are jealous gods
That would have the whole world flat because they are.

Eileen Aird says of Sylvia Plath that her originality

> lies in her insistence that what has been traditionally regarded as
> a woman's world of domesticity, childbearing, marriage, is also
> a world which contains the tragic. She draws from this female
> world themes which are visionary and supernatural; although it
> is a world which is eventually destroyed by death, her work is far
> from depressing because of the artistry with which she delineates
> her vision.[7]

This assessment is a very fair one. Again and again the bleakness of the content material of one of Sylvia Plath's poems is offset by the structure and the language which foregrounds the motif of survival. *Three Women* ends with the word 'life' and she arranged the poems for her *Ariel* collection in a deliberate sequence that began with the word 'Love' in 'Morning Song' ('Love set you going like a fat gold watch') and ended with the word 'spring' in 'Wintering' ('The bees are flying. They taste the spring'). Far from foregrounding death there is a conscious effort to foreground life, even when the poems speak of the greatest pain, and it is this characteristic of her poetry which marks Sylvia Plath as a survivor poet, a writer with a message of hope.

Shortly after *Three Women*, Sylvia Plath wrote *Crossing the Water*, a twelve-line poem divided into four stanzas of three lines each, which is, as the title indicates, a poem about transition. There is no I-speaker, instead there are references to us and the final verse is addressed to a you that may be an individual or may be the collective reader. The image of flatness, developed in *Three Women*, is strongly present here and the word 'black' or 'blackness' is repeated several times. The opening lines establish the tone of the poem:

> Black lake, black boat, two black, cut-paper people.
> Where do the black trees go that drink here?

The trees, humanised in this way, seem more alive than the people who are reduced to silhouettes, two-dimensional figures of blackness. In the second verse there is a shift of perspective; from the wide-angle image of the lake and the vastness of trees stretching out to 'cover Canada' down to the people in the boat looking at the water lilies whose leaves 'do not wish us to hurry'. But these leaves too are flat and they are also 'full of dark advice'. The people in the boat, like the flowers, trees, even the fishes in the lake are filled with darkness—'the spirit of blackness is in us'.

The ninth line of the poem introduces a whole new set of images: a snag in the water 'is lifting a valedictory, pale hand'. This is an image from Arthurian romance recalling the passing of Arthur, the moment when the white hand emerged from the dark lake to take back Arthur's sword, symbol of the now-lost unity of the Round Table. As in 'Lyonnesse', there is a deliberate reference to the end of idealism through the image of the end of Arthur's dream of an ideal society. The last verse of the poem goes beyond the lake, beyond the immediacy of the blackness, into a quasi-dreamlike state:

> Stars open among the lilies.
> Are you not blinded by such expressionless sirens?
> This is the silence of astounded souls.

Who is the you-figure, blinded by the silence of the lilies? Floating on the water's surface, the lilies seem to be inviting the people in the boat to join them and sink down beneath the black water. In Arthurian legend, the arm rising from the lake is evidence of the supernatural, of the fairy kingdom that finally takes Arthur back to live forever waiting for the moment to return. In this poem, the dark water remains an enigma; the stars among the lilies may be beckoning to death or to a state beyond death, a mystical point of stasis where no pain exists and all is silence.

Despite stylistic differences, there are close links with 'Winter Landscape with Rooks' from 1956. There is the same dark water, the same use of contrast with a flash of white (a swan in the first poem, lilies in the second), the same use of landscape to create a physical image of a state of mind. The close links between the imagery of these two poems is further evidence of the validity of Ted Hughes' analysis of her work as a unified whole, through which patterns of imagery, themes and symbols recur consistently. In the last year of her life, Sylvia Plath wrote several poems that have been described as mystical though whether this is evidence of a religious conversion, as some critics have suggested, is a debatable point. What seems most likely is that emotional crises through which she was passing caused her to reconsider various strands of her own existence. Earlier, in December 1958, she had noted in her journal that

> Writing is a religious act: it is an ordering, a reforming, a relearning and reloving of people and the world as they are and as they might be. A shaping which does not pass away like a day of typing or a day of teaching. The writing lasts: it goes about on its own in the world.

'Years' and 'Mary's Song', for example, both written in November 1962, are poems with a strong sense of mysticism as is an appropriately titled poem dated 1 February 1963, 'Mystic'. As with many of the poems from the last year, questions are asked and answers are not given. In 'Mystic', the question that is repeated over and over is 'what is the remedy?' Once one has seen God, the I-speaker asks, what is the remedy? How can the experience be put out of mind when memory brings it back continuously? The god, however, does not seem to be the Christian God, despite the many overtly Christian references to cathedrals, the communion tablet, even to Christ himself. Rather God is symbolic of something or someone that the I-speaker has encountered and loved and cannot forget. 'Meaning leaks from molecules', 'the air is a mill of hooks', the speaker of the poem cannot escape from the memories of the vision of perfection that she once believed was possible. Yet even here, despite the sadness, the poem ends on a hopeful note:

> The chimneys of the city breathe, the window sweats,
> The children leap in their cots.
> The sun blooms, it is a geranium.
> The heart has not stopped.

The suffering heart can still experience the daily life of a city, still reach out towards the energy of children and the colour of flowers. Whatever remedy is sought, the poem seems to answer itself. The remedy is living, it is continuing to experience those parts of life that are beautiful, despite the encounter in the past with God.

Besides the mystical poems, the poems in which the struggle for happiness competes with the forces that bring despair and hopelessness, there are also poems that show a strong awareness of the historical moment through which Sylvia Plath was passing. Just as she seems to have thought deeply about the significance of religious experience once the greatest pain was over, so she also seems to use images from the world to describe her own inner feelings. In an interview with Peter Orr she describes her new interest in studying history:

> I am very interested in Napoleon at the present: I'm very interested in battles, in wars, in Gallipoli, the First World War and so on, and I think that as I age I am becoming more and more historical. I certainly wasn't at all in my early twenties.[8]

Napoleon, 'The hump of Elba on your short back', provides one of the central images for 'The Swarm,' one of the five bee poems written in October 1962.

He fuses with the beekeeper, the 'man with gray hands', who comes to the village to catch and hive the swarm which is taken from the freedom of the high trees to its 'new mausoleum'. Susan Van Dyne has studied the bee poems in manuscript form, looking at the changes in the drafts, and she suggests a reading for 'The Swarm' that integrates the motif of the retreat from Moscow and Napoleons plundering of Europe, the details of the capture of the bees and the reference in the third line of the poem to jealousy—'Jealousy can open the blood'. In Van Dyne's reading, Sylvia Plath is linking her Napoleon with Ted Hughes, the 'little man', as she described him after the break-up, and there is a level of autobiographical statement running through the poem which utilises the historical references metaphorically. History, and everyday experiences became equally material sources for poetic expression. Susan Van Dyne states her view that the entire bee sequence of poems represents 'Plath's struggle to bring forth an articulate, intelligible self from the death-box of the hive'.[9] Her essay is very useful in shedding light on the way in which Sylvia Plath created her poems, carefully selecting words and phrases, listing her own alternatives. She shows, for example, the way in which the final, assertive line of 'Wintering' went through a series of stages of doubt, when the poet seemed unable to move beyond questioning. As it stands, that final verse reads as follows:

> Will the hive survive, will the gladiolas
> Succeed in banking their fires
> To enter another year?
> What will they taste of, the Christmas roses? The bees are flying.
> They taste the spring.

The questions remain unanswered in that last line but the sureness of these two short sentences gives the reader an impression of hope. That hope was certainly not so clear in the versions listed by Van Dyne:

> Snow water? Corpses? (Thin, sweet Spring.)
> (A sweet Spring?) Spring?
> (Impossible spring?)
> (What sort of spring?)
> (O God, let them taste of spring.)

The form of the question, the use of adjectives to qualify the noun 'spring', the wish form of the last alternative are all syntactically weaker than the final version with its short, tight statements. The bee poems bring together a complex web of narrative threads, from Sylvia Plath's autobiography and her other writing, but the clearest single line through them all is the exploration of the meaning of power and freedom. In the first of the sequence, 'The Bee Meeting', the I-speaker is met by a group of villagers who dress her in a beekeeper's veil. She appears to be their victim, unable to escape from the task they have imposed on her—'I could not run without having to run for ever'—and as the villagers hunt the old queen bee, so the I-speaker and the queen fuse together and the last verse of the poem might equally be spoken by either woman or bee.

In the second poem, 'The Arrival of the Bee Box', the I-speaker listens to the buzzing of the furious bees within the box and wonders what would happen if she were to let them loose. By the last lines of the poem she has decided. The bees will not attack her since she is 'no source of honey' so she will take on herself the power to release them:

> Tomorrow I will be sweet God, I will set them free.
> The box is only temporary.

In 'Stings', the third poem, the I-speaker states explicitly 'I am in control'. She and the old queen bee share past imprisonment; the one is old, 'her wings torn shawls, her long body / robbed of its plush', and the other has suffered from servitude: 'for years I have eaten dust / and dried plates with my dense hair'. Both woman and queen bee 'stand in a column / of winged, unmiraculous women'. But in the last verse of the poem, the queen comes out to claim her own like an avenging angel:

> Now she is flying
> More terrible than she ever was, red
> Scar in the sky, red comet
> Over the engine that killed her—
> The mausoleum, the wax house.

The battle continues in 'The Swarm' when the bees are captured and taken prisoner by the man with grey hands. For a time, it seems, the male power of the beekeeper has triumphed. But in the last poem, 'Wintering', that triumph is turned around, as female bees and the woman become the survivors of the winter cold and the bringers of new life:

> The bees are all women,
> Maids and the long royal lady.
> They have got rid of the men,
> The blunt clumsy stumblers, the boors.

Winter is for women—
The woman still at her knitting,
At the cradle of Spanish walnut,
Her body a bulb in the cold and too dumb to think.

'This is the time of hanging on for the bees' says the I-speaker in the fifth
verse of the poem and equally it is a time of hanging on for the woman with
her child and her knitting. Once through the winter they will share in the
coming of spring and new life. It is ironic that, despite this promise, Sylvia
Plath was not to see the next spring after all.

The battles of which she spoke in her interview rage through many
of the poems in the autumn–winter of 1962–63. 'The disks of the brain
revolve, like the muzzles of canon' she says in 'The Courage of Shutting-
Up'; in 'Daddy', the Polish town is 'scraped flat by the roller / of wars, wars,
wars'; the sleeping capsule in 'The jailer' is a 'red and blue zeppelin' that
drops the speaker 'from a terrible altitude'. Most potent of all, the image of
the concentration camps and the destruction of the Jews runs through many
poems, such as 'Daddy', 'Lady Lazarus' and 'Getting There'. This image is
linked to another central twentieth-century image of total devastation, that
of the nuclear holocaust. In 'Mary's Song', dated 19 November 1962, these
images combine with other motifs—the fears of the mother for her child, the
necessity of sacrifice, regeneration after suffering.

'Mary's Song' is a poem made up of seven three-line stanzas, linked by
the imagery which proceeds through a series of thought-leaps. The opening
line presents an image from everyday life: 'The Sunday lamb cracks in its fat'
but then immediately that sentence acquires symbolic overtones in the next
two lines: 'the fat / sacrifices its opacity...'. The lamb that is being cooked is
equated to the lamb that was Mary's child, the Christ child. The image of the
fat losing its texture and thickness and becoming translucent is taken up in
the second verse, where the golden colour of the fat is a 'holy gold'. The fire
that melts the fat, making it edible ('precious') also burns people—heretics
and Jews—and the fourth verse stresses the permanence of those historical
persecutions as symbols of man's inhumanity:

Their thick palls float
Over the cicatrix of Poland, burnt-out
Germany.
They do not die.

The past with all its horrors remains part of the present, the images of death
cannot be set aside. In the fifth verse the I-speaker appears for the first time

with an image of suffering—'gray birds obsess my heart'. The grey birds
that bear the message of death from the past move us on to the possibility
of future destruction in the next line—'Mouth-ash, ash of eye'—where the
word 'ash' carries connotations of nuclear death. The ashes of burned bodies,
the glowing ovens become the whole universe in the sixth verse and in the
seventh that universe turns into a psychic landscape:

> It is a heart,
> This holocaust I walk in,
> O golden child the world will kill and eat.

'Mary's Song' recalls the fears of the First Voice in *Three Women*, uncertain
how long she will be able to protect her child from the world's evils. Mary's
case should be different, since the death of her child is a symbol of human
regeneration, but the emphasis in this poem is on the power of history and
the horrors of the past to reach out and touch the present. Mary must accept
the inevitability of suffering.

Anne Cluysenaar discusses Sylvia Plath in terms of someone who is
a 'survivor' in the clinical sense of the term. She describes her as 'a typical
"survivor" in the psychiatric sense', arguing that 'as an element in this
complex of emotions, imagining death has a life-enhancing function'. The
fictionalising of death becomes an assertion of power over death. Anne
Cluysenaar sees the central message of her writing as being:

> The retention of discrimination and the will to speak, the will to
> communicate. Her determination not to accept relief from any
> ready-made dogma is admirable.[10]

The poems are a testament to struggle and the *Ariel* poems particularly
show a determination to survive that overrides all the imagery of death and
horror. In the event, *Ariel* was never published in the order that she had
wanted it and the collection was ultimately overshadowed by *Winter Trees*,
which contained the last poems she ever wrote, together with *Three Women*.
The disparity between her structure for *Ariel* and the volume that finally
appeared is most obvious in the different emphasis on hope and survival. Her
structure would have led the reader towards faith in the continuation of the
struggle. As we have received the poems since her death, the emphasis has
shifted onto a reading of the poems which perceives them as prefigurations
of her end. She has become a writer who wrote her own epitaph during her
lifetime.

Margaret Uroff sums up the achievement of *Ariel* in fitting terms:

Ariel must be read as several chapters of a creative autobiography, written by a woman whose purpose in the last years of her life was to come to terms with the various female roles and identities into which she had been split. It is full of wrong leads, frustrated efforts, obscure and private battles that attest to the difficulties she had to face and to the energy she expended on them. Her final poetic accomplishment was not to transcend these hardships, but to face them directly and to leave a record of that confrontation. In the image of the rising lioness/Virgin/red comet, she identified a female figure violent enough to triumph in a world that Plath imagined would reduce the woman to a jade statue—but a female also with creatively violent powers of her own.[11]

The poems read as epitaphs belong to the last days in February 1963. On 1 February she wrote 'Mystic', 'Kindness' and 'Words'. Three days later, on 4 February, came 'Contusion' and on 5 February the two last poems, 'Balloons' and 'Edge'. Two of these, 'Contusion' and 'Edge', are poems in which any semblance of struggle has been abandoned; they are perhaps the saddest of all her works. The four sparse verses of 'Contusion' offer, through the means of a distant third-person narrator, a vision of stasis and silence. The first two lines contrast the dull purple of the bruise with the whiteness of the deathly body:

> Colour floods to the spot, dull purple.
> The rest of the body is all washed out

The pearly whiteness of the body of the third line carries connotations of death; years before, Plath had described her father as Neptune with his conch shell ('On the Decline of Oracles'), which in turn was an image derived from T. S. Eliot and Shakespeare's *The Tempest* ('Full fathom five thy father lies'). Whose death, whose body are never defined in this poem but the very absence of clarification emphasises the sense of despair. The third-person narrator makes statements in a cold, detached manner that belies the content material. The last three lines are three simple sentences, each containing an image of ending:

> The heart shuts,
> The sea slides back,
> The mirrors are sheeted.

'Edge' continues from that image of the covered mirror. Narrated in the third person it describes someone only as 'the woman', whose dead body 'wears the smile of accomplishment'. Robed in a Greek toga, her dead children 'coiled' beside her, 'folded ... back into her body as petals/of a rose close', she is observed from a distance. The last two verses introduce the image of the greatest watcher of all, the moon:

> She is used to this sort of thing.
> Her blacks crackle and drag.

The dead woman is a kind of statue, a monument to herself, watched by the old moon in her hag phase. The woman and her children 'have come so far, it is over' and the poem seems to suggest that this decision of ending should be accepted for what it is—a statement of finality. The moon, ancient goddess and muse, need not grieve, for this is neither unexpected nor unusual. She has seen it many times before when a woman gives up the struggle to juggle the many facets of her life. And yet the woman who wrote 'Edge' also wrote the beautiful 'Balloons' on the same day, in which she compares the 'globes of thin air, red, green' to 'wishes or free / peacocks blessing / old ground with a feather'. Two such different poems, one rejoicing in the mobility of life and the other praising the dignity and silence of death.

Reading Sylvia Plath's Journal, the swings of mood show up very clearly. She records moments of ecstasy, enthusiasm, anger, pain and black depression. An entry for 13 October 1959 details one such depression:

> Very depressed today. Unable to write a thing. Menacing gods. I feel outcast on a cold star, unable to feel anything but an awful helpless numbness. I look down into the warm, earthy world. Into a nest of lovers' beds, baby cribs, meal tables, all the solid commerce of life in this earth, and feel apart, enclosed in a wall of glass.

Perhaps, on that morning of 11 February 1963, the glass walls descended round her once again and she was too exhausted to fight back. The last lines of 'Ariel' say all that needs to be said:

> And now I
> Foam to wheat, a glitter of seas.
> The child's cry
>
> Melts in the wall.
> And I
> Am the arrow,

The dew that flies
Suicidal, at one with the drive
Into the red

Eye, the cauldron of morning.

Notes

1. Ted Hughes, note in *Encounter*, October 1963.

2. A. Alvarez, *The Savage God* (London, Weidenfeld & Nicholson, 1971), pp. 28–29.

3. *The Bell Jar*, p. 1, see Chapter 1, Note 11.

4. Ibid., p. 250, see Chapter 1, Note 11.

5. Preface to *Johnny Panic and the Bible of Dreams* (London, Faber & Faber, 1977), p. 15.

6. Sylvia Plath is included in the section entitled 'Where Are the Women Playwrights?' in *Women in American Theatre*, eds Helen Krich Chinoy and Linda Walsh Jenkins (New York, Crown Publishers, 1981).

7. Eileen Aird, *Sylvia Plath* (London, Oliver & Boyd, 1973), p. 14.

8. 'Sylvia Plath' in *The Poet Speaks*, ed. Peter Orr (London, Routledge & Kegan Paul, 1966), pp. 167–172.

9. Susan R. Van Dyne, 'More Terrible Than She Ever Was', 'The Manuscripts of Sylvia Plath's Bee Poems' in *Critical Essays on Sylvia Plath*, ed. Linda W. Wagner (Boston, G. K. Hall and Co., 1984), pp. 154–170.

10. Anne Cluysenaar, 'Post-culture: Pre-Culture?' in *British Poetry since 1960: A Critical Survey*, eds Michael Schmidt and Grevel Lindop (Oxford, Carcanet Press, 1972), pp. 219–221.

11. Margaret Dickie Uroff, *Sylvia Plath and Ted Hughes* (Urbana, Chicago, London, University of Illinois Press, 1979), p. 169.

Chronology

1932	Sylvia Plath is born on October 27 in Boston, the first child of Aurelia Schober and Otto Emil Plath, a professor of biology.
1935	Brother Warren is born in April.
1937	Family moves to the seaside town of Winthrop, Massachusetts, close to Sylvia's maternal grandparents.
1940–1941	Father dies in 1940. Grandparents move in with the Plaths. Mother begins teaching.
1942	Family moves to Wellesley, Massachusetts.
1942–1950	Plath writes her first poems and short stories while attending public schools. In 1950 she wins a scholarship and begins attending Smith College.
1953	Goes to New York during the summer to work as a guest editor for *Mademoiselle* magazine. Returns home exhausted; becomes depressed and attempts suicide; is hospitalized in Belmont, Massachusetts.
1954	Returns to Smith. Is awarded scholarship to Harvard summer school.
1955	Graduates college *summa cum laude*. Travels to England to study at Cambridge University on a Fulbright fellowship.
1956	Meets Ted Hughes in February and marries him on June 16. After their honeymoon, Plath returns to Cambridge for second year.

1957	After receiving her degree, Plath and Hughes return to the United States where Plath becomes a visiting professor at Smith College.
1958–1959	Plath leaves her position at Smith and holds various part-time jobs. She audits Robert Lowell's poetry classes at Boston University and writes. Plath and Hughes travel across the country, spending some time at the Yaddo writers' colony. Eventually the couple moves to London.
1960	First child, Frieda Rebecca, born on April 1. *The Colossus and Other Poems* is published.
1961	Moves with family to house in Devon.
1962	Second child, Nicholas Farrar, is born on January 17. Separates from husband later in the year. In December, Plath moves to London with her children.
1963	Publishes her novel, *The Bell Jar*, using the pseudonym Victoria Lucas. On February 11, Sylvia Plath commits suicide.
1965	Hughes publishes his version of Plath's collection of poems, *Ariel*.
1971	Hughes publishes *Crossing the Water* and *Winter Trees*, collections of Plath's poetry.
1977	Hughes publishes *Johnny Panic and the Bible of Dreams and Other Prose Writing*, containing Plath's stories, essays, and some of her journal excerpts.
1981	Huges publishes *Sylvia Plath: The Collected Poems*, which wins the Pulitzer Prize for Poetry. *The Journals of Sylvia Plath, 1950–1962* is published only in the United States.

Contributors

HAROLD BLOOM is Sterling Professor of the Humanities at Yale University. He is the author of 30 books, including *Shelley's Mythmaking*, *The Visionary Company*, *Blake's Apocalypse*, *Yeats*, *A Map of Misreading*, *Kabbalah and Criticism*, *Agon: Toward a Theory of Revisionism*, *The American Religion*, *The Western Canon*, and *Omens of Millennium: The Gnosis of Angels, Dreams, and Resurrection*. *The Anxiety of Influence* sets forth Professor Bloom's provocative theory of the literary relationships between the great writers and their predecessors. His most recent books include *Shakespeare: The Invention of the Human*, a 1998 National Book Award finalist, *How to Read and Why*, *Genius: A Mosaic of One Hundred Exemplary Creative Minds*, *Hamlet: Poem Unlimited*, *Where Shall Wisdom Be Found?*, and *Jesus and Yahweh: The Names Divine*. In 1999, Professor Bloom received the prestigious American Academy of Arts and Letters Gold Medal for Criticism. He has also received the International Prize of Catalonia, the Alfonso Reyes Prize of Mexico, and the Hans Christian Andersen Bicentennial Prize of Denmark.

BRUCE BAWER has written on numerous subjects, and has published essays in *The New Republic*, *The Nation*, *The Wilson Quarterly*, and *the Hudson Review* among others. His books include *A Place at the Table*, *Stealing Jesus*, *Prophets & Professors*, *Beyond Queer*, *Diminishing Fictions*, and most recently *While Europe Slept*.

JACQUELINE ROSE has taught English at Queen Mary and Westfield College, University of London. She is the author of *The Case of Peter Pan*, *or the Impossibility of Children's Fiction* and other titles. She also has been a translator.

NANCY D. HARGROVE teaches twentieth-century American and British literature at Mississippi State University. In addition to her book on Plath's poems, she has published *Landscape as Symbol in the Poetry of T. S. Eliot* and many essays on Plath, Eliot, Yeats, and others.

SANDRA M. GILBERT teaches at the University of California, Davis. She is the author of her own books of poetry as well as other titles, among them work covering Virginia Woolf's *To the Lighthouse* and *Mrs. Dalloway*. She also is a co-editor of *The Norton Anthology of Literature by Women*.

CAROLINE KING BARNARD HALL has taught at Pennsylvania State University, Beaver Campus. She is the author of *Sylvia Plath* and *Anne Sexton* and also has published on Ellen Glasgow, twentieth-century American literature, and women's studies.

CHRISTINA BRITZOLAKIS teaches at the University of Warwick. She is the author of *Sylvia Plath and the Theatre of Mourning* and also has published on modernist poetry, fiction, and drama.

TIM KENDALL teaches at the University of Bristol. He is the author of *Paul Muldoon* and other titles and also has published his own poetry.

SUSAN GUBAR teaches at Indiana University. She is the author of *Poetry after Auschwitz: Remembering What One Never Knew* and *Critical Condition: Feminism at the Turn of the Century*. She has also co-authored and co-edited several titles, including *The Norton Anthology of Literature by Women*.

LINDA WAGNER-MARTIN teaches at the University of North Carolina at Chapel Hill. She has authored or edited titles on Plath and has authored more than forty titles on other writers as well. She also is a co-editor of *The Oxford Companion to Women's Writing in the United States*.

SUSAN BASSNETT has taught at the University of Warwick. In addition to her title on Sylvia Plath, she has published *Comparative Literature: A Critical Introduction* and other titles, as well as her own poems. She has also been a co-author and co-editor.

Bibliography

Anderson, Robert. *Little Fugue*. New York: Ballantine Books, 2005.

Axelrod, Steven Gould. *Sylvia Plath: The Wound and the Cure of Words*. Baltimore: Johns Hopkins University Press, 1990.

Badia, Janet L. "Viewing Poems as 'Bloodstains': Sylvia Plath's Confessional Poetics and the Autobiographical Reader." *A/B: Auto/Biography Studies* 17, no. 2 (Winter 2002): pp. 180–203.

Baldwin, Kate A. "The Radical Imaginary of *The Bell Jar*." A. *Novel: A Forum on Fiction* 38, no. 1 (Fall 2004): pp. 21–40.

Beer, John B. *Post-Romantic Consciousness: Dickens to Plath*.

Houndmills, Basingstoke, Hampshire; New York: Palgrave Macmillan, 2003.

Bloom, Harold, ed. *American and Canadian Women Poets 1930–Present*. Philadelphia: Chelsea House Publishers, 2002.

———. *Sylvia Plath*. Philadelphia: Chelsea House Publishers, 2001.

Boyer, Marilyn. "The Disabled Female Body as a Metaphor for Language in Sylvia Plath's *The Bell Jar*." *Women's Studies: An Interdisciplinary Journal* 33, no. 2 (March–April 2004): pp. 199–223.

Bundtzen, Lynda K. *The Other Ariel*. Amherst: University of Massachusetts Press, 2001.

Christodoulides, Nephie. *Out of the Cradle Endlessly Rocking: Motherhood in Sylvia Plath's Work*. Amsterdam; New York: Rodopi, 2005.

Curry, Renée R. *White Women Writing White: H.D., Elizabeth Bishop, Sylvia Plath, and Whiteness*. Westport, Conn.: Greenwood Press, 2000.

Davison, Peter. *The Fading Smile: Poets in Boston, 1955–1960, from Robert Frost to Robert Lowell to Sylvia Plath*. New York: Knopf, 1994.

Enniss, Stephen C., and Karen V. Kukil. "No Other Appetite": Sylvia Plath, Ted Hughes, and the Blood Jet of Poetry. New York: Grolier Club, 2005.

Frost, Laura Catherine. *Sex Drives: Fantasies of Fascism in Literary Modernism*. Ithaca: Cornell University Press, 2002.

Gagné, Laurie Brands. *The Uses of Darkness: Women's Underworld Journeys, Ancient and Modern*. Notre Dame, Ind.: University of Notre Dame Press, 2000.

Hannah, Sarah. "'Something Else Hauls Me through Air': Sound and Structure in Four Late Poems by Sylvia Plath.." *Literary Imagination: The Review of the Association of Literary Scholars and Critics* 5, no. 2 (Spring 2003): pp. 232–266.

Harrison, DeSales. *The End of the Mind: The Edge of the Intelligible in Hardy, Stevens, Larkin, Plath, and Glück*. New York: Routledge, 2005.

Hayman, Ronald. *The Death and Life of Sylvia Plath*. Stroud: Sutton, 2003.

Hungerford, Amy. *The Holocaust of Texts: Genocide, Literature, and Personification*. Chicago: University of Chicago Press, 2003.

Kendall, Tim. *Sylvia Plath: A Critical Study*. London; New York: Faber, 2001.

Keniston, Ann. *Overheard Voices: Address and Subjectivity in Postmodern American Poetry*. New York: Routledge, 2006.

Kirsch, Adam. *The Wounded Surgeon: Confession and Transformation in Six American Poets: Robert Lowell, Elizabeth Bishop, John Berryman, Randall Jarrell, Delmore Schwartz, Sylvia Plath*. New York: W.W. Norton & Company, Inc., 2005.

Levin, Dana. "The Heroics of Style: A Study in Three Parts." *American Poetry Review* 34, no. 3 (May–June 2005), pp. 20–21.

Macpherson, Pat. *Reflecting on* The Bell Jar. London; New York: Routledge, 1991.

Malcolm, Janet. *The Silent Woman: Sylvia Plath & Ted Hughes*. New York: Knopf: distributed by Random House, 1994.

Marsack, Robyn. *Sylvia Plath*. Buckingham, England; Philadelphia: Open University Press, 1992.

McQuade, Molly, ed. *By Herself: Women Reclaim Poetry*. Saint Paul, Minn.: Graywolf Press, 2000.

Moses, Kate. *Wintering: A Novel of Sylvia Plath*. New York: St. Martin's Press, 2003.

Oates, Joyce Carol. *Uncensored: Views & (Re)views*. New York: Ecco, 2005.

Parmet, Harriet L. *The Terror of Our Days: Four American Poets Respond to the Holocaust*. Bethlehem, Pa.: Lehigh University Press; London; Cranbury, NJ: Associated University Presses, 2001.

Peel, Robin. "The Ideological Apprenticeship of Sylvia Plath." *Journal of Modern Literature* 27, no. 4 (Summer 2004): pp. 59–72.

———. *Writing Back: Sylvia Plath and Cold War Politics*. Madison, N.J.: Fairleigh Dickinson University Press; London; Cranbury, N.J.: Associated University Presses, 2002.

Saldívar, Toni. *Sylvia Plath: Confessing the Fictive Self*. New York: Lang, 1992.

Strangeways, Al. *Sylvia Plath: The Shaping of Shadows*. Madison, N.J.: Fairleigh Dickinson University Press; London; Cranbury, N.J.: Associated University Presses, 1998.

Swiontkowski, Gale. *Imagining Incest: Sexton, Plath, Rich, and Olds on Life with Daddy*. Selinsgrove, Pa.: Susquehanna University Press; London; Cranbury, N.J.: Associated University Presses, 2003.

Tytell, John. *Passionate Lives: D. H. Lawrence, F. Scott Fitzgerald, Henry Miller, Dylan Thomas, Sylvia Plath—in Love*. Secaucus, N.J.: Carol Pub. Group, 1991.

Van Dyne, Susan R. *Revising Life: Sylvia Plath's Ariel Poems*. Chapel Hill: University of North Carolina Press, 1993.

Vendler, Helen Hennessy. *Coming of Age as a Poet: Milton, Keats, Eliot, Plath*. Cambridge, Mass.: Harvard University Press, 2003.

Vice, Sue. *Representing the Holocaust: In Honour of Bryan Burns*. London; Portland, Ore.: Vallentine Mitchell, 2003.

Wagner, Erica. *Ariel's Gift: A Commentary on* Birthday Letters *by Ted Hughes*. London: Faber and Faber, 2000.

———. *Ariel's Gift: Ted Hughes, Sylvia Plath, and the Story of* Birthday Letters. New York: Norton, 2001.

Wagner, Linda W., ed. *Sylvia Plath: The Critical Heritage*. London; New York: Routledge, 1997, 1988.

Wagner-Martin, Linda. The Bell Jar, *a Novel of the Fifties*. New York: Twayne; Toronto: Maxwell Macmillan Canada; New York: Maxwell Macmillan International, 1992.

Acknowledgments

"Sylvia Plath and the Poetry of Confession" by Bruce Bawer. From *The New Criterion* 9, no. 6 (February, 1991): pp. 18–27. © 1991 by *The New Criterion*. Reprinted by permission of the Gale Group.

"'Daddy'" by Jacqueline Rose. From *The Haunting of Sylvia Plath*: pp. 205–238. © 1991 by Jacqueline Rose. Reprinted by permission of Harvard University Press.

"The Poems of 1957" by Nancy D. Hargrove. From *The Journey Toward Ariel: Sylvia Plath's Poems of 1956–1959*: pp. 99–133. © 1994 by Nancy D. Hargrove. Reprinted by permission.

"A Long Hiss of Distress: Plath's Elegy on the Beach at Berck" by Sandra M. Gilbert. From *Field* 59 (Fall 1998): pp. 30–38. © 1998 by Oberlin College. Reprinted by permission.

"Transitional Poetry" by Caroline King Barnard Hall. From *Sylvia Plath, Revised*: pp. 67–82. © 1998 by Twayne Publishers. Reprinted by permission of The Gale Group.

"Gothic Subjectivity" by Christina Britzolakis. From *Sylvia Plath and the Theatre of Mourning*: pp. 101–134. © 1999 by Christina Britzolakis. Reprinted by permission of Oxford University Press.

"From the Bottom of the Pool: Sylvia Plath's Last Poems" by Tim Kendall. From *English* 49 (2000): pp. 23–38. © 2001 by The English Association. Reprinted by permission.

"Prosopopoeia and Holocaust Poetry in English: Sylvia Plath and Her Contemporaries" by Susan Gubar. From *The Yale Journal of Criticism* 14, no. 1 (Spring 2001): pp. 191–215. © 2001 by Yale University and The Johns Hopkins University Press. Reprinted by permission of The Johns Hopkins University Press.

"Plath's Triumphant Women Poems" by Linda Wagner-Martin. From *Sylvia Plath: A Literary Life*: pp. 106–118. © 1999, 2003 by Linda Wagner-Martin. Reprinted by permission of Palgrave Macmillan.

"Poetry and Survival" by Susan Bassnett. From *Sylvia Plath: An Introduction to the Poetry*, second edition: pp. 117–138. © 2005 by Susan Bassnett. Reprinted by permission of Palgrave Macmillan.

Index